THE DEEPENING STREAM

A History of the
New Zealand Literary Fund

THE DEEPENING STREAM

A History of the
New Zealand Literary Fund

ELIZABETH CAFFIN

& Andrew Mason

VICTORIA UNIVERSITY PRESS

TE WHARE WĀNANGA O TE ŪPOKO O TE IKA A MĀUI
VICTORIA
UNIVERSITY OF WELLINGTON

VICTORIA UNIVERSITY PRESS
Victoria University of Wellington
PO Box 600 Wellington
vup.victoria.ac.nz

First published 2015

National Library of New Zealand Cataloguing-in-Publication Data

Caffin, Elizabeth, 1941-
The deepening stream : a history of the New Zealand Literary Fund / Elizabeth Caffin and Andrew Mason.
Includes bibliographical references.
ISBN 978-1-77656-036-3

1. New Zealand Literary Fund—History. 2. Authors—Salaries, etc.—New Zealand—History—20th century. 3. Authors—New Zealand—Social conditions—20th century. 4. Literary prizes—New Zealand—History—20th century. I. Mason, Andrew, 1950-2009. II. Title.
NZ820.9—dc 23

Index by Tordis Flath

Published with the assistance of a grant from

creative nz
ARTS COUNCIL OF NEW ZEALAND TOI AOTEAROA

Printed by Printlink, Wellington

To the memory of Ian Gordon, Roly Frean,
Ray Copland and Terry Sturm
and especially of Andrew Mason

CONTENTS

ACKNOWLEDGEMENTS

A study such as this could not have been written without help from many, many people. Foremost among them of course is Andrew Mason himself, whose rigorous standards were an inspiration, and Malcolm McKinnon, his executor. I would also like to thank warmly several members of the Literary Fund Advisory Committee: Ann Mallinson, Wendy Harrex and Elizabeth Alley, and some of the public servants who worked with the committee: Mike Jarman, Pat Stuart, Jane Kominik, Rosemary Wildblood, Jock Vennell. All put themselves out to help me. The same is true of many writers: C.K. Stead, Elizabeth Smither, Ian Wedde, Maurice Gee, Fiona Kidman, Witi Ihimaera, Vincent O'Sullivan, Ray Grover, Tony Simpson. Others whose help was essential were Linda Cassells, Rachel Barrowman, Helen Bones, Adam Dudding, Kate Fortune, Marion Kelsall at Creative New Zealand, Maggie Tarver at the New Zealand Society of Authors, Cecilia Johnson, Cathie Gordon, Louis Changuion at Massey University Library, Deborah Gale at the Hocken Library, and my brother Jock Phillips. Melanie Lovell-Smith helped me expertly with finding illustrations. Peter Simpson produced overnight a brilliant selection of likely cover images. Creative New Zealand kindly passed on to me what remained of the grant awarded to Andrew and also supported the publication of this book. I am also grateful to Victoria University Press, Ashleigh Young and Fergus Barrowman. Brian Easton constantly supported, encouraged and provoked me. Thank you all.

Elizabeth Caffin
Wellington, September 2014

INTRODUCTION

This book was begun by Andrew Mason, who chaired the Literature Committee of the Queen Elizabeth II Arts Council for its last years, in which it still bore some resemblance to the Literary Fund Advisory Committee. Andrew, assisted by a grant from Creative New Zealand, had covered the period up to 1955 when, sadly, he died in 2009. I had served on the advisory committee twice, once in the 1970s and again in the 1980s leading up to its absorption by the Arts Council. Remembering how dedicated Andrew had been to this project and remembering also the late Professor Terry Sturm's wish for such a history to be written, I took it over.

The first three chapters thus are largely Andrew's own work, though they have been significantly shortened. It was also his idea to call the book *The Deepening Stream*, adapting Monte Holcroft's title to a new and happy use. I can only hope Andrew would have been satisfied with the completed story.

The title is apt because this is the story of the evolution of New Zealand's literary culture over forty years, from 1947 to 1988. Starting with a small sum of public money and a large committee, the Literary Fund played a part—often overlooked but actually crucial—in increasing the confidence and skills of writers and the openness and enthusiasm of readers.

By using its always modest allocation to encourage, maintain and reward literary talent it assisted almost every serious writer at some time or other; it also attempted, perhaps with less deftness, to support the passage of their work out into the world.

I was an inexperienced editor at the publisher A.H. and A.W. Reed when I became a member of the committee in 1977. Fortunately the chairman, Professor Roly Frean, had taught me at the University of Canterbury, and was an old friend. The other members were daunting grand old men of letters: Bruce Mason, David Ballantyne and Professor James Bertram. There was also the young, nervy and talented Ian Wedde. I was the only woman. Two academics, three writers and a publisher. We read every submission: each one came by post with a stamped and addressed envelope so that you could send it on to the next member. It was an odd group to be in, considering the irreverent, baggy, energetic writing of that time, but I recall no major disputes or disagreements.

Assessment of this type is not a precise art. There were inevitable complaints of injustice or inconsistency, and mistakes were sometimes made. None of this was easy, especially in a small society with a literary community in which everyone knew everyone else. But once such a fund was established it was better that decisions be made by a group rather than by a single judge; that the group not be politicians or bureaucrats but people with relevant expertise; and that the group possessed shared knowledge but different perspectives.

I served on the committee a second time from 1985 to 1989. By then the Literary Fund programme was complex and extensive, meetings took several days and the annual allocation was much larger. Submissions were photocopied and arrived in huge packages. But the structure and practice of the committee was unchanged, and Professor Sturm took extraordinary care that all opinions were heard and considered. This inclusiveness was essential at that time of change and almost impossible to achieve, given the articulate, opinionated, combative character of the literary community. But a difficult transition was finally achieved.

It was a privilege to be a member of that committee. I always thought how lucky we were to see the current state of writing in New Zealand (or a large part of it) spread out before us. We were confronted, challenged and excited. People trained in literary judgement and knowledgeable about literary tradition and context were balanced with working writers familiar with local contemporary conditions, allowing for a valuable range of opinions. This went along with the fact that the committee was pretty much left alone to determine policy and to be open to the views of both writers and publishers. From the perspective of the early twenty-first century, it is moving to see how the state worked modestly but determinedly in cooperation with publishers of magazines and books to allow writers and writing to flourish.

On the acknowledgements page of his second novel, Barry Crump wrote:

> The New Zealand Literary Fund came across with some dough to help me write this. Not a bad bunch. The publishers came in handy once or twice.

The writing world is much larger now, more sophisticated and more diverse. The literary arts are widely respected and honoured. There are of course many reasons for this, but the Literary Fund, not a bad bunch, must be one of them.

1

AN IDEA TAKES ROOT

1936–1947

On Monday, 27 November 1944, as the Allies liberated Strasbourg and heavy air raids began on Tokyo, the New Zealand Minister of Internal Affairs, W.E. Parry, prepared to receive a deputation from the local centre of PEN, the international writers' organisation. The deputation was led by Colonel C.A.L. Treadwell, the president of PEN New Zealand, supported by the Parliamentary Librarian, Dr Guy Scholefield, Professor Ian Gordon of the English Department at Victoria University College and O.N. Gillespie, a journalist then on the information staff of the Prime Minister's Department. They had a grand objective: to persuade the Labour Government to establish a New Zealand Literary Fund for the purposes of:

> 1. assisting in the publication of books, which, owing to the 'limited field' in New Zealand, would not find a popular sale—such as biographies and histories;
> 2. subsidising any 'worth-while' book;
> 3. republishing of New Zealand classics.[1]

Their model was Australia's Commonwealth Literary Fund, a summary of whose operations the deputation helpfully provided. The Australian fund at that time had a budget of £6000 a year, and made its decisions on the recommendations of an advisory board comprising mainly academics and representatives from the Fellowship of Australian Writers. From its establishment in 1908 until 1938, the fund had concentrated on awarding pensions to elderly or sick writers and their families; in 1939 it had extended its role to include awarding fellowships to writers 'of proven literary ability' to enable them to devote their time and talents to producing specified works. Financial assistance towards the publication of works of 'literary merit' that would otherwise probably not be published, and towards reprinting approved local 'standard works'—the New Zealand PEN's main concern too—was added to the Australian fund's list of purposes at the same time.[2]

Treadwell considered that, given the comparative populations, a fund of £1200 would be appropriate for New Zealand. He stressed that in the past New Zealand writers seeking publication had gone to America, England or Australia, where the markets were larger, and that a New Zealand literary fund would be a 'service to the country—not only to the authors but also to those who read books about their country'. Treadwell, a lawyer with literary ambitions who had become president of PEN on the strength of his popular 1936 book, *Notable New Zealand Trials*,[3] said that there were many good New Zealand manuscripts awaiting publication, but that publishers required authors to subsidise the cost of publication—and most authors could not afford that sort of money.[4]

Parry agreed it was 'imperative' that New Zealanders write about their country if its history and culture were to be preserved, and it was 'just as essential for such writings to be undertaken and to be available to the people of the

Dominion as it was to have written up current information of the war'. He hoped that 'writings by the Maoris and of the Maoris' would be encouraged. As evidence of the government's sympathetic treatment of the arts, he itemised the amount of money it had given to 'literary art' associated with New Zealand's centenary four years before, including £30,000 for the Department of Internal Affairs' own centennial publications.[5] However, a champion of physical rather than cultural activities,[6] he felt that the best way forward would be for the deputation to meet with the Prime Minister, Peter Fraser, 'a keen and wide reader and deeply interested in the encouragement and extension of literary and other arts', and possibly also with the Minister of Finance, Walter Nash, another 'great reader' who was 'keenly interested in literature'.[7] Gillespie, as a member of the Prime Minister's staff, undertook to arrange such a meeting.

Much has been written on the emergence in the 1930s in New Zealand of a distinctive literary culture. It is certainly true that a literary infrastructure was slowly beginning to take shape: publishers like Caxton with a commitment to the local and the imaginative; journals likewise, from *Tomorrow* to *Art in New Zealand* to *Kiwi*; bookshops like Paul's Book Arcade. Serious creative writing hitherto largely associated with journalism or as an amateur activity was moving towards the universities, the more deliberate concern of students and scholars. In Wellington a new breed of politicians, often earnestly educated at the Workers' Educational Association, were bookish and idealistic.[8]

The New Zealand Literary Fund can be seen as one of a group of cultural initiatives and investments by the state in the years following the Second World War. They include the National Film Unit, the National Library

Service and the National Orchestra. Most of them had been suggested in the 1930s in the atmosphere of change and reform characteristic of the new Labour Government; they represented an important aspect of the socialist state and a sensitivity to the cultural nationalism stirring in those years. But they were delayed by the war.

PEN's campaign for a New Zealand literary fund seems to have had its origins in the inaugural New Zealand Authors' Week in April 1936, the brainchild of PEN's indefatigable and ubiquitous founder and secretary, Pat Lawlor. Shortly before the general election in November 1935, Finance Minister Gordon Coates granted the week's organising committee, chaired by Treadwell, £100 to help defray exhibition costs. Later, Parry funded the full publication cost of £200 of the first bibliography of books by New Zealand writers, *Annals of New Zealand Literature*, compiled by the Alexander Turnbull Librarian Johannes Andersen, as part of the festival. He told the organisers that no public announcement would be made and, in return, took the unsold copies of the bibliography and had them distributed gratis to libraries in New Zealand and around the world.[9]

The week itself was a resounding success, with well-attended public lectures, readings and displays in the four main centres, and one of the conditions of Parry's grant was that the movement for promoting New Zealand writing be continued. A PEN committee soon came up with a scheme that was enthusiastic and hopeful, rather than practical, involving a proposal to hold monthly meetings in the main centres for readings of new work. This plan came to nothing, but the impact of these events was longer lasting. It was becoming clear to PEN members that a more systematic, independent and transparent way of providing state assistance for literary activities—one less dependent on ministerial whim or bureaucratic favour—needed to be devised. In its *Gazette*, PEN highlighted from time to time the arrangements in other countries, finding particular relevance in the Canadian and Estonian, as well as Australian, examples.[10]

The idea of a government fund to assist literature had been present in the official mind too for some time, beginning with Dr Angus Harrop. Harrop is remembered as a London-based historian and the founder in 1927 of *New*

Inauguration of the New Zealand Authors' Week, 1936. Standing far right, Pat Lawlor; sitting far right, O.N. Gillespie, beside him Johannes Andersen, centre Sir Harold Beauchamp.
S.P. Andrew Collection, ATL, F-18634-1/1

Zealand News, a weekly digest of local news for homesick expatriates. However, through his 'long-term persecution' (as J.C. Beaglehole called it) of the New Zealand government in the 1930s, Harrop must be credited with inspiring the idea of a literary fund in government circles.[11]

Unable to find a British publisher for his book *England and the Maori Wars*, a compilation of official documents and newspaper reports based on records in London, Harrop decided to publish it himself, and in March 1936 he wrote to the Prime Minister, Michael Joseph Savage, offering to dedicate the book to him and asking for a subsidy of £80 from the Maori Purposes Fund Board. The government was reluctant to agree to either request without having seen the text, but Harrop persisted, eventually offering his book as a candidate for the proposed series of centennial historical surveys. The Under-Secretary for Internal Affairs, Joseph Heenan, then had to refer his request for a subsidy to the newly established Centennial Historical Committee. While strongly supporting financial assistance for the publication of 'works of scholarship', the committee quickly reached the opinion that such grants 'should be made only in accordance with a declared and regular policy, public in its nature. The making of piecemeal grants . . . is likely to lead to the establishment of undesirable precedents.' Doubtful about the merits of Harrop's book, which still had not been seen, the committee also recommended that such works 'should reach a reasonable standard of scholarship as determined by competent authorities in the special field dealt with'.[12] Harrop went ahead and published the book anyway, and when a copy finally reached the government, the opinion of the 'competent authorities' was scathing: 'practically unreadable . . . a vast notebook of raw material' (Professor Fred Wood); 'a very long necklace, composed of rough and uncut stones, some of them showing authentic sparkle, some just plain ordinary rock—strung on a very thin string of Harrop' (J.C. Beaglehole).[13] No grant was given.

Reflecting on the whole situation, which had taken up a great deal of official time to no good purpose, Beaglehole wanted to prevent a recurrence. He told Heenan: 'A Government fund should be set up, from which assistance should be granted towards the publication of work deemed worthy of aid, on conditions clearly understood'. Those conditions included:

1. The possibility of such grants-in-aid should be generally known.
2. The grants must be made on the advice of a competent person or committee.
3. The person or committee must have read the work before publication.

(This last was to 'avoid the absurd situation which tends to arise in the case of an author like Dr Harrop who, with a great fanfare of trumpets, produces a baby, and then, on his assurance that it is a very good baby, expects the Government to rush forward to help hold it'.) The main point, Beaglehole went on, 'is that the whole system needs to be regularised'. New Zealanders who produce 'really good work' should have a claim on the public purse if there was no other way of getting that work published because it was not a commercial proposition. 'But there ought to be some recognised and decent mode of procedure, not a course of siege-warfare on every occasion when a man deems he has a claim; or, alternatively, a refusal to a deserving scholar of less pertinacity.'[14]

Such a system, which implied an independent advisory board as in Australia, must have seemed anathema to

Heenan, who preferred to work unencumbered by formal structures. Rather, he relied on advice from a few trusted colleagues or friends and then making recommendations to his Minister himself. (For grants of up to £250 he needed only the approval of his Minister, not from Cabinet.)[15] Beaglehole had caught his attention, however, and in 1939 Heenan, having read an article about it in the *Christian Science Monitor*, obtained from the Australian Prime Minister's Office a detailed account of the recently reconstituted and extended Commonwealth Literary Fund. This must have set him thinking, for three years later, when onetime Minister of Internal Affairs Downie Stewart asked him whether the government would fund the publication of the winning novel in the Centennial Literary Competition (its author was an 'old friend' of Downie Stewart), Heenan replied that he had not contemplated publishing the prizewinners, as the centennial funds were being used to produce historical works only. However, he went on, 'Nothing would please me more, personally, than to have on the vote of our Department an item which would be roughly the equivalent of the Commonwealth Literary Fund'. He had discussed the matter with his Minister, he said, and had 'every hope' of establishing a literary fund after the war.[16]

PEN had submitted an outline of its projected literary fund in preparation for its meeting with Parry in November 1944. Heenan passed this on for comment to Beaglehole, who pointed out that it was actually similar to his earlier suggestions. PEN wanted the fund to be administered by a committee of seven, comprising three of its own members, plus representatives from the government, the Senate of the University of New Zealand and possibly the Supreme Court. Beaglehole responded: 'God preserve us from the University Senate. And why a Supreme Court judge?' Commenting on the revamped Australian model, Beaglehole made his own priorities clear: a New Zealand fund should be kept 'primarily for assisting publication'. His opinion of the standard of commercial New Zealand publishing was clearly low, for he added, 'Private publishers be damned—except under careful supervision' and declared that 'Reprinted "classics" should be properly edited'.[17]

In view of Heenan's and Beaglehole's wish to retain control over state-assisted publications, it is worth examining the state's own record in this area outside the centennial historical surveys. In his briefing paper to the Minister, Heenan mentioned three works of 'national importance' that the department had produced since the centenary. One was the booklet commemorating the 300th anniversary of Tasman's visit in 1642, which contained Allen Curnow's poem 'Landfall in Unknown Seas', commissioned on Beaglehole's suggestion to mark the occasion—a very rare instance of the state commissioning creative literature.[18] The booklet was a triumph: although it was not printed for sale, the department received so many inquiries from people wanting to buy it that Heenan suggested they make a donation to their local patriotic fund instead.

Another of Heenan's works of 'national importance' was *The Gael Fares Forth*, by N.R. McKenzie, a history of the Nova Scotian settlement at Waipu first published privately in London in 1935.[19] When the author approached Internal Affairs for a subsidy for a second edition in New Zealand in 1940, the Prime Minister, Peter Fraser, a friend of the author and a fellow Scot, insisted that 'the most generous assistance should be offered'.[20] Cabinet approved a subsidy of up to £450, anything over £200 of which was to be recouped from sales. Although Beaglehole remarked that, given the wartime shortages of paper and of everything else, 'the republication of this volume inspires me with dismay',[21] the newly formed Historical Branch, which Heenan had fashioned from the Centennial Branch, put its weight behind the production, which featured an elegant design by Beaglehole and photographs of Waipu and its denizens by J.D. Pascoe. Fraser was so pleased with the book that he used it for official Christmas presents, and even had a specially bound copy presented to President Roosevelt. Although the final production bill came to £550, the second edition sold well and was out of print within two years.[22]

Another example of the ad hoc nature of the state's sponsorship of publishing was the request by the 74-year-old W.K. Howitt of Taranaki for money to help publish his reminiscences of pioneering life, *A Pioneer Looks Back: Days of Trials, Hardships and Achievements.* Heenan recommended to Parry that a grant of £50 could be made 'by way of a gesture to an old citizen', but Parry, carried away by his enthusiasm, gave Howitt £100. The book was eventually published in 1945. Howitt asked for another grant for his second volume of memoirs but met a stony rejection.[23] Enthusiasm outran merit also in the grant to journalist Sidney Baker, who had written a book on New Zealand slang, to compile 'A Dictionary of the Australasian Language: Australian and New Zealand contributions to colloquial and unconventional English'. Heenan, who was interested in the study of language, gave Baker £100 in 1942; when Baker confessed in 1945 that he needed at least £10,000 to complete the project, Heenan told him to 'keep up the good work' and was sorry that he had been able to make only a 'token grant'.[24]

State assistance for writers was similarly haphazard. In Australia, the Commonwealth Literary Fund had up to 1938 granted pensions to writers who, because of age or infirmity, were unable to support themselves, and to families of 'literary men' who had died poor; the maximum pension was £1 a week and, for 'outstanding men of letters', £2 a week.[25] In New Zealand, there was nothing so systematic. The newly founded PEN campaigned in 1934 for a state pension for the journalist and historian James Cowan, because of his failing health and because 'he had never made any money out of his historical books but had done very good work for the country'. The campaign was unsuccessful, but the deputation to the Minister of Internal Affairs included Peter Fraser, a great admirer of Cowan, and after the Labour victory in 1935 PEN found the new Minister of Finance, Walter Nash, more sympathetic. Cowan was granted an annuity of £100 from the Civil List in May 1936.[26] So too was the frail 72-year-old poet Jessie Mackay, who, on receiving her pension, hoped that the government 'might even desire to extend this amazing generosity on behalf of young and vigorous writers'.[27] The elderly William Satchell, whose best-known novel, *The Greenstone Door* (first published in 1914), enjoyed a revival after 1935, was granted a Civil List annuity in 1939. The poet Eileen Duggan, though not yet 50, was also granted an annuity in 1942, presumably on the ground that she was 'generally understood to be a lady of a retiring and delicate character'.[28] After Cowan died in 1943, his widow was given a special pension at the instigation of Fraser.

Assistance to Jessie Mackay's 'young and vigorous writers' was another matter, however. When the Labour Parliamentary Under-Secretary for Housing, John A. Lee, himself a writer, sought help from Heenan in 1936 for the penurious poet and critic of New Zealand society D'Arcy Cresswell, then barely 40, Heenan regretted that there was no provision for an annuity in such a case. Lee found the poet a job in a state forest at Riverhead, near Auckland, but Cresswell lasted only a few months there and soon returned to England.[29]

The singular case of Frank Sargeson is instructive in revealing Heenan's characteristic modus operandi. In mid-1940, Sargeson, then in his late thirties, had an operation for tuberculosis, but was then told he was ineligible for a sickness benefit. He outlined his plight in a letter to his poet and printer friend Denis Glover, who sent it on to Heenan asking him to help.[30] Heenan promptly arranged an emergency benefit until Sargeson's application for a permanent invalid's benefit could be processed. When by 1947 Sargeson's recovery had put this benefit (by now worth £3 a week) at risk, Eric McCormick, who had been hand-picked by Heenan to be the first member of his Centennial Publications staff, got in touch with his former boss. Heenan then arranged for Sargeson to receive instead a permanent 'literary pension' of £4 a week, tax free (the average wage was just over £6 a week), to be drawn from state lottery profits under Heenan's control. He and Sargeson sorted out the details over a drink at the Grand Hotel in Auckland, and the lack of formal documentation created problems for Sargeson later when he could not prove that the pension was intended to be tax free.[31] Dennis McEldowney commented that this pension 'to an active writer was a precedent which an Arts Council might well have hesitated to make'.[32] Historian Rachel Barrowman observed that it was not only unprecedented but unique, and could 'probably only have been devised at this time by someone with Heenan's personal enthusiasm for literature, his imaginative approach to the spending of government funds, his dislike for the constraints of advisory committees and other bureaucratic obstructions, and with the ear of his minister, the Prime Minister and the Minister of Finance'.[33]

* * *

Others saw a similar need for a system of state aid to literature. Beaglehole deplored the 'painful negotiation and bargaining' involved in getting state assistance for publications.[34] Monte Holcroft, whose reputation as an essayist was then at its height, took a writer's perspective. He was incensed that, of the dozen novels that the judges of the Centennial Literary Competition had said were 'well worthy of publication and in fact it would be a loss to New Zealand if they remained unpublished', not one had been published—not even the winning entry. '[S]urely', he wrote in his 1943 essay *The Waiting Hills*, 'the Government could have subsidized the publication of at least two or three of these books—which must now, it seems, remain forever unknown to the people of New Zealand.'[35] Foreshadowing the argument PEN put to the Minister a year later, that writers were required to subsidise commercial publishers in order to have their books published, Holcroft felt that this system meant that 'books of inferior quality have been published, while promising work has been excluded simply because the authors could not afford to pay a printer's bill. . .'. The solution, he went on, was to place a 'selective agency' between the writer and his public in the form of a state editorial board. This board should be confined to the 'selection of promising work, which could then be placed on the market at a nominal price by means of Government subsidies'.[36] Foreshadowing also PEN's request for the government to reprint New Zealand 'classics', Holcroft advocated making 'outstandingly good' works of New Zealand literature, otherwise obtainable only in reference libraries or in expensive secondhand copies, readily available in cheap editions.[37]

It is not clear whether Holcroft's essay was the spur needed to prick PEN into action.[38] Certainly, soon after it appeared Lawlor let him know that PEN was working along the lines he had suggested, although in his autobiography, Holcroft disclaimed 'any significant part in the creation of the Literary Fund':

> When I was writing *The Waiting Hills* I believed myself to be advocating a new and radical step towards State patronage. I had seen no similar argument in print, had heard nothing of it in private discussion. The proposal came straight from my own hard experience as a writer. But ideas of this sort are not afloat until people are ready for them, and then they come as if spontaneously from different sources.[39]

Holcroft returned to the idea a year later when, as acting editor of the *Southland Times*, he applauded in a leading article the suggestion by the Labour MP for Invercargill, W.M.C. Denham, that the government establish a 'State examining committee' to perform precisely the function he had been advocating. It is presumably no coincidence that Holcroft had since joined PEN, that Denham was Holcroft's local MP, and that Denham made his suggestion in Parliament on 28 November 1944, the day after PEN's deputation to Parry.[40]

In the event, PEN's hoped-for meeting with Peter Fraser at the end of 1944 had to be postponed, as the Prime Minister was in San Francisco helping to found the United Nations. But PEN had already announced its proposals in its November 1944 *Gazette*, and used the time gained to refine the concept. When it renewed its assault on the government a year later, PEN was proposing something altogether more confident, extensive, writer-oriented and self-interested—even self-important. (When Charles Brasch attacked PEN in *Landfall* as representing 'no one but its own members' and certainly not the writers of New Zealand, 'most of whom do not belong to it', the organisation responded that in its initial approach to the minister it had 'presumed' to represent the interests of all writers.)[41] The fund's annual grant should be used, it said, for:

1. subsidies for the publication of worthwhile historical works (such as the Richmond Papers, the Sinclair Papers and the work of such writers as M.C. Keane);[42]
2. subsidies for the publication of belles-lettres, poetry or prose, which are not capable of profitable production on a commercial basis;
3. grants to authors engaged on promising fiction or other creative writing;
4. prizes for young writers;
5. reprinting New Zealand classics in cheap editions;
6. lectures on New Zealand literature at the university colleges;
7. a subsidy to PEN for publication of its *Gazette* and for cooperation in a National Book Week;
8. a second subsidy to PEN for providing professional assistance and advice to authors.

As for pensions to deserving writers, PEN was confident that they would be continued, but left it to the government to decide whether they should be paid out of the Civil List or the literary fund's annual grant. In support of the subsidies to itself, PEN adduced the example of the Canadian Authors' Association, which sponsored the publication of a quarterly magazine called *Poetry* and published its own quarterly bulletin of advice to authors; PEN New Zealand wished to enlarge its *Gazette*. Reiterating its proposals for a seven-member advisory committee (including three of its own representatives), PEN noted that the Commonwealth Literary Fund's advisory board had only four members plus the chairman, and there had been complaints that 'professional jealousy keeps the benefits of the fund restricted to a circle'.[43]

It was this last matter that was obviously bothering Heenan, himself a member of PEN.[44] The irrepressible Heenan had, since 1935, shown himself an imaginative and creative public servant who, working well with Fraser, had sought to make his department 'the cultural hub of the Government wheel'[45] and dispensed state patronage of the arts in ways that were coming to seem more like personal patronage. He was particularly proud of the centenary projects which he had masterminded and especially the successful historical surveys. Reluctant to disband his department's publishing unit as its centennial publication programme neared completion, he had converted the temporary Centennial Branch into a permanent Historical Branch in 1941, with historian and scholar J.C. Beaglehole in charge, working on books published either by or with the assistance of the department. He had of course been present at the meeting between PEN and Parry and had characteristically argued for continuing the government's present policy of producing books itself—through his own department, of course—or making grants towards the objectives the deputation sought—also through his own department, of course. In fact, Heenan had urged this course on his Minister in his briefing notes before the meeting, declaring it to be 'preferable to establishing a fund to be administered by a separate body'.[46]

In July 1945, J.H.E. Schroder, then assistant editor in charge of the literary pages of the Christchurch *Press*, had implored him 'for the fifth time, on my bended knees, to give me your views about . . . the possible development of something like the Commonwealth Literary Fund'. Heenan responded frankly, repeating his views on 'the impossibility, to my mind, of getting a suitable body to administer it. New Zealand has so many mutually intolerant cliques, each of which claims in all fields of art to have the monopoly of knowledge and taste'. In essence, he felt he was 'achieving the same object by having the matter more or less in my hands here at Internal Affairs'.[47] Heenan may have envisaged, as Rachel Barrowman tartly observed, a much larger role for his department in literary patronage than 'simply doing the bookwork for a committee of PEN members'.[48] But he may also have been genuinely—and presciently, given accusations of 'provider capture' in the 1980s and 90s—concerned that the administering body would be captured by a particular group of literary interests, in this case PEN.

Heenan repeated his concerns when PEN came to see him in November 1945 about getting action on its new proposals. The deputation was led by the organisation's new president, Sir James Elliott (a surgeon who had published an autobiography, *Scalpel and Sword*, and a biography of the Wellington College headmaster Joseph Firth), accompanied by Professor Gordon and Pat Lawlor. Heenan advised them to try the Prime Minister again, but repeated his preference for a government-administered fund, with the Department of Internal Affairs seeking 'appropriate advice' from PEN 'and other reputable bodies'.[49]

PEN took Heenan's concern to heart, for when Elliott wrote to the Prime Minister seeking a meeting, he was quick to reassure him that PEN, while being the 'prime mover', did not wish to have control. The 'board of control' should be selected from PEN, the university and, 'of course', the state.[50] This time, however, Fraser was off to London for the inaugural meeting of the United Nations General Assembly, and it was Heenan who took up PEN's proposals with him informally after his return in February 1946. Elliott contented himself with sending Fraser a further encouraging letter.[51] There were other political factors at work, too. Later that year Fraser was facing an election which he knew would be closely fought,[52] and in March the Labour Party's own newspaper, *Southern Cross*, had stated editorially that a literary fund 'to ensure cheap reprints of New Zealand literature' could be established 'to some advantage': such a proposal 'would be sure of the backing of the whole Labour movement'.[53] Furthermore, Heenan had found an inspired way around his own objections. Fraser was persuaded, and on 10 July 1946 Heenan sent his Minister a memorandum that in effect established the New Zealand State Literary Fund.[54]

He claimed that establishing the literary fund would be a 'public gesture' which would definitely be appreciated, not only by PEN, but by 'all others interested in encouraging the development of a national New Zealand literature'. So enthusiastic was he now about the proposal that he thought an annual grant of £2000, rather than the modest £1200 that PEN had sought, would be a 'more worth-while gesture'. The 1946/47 grant would be taken out of the supplementary estimates.

Heenan based the fund's administrative structure directly on the Commonwealth Literary Fund, adapted only slightly to meet his needs. At its inception, the Australian fund had been administered by the Prime Minister and the Leader of the Opposition, assisted by an advisory board, though its composition was subsequently changed. In New Zealand, he thought, there was no need to include the Leader of the Opposition, and that a Cabinet committee comprising the Prime Minister, the Minister of Finance and the Minister of Internal Affairs—Heenan's favourite triumvirate—would be appropriate. They would have the power to question, or even veto, any of the advisory board's recommendations. The personnel of the advisory board could be decided later, along with the question of whether literary pensions should be paid out of the fund's income. The cost of administering the fund would be part of Internal Affairs' ordinary expenses.

Parry was asked to take the matter to Cabinet where in spite of predictable attempts by Treasury to reduce the annual grant, Heenan's original recommendations passed unaltered on 16 August.[55] Heenan also gained ministerial approval for an advisory committee of seven members, including three representatives from PEN. Advising Elliott, Gordon and Lawlor of the new arrangements at a meeting in his office on 29 October, Heenan noted that the annual grant of £2000 would be appropriated each year but that any money not spent would *not* be added to the funds for the following year. He hoped to get the committee set up and underway as soon as the forthcoming election was over, with a view to spending as much as possible in the 1946/47 financial year. He recorded that the PEN members were 'well satisfied' with what the government had done.[56]

What had prompted Heenan's sudden change of heart about an independent literary fund? The most likely reason is that he had devised a way of extending his own ad hoc system of literary patronage, and was less concerned about what the Literary Fund might get up to. Earlier, on 4 June 1946, he had received Cabinet approval to set up a Cultural and General Arts Fund with an annual income of £20,000, derived from the surplus profits of the Art Union, or state lottery. In making his case for this fund to Fraser and Nash, Heenan specifically excluded the Literary Fund, and pointed out that under his new proposal the government of the day would 'still have *at its own disposal* a fund out of which to make grants in meritorious cases for the publication of books or to help other artistic effort' (emphasis added).[57] Cannily, he cited the much-lauded production of McKenzie's *The Gael Fares Forth* as a justification, and appended an ecstatic memorandum from Beaglehole, waxing lyrical about the proposed fund ('one of the intellectually most exciting things ever to have happened in New Zealand') and advancing an extensive list of projects, including historical and art publications, music publishing, and even an annual prize for typography, as candidates for patronage.[58] In approving Heenan's recommendations, Cabinet added 'subsidies to authors or publishers' to the purposes of the Cultural and General Arts Fund, and it was from this fund that Heenan took Frank Sargeson's 'literary pension' of £4 a week.

The trustees of the Cultural and General Arts Fund were the Minister of Internal Affairs and the Prime Minister, acting on the recommendation of the Department of Internal Affairs—that is, Heenan, who would make the selection. 'It would be our duty to bring to your notice only such objects as in our considered judgment were worthy of your approval,' he explained.[59] There was to be no nonsense about advisory committees here. Moreover, as there would be no item on the Internal Affairs vote, there could be no scrutiny by Parliament; nor would there be any publicity about the fund, or announcement of the recipients of its largesse, ostensibly to prevent a deluge of applications.

This highly secretive arrangement was soon questioned. The poet A.R.D. Fairburn claimed that Heenan, in discussing Sargeson's pension in July 1947, had described the Literary Fund as 'the facade fund' behind which he intended to 'hand out much more substantial sums for the encouragement of literature'.[60] When Sargeson told Fairburn in November 1947 that he intended to nominate the poet for a 'literary pension' like his own, Fairburn rejected the offer: 'I don't want to accept any money from the state unless it is under public scrutiny.'[61] Elaborating a few days later, Fairburn wrote to Sargeson: 'By "public scrutiny" I mean that . . . neither Parliament nor the public nor the Literary Fund Committee knows anything about Heenan's disposal of the money in his kitty. . . . I think it's wrong for a Government employee to be dishing out public funds without the public being made aware of what he's doing.'[62] It was with this letter that Fairburn enclosed a copy of his celebrated 'Note on the State Literary Fund':

> Here is a piece of wisdom
> I learnt at my mother's knee:
> The mushroom grows in the open,
> The toadstool under the tree.[63]

This much-quoted quatrain was apparently written at Denis Glover's kitchen table in Sumner during Fairburn's visit to the South Island in October–November 1947, and was published by Glover as a folded quarto sheet.[64] Fairburn had been discussing both the Literary Fund and Heenan's 'secret' fund with Glover, Brasch, Holcroft and others during his visit, and it appears that the title of the quatrain may be a misnomer: Fairburn's correspondence suggests that his real target was the Cultural Fund—and, Sargeson's biographer Michael King speculates, Sargeson's homosexual lifestyle—not the State Literary Fund.[65] As Fairburn wrote to Brasch in December 1947: 'The notion of having Heenan (or anybody else) acting as a secret arbiter of letters— backing horses off the course, so to speak—doesn't appeal to me much. If I were a member of that Committee [the Literary Fund Advisory Committee] I should feel an awful fool.'[66]

* * *

The State Literary Fund may have been agreed to and the funding set aside, but there were still the questions of its purposes, and the membership of the Advisory Committee, for Heenan to resolve. Monte Holcroft had given some thought to these issues in 1943, and considered that a board or committee along the lines of the National Historical Committee 'could be trusted to administer a fund without any hint of political bias'. (This committee, set up to organise the centennial publications, had comprised the professors of history of the four university colleges, two university lecturers known for their radical opinions, three politicians, three journalists and two civil servants, with Eric McCormick as secretary.[67]) Holcroft's ideal committee would have academic and departmental interests represented, and preferably the assistance of a writer 'whose experience would allow him to understand the difficulties of authorship'.[68] The committee's early function might have to be confined to the republication, 'in good but cheap editions', of standard New Zealand works, he thought, but as it began to introduce 'new work of high merit', public interest might open up a wide field of activity—even a journal devoted entirely to the arts might be possible, and become a 'central organ of discussion'. In sum:

> This State enterprise, introducing books of intrinsic value, new and old, would bring hope and encouragement to neglected writers. By fostering the discussion of books among those who read as well as those who write them, it would lift the standards of authorship beyond their present levels

> of artificial or imitative mediocrity, and at the same time it would educate the reading public to new standards in literary taste. All of this could be done at a money cost which, in terms of our national outlay, would be contemptibly small.[69]

Eric McCormick, in an address to the New Zealand Library Association in March 1946, took a more pragmatic view.[70] In an engaging fantasy born out of wide bureaucratic experience, he imagined the kind of committee that would be capable of recognising the 'forerunner of a masterpiece'—a *White Peacock* as well as a *Sons and Lovers*, say. Its members would have to be people of 'great critical discernment, free from stifling preconceptions', preferably practising writers and without strong ties or obligations to any interest. His ideal committee would consist first of Holcroft, as a 'practised critic', then Sargeson, as New Zealand's 'most accomplished' writer of fiction, then poet Eileen Duggan (so that both Wellington and women were represented), and finally, because Christchurch was not yet represented, Allen Curnow, as a 'poet and critic of distinction'. There would be no civil servants, as they have 'a tacit agreement to respect the standards and the opinions of the many'.

Having appointed his committee, McCormick imagined how its members would view *Cliffs of Fall* (Dan Davin's first novel, published in London the year before). Although it had its faults—the committee found it overwritten, with implausible dialogue and a strained and unconvincing dénouement—they nevertheless recognised a 'powerful and original talent which should be encouraged', and granted the novel a subsidy towards publication. There was an immediate outcry against 'this outrageous slur on the character of New Zealand women' and 'this flagrant abuse of taxpayers' money'. McCormick's point was that a book which would have 'excited no comment' if published in the usual way, once it had acquired some sort of official status, 'immediately becomes the concern of any payer of taxes who cares to make it such'. However, because the state had a 'highly developed instinct for avoiding trouble', a state literary board would be 'largely composed of people with standing in the community—of dignitaries who would sit on the committee not by virtue of their talents and capacity but because of the positions they occupied'. The result, McCormick feared, would be 'the encouragement of the safe and second-rate'.

Unlike Holcroft, he concluded that 'it would not be doing a service to serious writers for the state to interfere on their behalf' and could even do them some harm. He did see a role for the state in publishing 'serious and scholarly works'—historical records, collections of manuscripts, bibliographies, scientific manuals and reprints of New Zealand classics (history he would leave to the fledgling New Zealand University Press)—but felt that there was no satisfactory solution for writers of 'imaginative literature', and no solution at all for writers like Fairburn.

Holcroft in turn wondered aloud, in an address to the Dunedin Workers' Educational Association at Otago University, 'Are there likely to be many cases of the kind mentioned by Mr McCormick? And would the possibility of occasional rejections—even if they are rejections to be lamented—destroy the value of the Literary Fund as an incentive to good writing?' Mentioning four 'outstanding books' published in the previous few years—Allen Curnow's *A Book of New Zealand Verse*, Frank Sargeson's collection of stories *A Man and His Wife*, Eric McCormick's *Letters and Art in New Zealand* and Ernst Plischke's *Design and Living*[71]—Holcroft considered these books to be '"safe" in the sense that nobody could challenge the use of State funds for their publication without making himself ridiculous. Yet they are also creative and influential.' Holcroft thought that poetry, essays and a wide range of fiction could be served 'more or less safely' by the State Literary Fund. Mistakes would be made—books which later became famous might be excluded by 'an over-cautious policy'—but a 'deeper stream of writing will come from our publishing houses'. It would be a 'stimulus to authorship if writers know that they are not dependent on one or two over-worked presses in private hands for the publication of good books', and publishers would take risks 'from which they now draw back in alarm'.[72]

Holcroft also addressed McCormick's question of whether grants should be made direct to writers. For a

Denis Glover and Allen Curnow, 1946.
Gordon Ogilvie Collection, ATL, PAColl-7404-2-23-1

writer who 'has succeeded in establishing himself', he thought, '[l]eisure is undoubtedly desirable': 'A man who has shown himself capable of overcoming the difficulties of an unfavourable environment, and who has developed a talent which promises still better work in the future, deserves all the assistance the State can give him.'[73] However, because 'a man's talent is hardened by adversity', he saw no need to provide younger writers with 'abundant leisure', believing that 'The struggle against difficulties is an indispensable part of the creative process, especially in the formative years.'[74]

Fairburn too had doubts about direct state assistance to creative writers. He took a very personal view of the issue, as expressed in the letter to Sargeson that accompanied his squib about the State Literary Fund:

> I'm not entirely against State assistance to writers—but the possible limits of its usefulness are very narrow, and the dangers are huge. I'm willing, in fit circumstances, to enter into a business relationship with the State—to contract to write a book for a certain amount of money. But the State can't (and won't want to) help me in the sort of writing I consider to be of most importance.

Coming to the point of his letter, which was to reject Sargeson's efforts to get him a 'private income' from Heenan's Cultural Fund, Fairburn wrote that his main objection to state patronage was that it 'allows the State to get a foot inside my door. It destroys my right to criticise and oppose the Government.' A state literary pension would be acceptable when 'one is old, and has done one's work', but not 'while one is still down in the arena. The psychological consequences are likely to be bad.'[75]

Writing to Charles Brasch a week later, Fairburn pictured

the kind of writers who would be acceptable to the State Literary Fund:

> The qualifications for patronage at present would appear to be these: (1) Bachelordom; (2) Poverty; (3) Neutrality on all important religious, political and economic issues; (4) Some sort of achievement already; (5) Acceptability to Mr Fraser, Mr Heenan, Mr Lawlor, Sir James Elliott, etcetera . . .
>
> I invite you to imagine what type of man of letters we shall evolve after a few decades of 'conditioning' on the standard set out. Think what a degree of romantic detachment from society—biologically, socially and in every other way—is implied.[76]

While all these opinions were in the air, PEN had wasted no time in trying to set its own stamp on the State Literary Fund. Its executive committee met the same day as its representatives were told by Heenan that the fund was to go ahead, and sent the names of its three nominees to the Advisory Committee off to him the next day. They were: Sir James Elliott, Dr G.H. Scholefield and Professor Ian Gordon, with PEN secretary Pat Lawlor proposed as the committee's secretary. Heenan had asked for PEN's advice on the other four members, and the organisation suggested Ngaio Marsh, J. Hight, J.C. Beaglehole, Alan Mulgan, S. Eichelbaum, Denis Glover and Eric McCormick.[77]

Advising his triumvirate of ministers on the fund in December, Heenan recommended that the PEN nominees be accepted. As for the other four members, he thought that the majority should live in Wellington, and that the people chosen should not be likely to seek help from the fund themselves, 'though this may narrow the scope of selection'. He himself put forward two names: Oliver Duff, formerly his head of Centennial Publications and now the editor of the *Listener*, and Schroder.[78] PEN was also becoming anxious that the Advisory Committee would not be set up in time to avail itself of the funding earmarked for the 1946/47 financial year, and wrote urgently to Fraser himself in mid-March 1947 to ask about progress. Thus reminded, Fraser suggested to Heenan that he might add Dr C.E. Beeby, the Director of Education, and perhaps his own information staff member, O.N. Gillespie, to the list. If it was 'considered desirable to appoint a lady', he recommended Ngaio Marsh, then at the front rank of writers of crime fiction.[79] Heenan accepted Fraser's suggestions, and added that Gillespie (whom Holcroft remembered as being 'well known on the fringe of literary life in New Zealand')[80] would bring 'a different angle of vision to bear from most members' and would be worth appointing, even at the cost of increasing the membership to eight. Heenan's main concern was that the membership as now proposed was confined to residents of Wellington and Christchurch, and he could think of no suitable person in Auckland or Dunedin.[81]

There was presumably some discussion among the politicians, and there may have been a desire to dilute the PEN influence. For the committee as finally advised to PEN in June 1947 had *nine* members plus the secretary[82]—'an amazing Literary Parliament', John A. Lee called it[83]—and contained some surprises from a literary perspective. The three PEN nominees (Elliott, Scholefield, Gordon) were there, plus Lawlor as secretary, and Ngaio Marsh, O.N. Gillespie and J.H.E. Schroder as expected. However, there was also Ormond Wilson, a somewhat patrician Labour MP who was the 'unofficial representative of the literary community in Parliament',[84] Pei Te Hurinui Jones, the Maori scholar, translator and adviser to the King Movement, and Mrs Craig (Mary) Mackenzie, a member of Fraser's circle of unofficial advisers and a close friend and neighbour of

Walter Nash in Lower Hutt.[85] As Brasch noted, only four of the nine members had some professional connection with letters, and only one of these four was a practising writer.[86] They were mostly, as McCormick had predicted, 'people of standing in the community', but their decisions—which were, of course, subjected to close scrutiny—were to prove sometimes surprisingly bold. The Advisory Committee was given no formal brief, and was left to devise its own policies and priorities at its first meeting, in July 1947.

2

A DELICATE AND DIFFICULT TASK 1947–1951

The Literary Fund had been established in a period of new energy after the war: writers were returning to their pens, publishers were refreshed by the enthusiasm and experience of key figures now back at their desks. A pioneering Labour government was again in charge after a narrow election in 1946 and keen to continue and develop the nationalism enhanced by war and by the centenary. Committed to the beneficial effects of state intervention, Peter Fraser's government saw patronage of literature as compensating for the limitations of the small and isolated market and allowing publishers to be bold and writers to thrive. It was a modest investment which, if well managed, might produce widespread enlightenment, understanding and entertainment and the growth of a local literary tradition.

The task confronting the Literary Fund Advisory Committee seemed, on the face of it, to be a simple one. The government had set up a fund of £2000 (about $160,000 in 2015 prices) to foster the growth of New Zealand literature, and the committee's job was to advise the trustees on the best ways to spend the money. The inaugural chairman foresaw no difficulty in doing this.[1] In practice, however, the task proved anything but straightforward. Having no precedent to follow, the committee was feeling its way, and its early patronage seems almost as disorganised as that of the regime that preceded it. The types of literary work to be assisted, the types of activities to be subsidised, the exact roles of the committee and the scope of its power—all these were still to be settled.

At the first meeting of the Literary Fund Advisory Committee, held in Wellington on 10 July 1947, the members discussed at length PEN's extended 1946 proposals and, aware of the niceties of their formal advisory capacity, eventually formulated their own statement of policy for submission to the government.

> The committee is of the opinion that under present conditions many works worthy of publication cannot be produced on a commercial basis and recommends that assistance be given:
>
> 1. By grants towards publishing costs (or by other appropriate means) to enable the publication of such writings as historical works, contemporary creative literature, reprints of New Zealand classics, and Maori literature.
> 2. By grants to New Zealand authors undertaking creative work on approved projects.
> 3. By encouraging the reading and study of New Zealand literature by means of grants towards the cost of publication (or by other appropriate means) of critical books and studies.
> 4. By such other means as the committee with fuller knowledge gained from its experience may deem desirable.[2]

The committee here clearly identified constraints on publication as the fundamental problem which a literary fund could correct. Access was the issue and the perspective seemed to be that of readers rather than of writers. However, this marked 'a sensible and cautious beginning', as Charles Brasch noted in *Landfall.* He hoped that the last clause would enable the committee 'to do something more especially for imaginative work as opposed to the works of scholarship and history which are likely to engage much of [its] attention',[3] taking a dig perhaps at the 'bookmen' of the committee, who were mostly 'not active as creative writers'.[4]

The meeting was chaired initially by Heenan, and all members were present except Ngaio Marsh. It was agreed that each year the committee would elect the chairman. Sir James Elliott was elected unanimously. Heenan outlined the origins of the fund and the general machinery for its work. He noted that literary pensions (such as he was then arranging for Frank Sargeson) would be outside its scope, and stressed that some potential committee members had been eliminated because they might be embarrassed if they became beneficiaries of the fund. Similarly, public servants had been deliberately excluded. The Prime Minister had decided that the committee would have an independent secretary, who would be allowed full freedom of discussion but no vote. Heenan then left the committee to its own devices.

Members decided to hold quarterly meetings of the full committee and set up a subcommittee of Wellington members, which subsequently produced a careful and comprehensive framework for dealing with applications for assistance. Grants to assist publication were expected to benefit both publishers, by reducing the cost and therefore the price of a book, and authors, through increased royalties. Such a grant would 'be prized as a mark of scholarship, literary achievement or substantial promise',[5] a clear, if unconscious, sign that the committee saw itself as defining reputations and establishing a local canon.

Writers, publishers and organisations of authors could all apply for assistance, but the committee would not itself act as a literary agent or publisher. Manuscripts submitted should, where possible, be accompanied by an opinion from a suitable publisher and if possible a reader's report, and all author applications should list qualifications and publication history. The committee, focused so clearly on publication assistance, generally expected to see complete manuscripts rather than proposals. Publishers were required to provide information on the format and style of the book, the likely print run, the selling price, the author's royalty and the amount of subsidy required.

Applications received and formally acknowledged, the next step was assessment and selection. With such a large committee submissions could not be read by each member. In the absence of a publisher's reader's report, manuscripts would be sent to an outside reader unless the committee was unanimously favourable. The names of readers and their reports would be confidential to the committee; the contents of a report would not be communicated as of right to the author, although helpful excerpts could be. Readers' fees would vary from 2 to 5 guineas according to the length and character of a manuscript.

* * *

With nine members the composition of the committee was unsurprisingly rather fluid in these early years, especially as no limit had been set on terms of appointment. Sir James Elliott resigned in April 1948 and Dr Scholefield was unanimously elected chairman in his place. To fill the vacancy PEN quickly nominated George von Zedlitz, the former professor of modern languages at Victoria University College and a well-known literary identity about Wellington, who had already been used as a reader by the committee.

Ngaio Marsh never attended an advisory committee meeting and early in 1949 she advised that she would be leaving for an indefinite period abroad. Wanting another senior writer among its members, the committee proposed to co-opt Monte Holcroft during her absence. However, Holcroft's appointment to the editorship of the *Listener* in April rendered him a public servant, ineligible to serve, according to the government. Instead, the government treated Marsh's advice as a resignation and appointed Joe Heenan, now retired—and knighted—to replace her. From one point of view of course this was an inspired choice; he was not a writer, however, and, although respected by the literary community, he was yet another elderly white male from Wellington.

These moves raised the whole question of public service members. Was Gillespie, as a member of the Prime Minister's information staff, no longer eligible? And what about Schroder, who had just been appointed Assistant Director of the New Zealand Broadcasting Service and was now technically Holcroft's boss? Heenan had to employ a degree of sophistry to get around this. At the first advisory committee meeting he attended as a member, he explained that Gillespie was not regarded as a public servant and that Schroder's position on the committee was unaffected by his new appointment, adding that Holcroft as editor of the *Listener* should be in an 'independent position'. 'If it should happen', he went on, 'that a public servant was required as a member of the Committee an exception might be made.'[6] By this time there was another vacancy on the committee, for George von Zedlitz had died unexpectedly in May 1949. On learning that the government had not accepted its recommendation of Holcroft to replace Marsh, the committee recommended to PEN that it nominate Holcroft to replace von Zedlitz instead.[7] PEN did as asked, but the Labour Government let the nomination languish until it was defeated in the general election.

However, the new Minister of Internal Affairs, W.A. Bodkin, saw 'no necessity for this restriction', the only effect of which was 'to keep good men and women off the Committee'. He had no objection to the appointment of 'suitable Government officers'.[8] Holcroft's nomination was accepted and he took his seat at the committee table in May 1950. Scholefield also recommended fixing the term for which members were appointed: he thought a term of two years would be most appropriate.[9] Bodkin agreed to consider the matter.

It soon became clear that Pat Lawlor was not an efficient secretary and by early 1949 the committee was tiring of his stridently voiced opinions, not to mention his sloppy administration, and had indicated privately to the new Under-Secretary, Arthur Harper, that it wished to relieve the secretary of his duties.[10] In the event, Lawlor lasted another six years in the position, to the general detriment of the Literary Fund's reputation.

* * *

Ironically, after Heenan's cautions about possible conflicts of interest, two of the three applications submitted at the first meeting raised this very issue. Elliott put forward a proposal for a publication subsidy for a new edition, rigorously edited, of the two-volume biography of the early missionary Henry Williams by his son-in-law, Hugh Carleton, published in 1874. Elliott had apparently already done much of the editorial work himself.[11] However there was some disquiet among committee members about the

Pat Lawlor, 1946. First secretary of the Literary Fund Advisory Committee.
Patrick Lawlor Collection, ATL, PAColl-6260-4-03

chairman's approach, which annoyed Elliott, and although the committee finally agreed to 'favourably consider' an application from Reeds, he chose not to stand for re-election as chairman and resigned from the committee.

In a rather similar case Scholefield described the Richmond–Atkinson letters which had come into his hands as Parliamentary Librarian. These covered the personal and political lives of some central figures in mid-nineteenth-century New Zealand politics and were, he believed, 'the finest corpus of historical source material in the country'.[12] The Prime Minister favoured their publication, he said, whereupon Elliott suggested that Scholefield might edit them. Members endorsed this 'major undertaking' and thought the committee should take charge of it, as its very first recommendation for assistance. Scholefield said that he could undertake the editing after he retired from the General Assembly Library the following year, so the question of an honorarium would not arise; however, the committee authorised a preliminary grant of £20 for typing and stationery.

The idea was revived at the end of 1949, when Reeds asked for a massive subsidy of £1000 to publish a two-volume edition of the letters under the editorship of Reeds chairman, A.H. Reed. Protracted negotiations between the committee, Reeds, the Minister and the Richmond family then followed. The committee, and especially Scholefield, were anxious that if left to Reeds, the editorial task would not be up to scholarly scratch and insisted that a state subsidy was essential. However, if it turned down the Reeds' application and then appointed its own chairman to the editorship and took on the publication itself, this could be construed as a form of nepotism and an abuse of power. A special committee, comprising two members of the advisory committee, two from the history department at Victoria University College and a PEN representative, finally recommended that Scholefield be appointed general editor on a salary of £750 a year, with another bright young Victoria graduate, Frances Porter, as part-time assistant editor and researcher. Schroder undertook to prepare a broad direction for the editor and a statement for the Minister, and the advisory committee agreed that he and Heenan (and after his death Gordon) would form a subcommittee to keep a watchful eye on the project.

At the committee's annual general meeting on 26 April 1951, Scholefield was re-elected chairman. At his request, the committee agreed to the proviso that, if the Minister accepted the committee's recommendation that he be appointed editor of the letters, members would consider the election of another chair. Not surprisingly, the minister agreed, and Scholefield duly resigned at the next meeting, on 20 June. Professor Gordon was elected chairman, and remained so for the next twenty-two years.

Scholefield's editing did come under question, but the Richmond–Atkinson papers were eventually published in two volumes by the Government Printer in 1960. The edition was criticised for inexplicable omissions and other editorial failings, in part because Lawlor had failed to pass on instructions drawn up by Schroder and Gordon. The project did not assist the Fund's reputation; and sailed close to the wind in terms of the principle laid down by Heenan that members of the committee should not stand to benefit from its decisions. By 1950 it had been confirmed as an 'essential condition' that members would not be eligible to receive assistance from the Literary Fund.[13] In a small literary community, where the pool of suitable members was tiny anyway, this condition was to prove a perennial problem.

* * *

As the advisory committee's existence became more widely known, the number of applications increased rapidly. In the first nine months (to the end of the 1947/48 financial year), it received 32 manuscripts to consider for grants in aid of publication, 4 applications for reprints and 10 applications for other forms of assistance, including travel and typing grants for writers, 46 applications in all. By the 1950/51 year there were 98 applications, 58 for publication assistance, 6 for reprints and 34 other.

As intended, requests for publication assistance were by far the largest group and required careful sifting. In the first year publication grants for works by well-known authors were deftly despatched. The committee quickly approved publishing grants to the Caxton Press (£300) for reprinting *Discovered Isles*, Monte Holcroft's three essays on New Zealand culture; to Paul's Book Arcade (£175) for a reprint of John Mulgan's 1939 novel *Man Alone*; and to Reeds (£100 conditional on a royalty) for *The Pioneers*, a collection of verse by Professor Arnold Wall. In general it was cautious and only 16 publishing grants (out of approximately 150 applications) were awarded in the first four years.

The committee appeared at times to be floundering on the flood tide of applications. Its original brief, 'to enable the publication of such writings as historical works, contemporary creative literature, reprints of New Zealand classics, and Maori literature', proved to be no filter at all. Applications included war memoirs and letters, family and local history, agriculture, philosophy and religion, along with a range of scientific subjects, mostly in natural history. As early as 1948 the committee was tending to use the test of 'definite literary quality, regardless of the subject matter',[14] but this led it into specialised areas that were well beyond its expertise and also, its critics felt, beyond its brief. But its approach remained conservative like its members. The kinds of books that met with their approval were history, memoir, collected letters, biography, and some poetry; they were largely retrospective in character and did not suggest that a lively inventive creative spirit was abroad.

With fiction, the good novels were still being published overseas and the standard of writing in those submitted to the committee for publication grants was 'disappointingly low'.[15] Not surprisingly in the early years, the committee had to deal with much bottom-drawer material, so one member would make a quick preliminary scan to see whether the work should be reported on, submitted through a publisher, or simply returned. In practice this meant that would-be authors of fiction tended to submit their work directly to the committee. In 1950/51, for instance, only five works of fiction out of about 25 were submitted by publishers: three from Reeds and two from Ron Holloway's Griffin Press (his first applications).

The most controversial work was from Reeds: Brian Sutton-Smith's collection of linked stories, *Our Street*, the first three of which had already appeared in the *School Journal* before the series was stopped after a public outcry. Sutton-Smith's hard-hitting portrayal of the social alienation of boys in a working-class urban environment was based on his experience of teaching at a Wellington school, and intended to provoke discussion of the growing social problem of juvenile delinquency. Agreeing with Holcroft's view that a collection of plain stories should not be 'so heavily freighted with explanation and endorsement'—it had four separate defensive prefaces—the committee agreed to a subsidy of £100 provided these were heavily reduced.[16] These terms were unacceptable to Reeds, who to their credit declined the subsidy and published the book anyway.

The applications were a motley lot. So were the applicants, who were aspiring authors, friends and relations of authors, interested dignitaries as well as publishers. In this situation the well-meaning committee coming across a halfway decent manuscript tended to bend over backwards to assist it. The committee seemed sometimes to be acting as literary agent or as publishing advisor, roles for which it had no mandate and little expertise. Literary Fund intervention in the publishing process, while intended to be helpful, led to some uncomfortable tensions with publishers, took up a lot of time and could be construed as inappropriate.

For example, in response to a request from Mrs Frank Hutchinson seeking publication assistance for her late husband's essays on the natural history and station life of Omatua in Hawke's Bay, *At Omatua's Fireside*, which had received a favourable report from Alan Mulgan, the committee managed to interest Harry Tombs of the Wingfield Press. When he offered to publish 2000 copies at 10s 6d with a royalty of sixpence a copy for a subsidy of £400, the committee granted him £100 provided he paid a royalty of one shilling a copy. Tombs balked, but agreement was reached for a subsidy of £200, with a retail price of 12s 6d.[17] Likewise, following a favourable report on Sheila Crawford's *Sheep and Sheepmen of Canterbury*, the committee urged the proposed print run of 1000 to be increased to 1500; eventually the publishers, Simpson & Williams, agreed to 1250, to keep the type standing for a year in case a reprint was required and to reduce the retail price. Only then was a subsidy of £200 provided.

In mid-1950, as another instance, novice writer Temple Sutherland submitted a semi-fictionalised account of his experiences trying to earn a living off the land after the Great Depression. Schroder was astonished that the manuscript had been turned down by both Whitcombe & Tombs and Reeds. After several attempts to find a publisher, members of the committee finally persuaded Michael Joseph to publish the book, provided a New Zealand publisher took a substantial portion of the edition. Schroder persuaded Whitcombe & Tombs to take 2000 copies, on the understanding that the advisory committee would help it procure from the Reserve Bank sufficient overseas funds to meet the cost (£600). The manuscript was published very successfully in 1952 as *The Golden Bush*, a new edition by Reeds following in 1964. This saga, however laudable, again raises questions about the appropriate role of the committee and the amount of time devoted to a book that did not need a subsidy.

Even more extensive efforts were made on behalf of various works by Reweti T. Kohere, a Maori journalist and Anglican minister. Here at least the advisory committee was within the brief it had set itself, and was able to defend its actions on the grounds of literary and historical merit (though not all were agreed on those merits).[18] Kohere's *The Story of a Maori Chief*, a life of his grandfather, the nineteenth-century Ngati Porou leader Mokena Kohere, received a subsidy of £150 in July 1948, provided the publishers (Reeds, again) revised the text to meet Scholefield's objections.[19] Kohere then applied for a typing grant for *Taumata Korero*, his collection of the best of his own and others' contributions to Maori-language newspapers. In spite of efforts to help Kohere achieve a properly edited and annotated manuscript in Maori, he would not agree to the revisions sought.[20] When he submitted his autobiography for consideration in 1950, however, Kohere did accept the deletion of 'current political references' which Pei Te Hurinui Jones thought were unsuitable.[21] Reeds agreed to publish this work for a subsidy of £250, but rejected Schroder's suggestion of a print run of 2000.[22] In the amount of attention—and funding—the committee devoted to Kohere's work, especially that in Maori, the advisory committee was forty years ahead of its time, but again its efforts were excessive for the fledgling institution.

Mindful of its reputation and anxious to support quality, the committee was reluctant to be seen to assist shoddy work. Reeds applied for assistance in publishing Graham Bagnall and George Petersen's biography of the early missionary and botanist William Colenso. J.C. Beaglehole had worked on the manuscript, and Reeds stated in their application that he thought highly of it, although Beaglehole later told the committee that the text had 'some very good material in it' but needed 'a good deal of revision & pulling together, even rewriting in places'.[23] Other readers were equally critical. The committee recognised both the importance of the work and the need for a significant subsidy to enable its publication, but did not want to support a sub-standard production. In the end they granted £300 while urging the publishers 'to remove if possible grave defects mentioned by the reader'.[24] The book was published for Christmas 1948, at the high price of 30 shillings a copy, with errata listed, and bearing on the half-title page the acknowledgment 'Published with the aid of the New Zealand State Literary Fund'. It was one of the first works to do so, following a suggestion by Schroder.[25]

Reeds' general editorial and production standards were a concern, along with its last-minute applications, as Lawlor made clear to A.W. Reed. Paul's Book Arcade, by contrast, had made three applications in the first year and got them all, receiving the full subsidies sought for the reprint of *Man Alone*, for Helen Wilson's reminiscences, *My First Eighty Years*, and for Jess Whitworth's novel *Otago Interval*. Paul's Book Arcade was also praised for the quality of its submissions. The complaints about Reeds' standards prompted Scholefield's stricture in the committee's second annual report that manuscripts should be submitted as early as possible in the publishing process, because 'Some proposals which we would like to have subsidised have had to be declined owing to defects in style or form . . .'.[26] A.W. Reed, frustrated at repeated rejections, wondered about including a special note, 'Subsidy refused by Lit Fund Comt', on some of them.[27]

Publishers had not proved to be an adequate filter. There was only a handful of major publishers in New Zealand at this time—Reeds, Paul's Book Arcade, Whitcombe & Tombs, and Caxton, with Albion Wright's new Pegasus

Press—and most were careful about the work they chose to submit. The entrepreneurial Reeds, however, seem to have tried out on the committee almost every manuscript they thought had even a remote chance of a grant. Although in its first two years the company received six subsidies towards publication, it had applied for nearly three times that number.[28] In 1950/1 they or their authors submitted a dozen proposals for publication grants, for a total of more than £3000, when the committee's annual budget was just half that sum; only two eventually received grants. Moreover, by weight of numbers Reeds received the bulk of the Literary Fund's publishing grants and the quality of subsidised books reflected well or badly on the fund. Close monitoring of Reeds' editorial standards continued, and concern about their cheap and cramped productions led the advisory committee to set up a subcommittee to approve dummies and specimen pages of all subsidised books before publication.

At the other extreme the committee declined to subsidise expensive limited editions with high production values. One case was D'Arcy Cresswell's verse play *The Forest*, for which a subsidy was given for a run-on 'ordinary' edition. An application from Pegasus Press in 1951 to subsidise a collection of Louis Johnson's poems was declined because it was to be an expensive or 'precious' edition. The committee continued to hold up Denis Glover's Caxton Press books as models of simple, elegant and inexpensive production.

The advisory committee's vetting procedures had also on occasion served it badly. Commissioning reports from outside readers—perhaps a dozen times a year—meant that members sometimes considered a manuscript that none of them had read carefully, reaching a decision based on the views of a single outside reader. As the problems with this emerged, members were increasingly being asked for a supplementary report, which added to their workload and delayed the final decision. Aggrieved authors often complained about a negative decision, either to the committee itself or to the minister, which led to the commissioning of yet more reports, usually to no avail.

The vetting procedures could also lead to an unduly prolonged process of consideration and revision, as with E.H. Audley's *Islands Float at Eleven*. This semi-autobiographical novel of a boy growing up in a colonial gold-mining town was first submitted by the author early in 1949 and passed to Reeds for an opinion. Reeds reported negatively and the manuscript was returned to Audley. The author must have revised the text, for it was resubmitted by Reeds a year later seeking a grant of £200. Three more sets of revisions and four more reports followed before a subsidy of £200 was finally granted in October 1951, nearly three years after Audley's first submission. This protracted revision process should have been the publisher's job, not the committee's.

Holcroft attempted to regulate the situation at the end of 1950 by proposing set terms of reference for all reports. These were intended to produce a clear impression of the work, its quality of writing, and its success or failure, but to refrain from making any recommendation, which should be left to the committee. These guidelines were endorsed by the committee, but it is not clear how closely they were followed.

Care of a different kind was required in dealing with an application from the political maverick John A. Lee. Keen to reprint his earlier literary works, Lee applied in January 1948 for a subsidy of £350 to reprint his 1934 novel *Children of the Poor*. The committee responded cautiously, pointing out the success of this title but then rejecting it.[29] Lee then asked for £400 on the understanding that he would also reprint his *Shining with the Shiner* yarns that year. A carefully worded letter composed by Scholefield, Gordon and Lawlor offered him a grant of £200 for *Children of the Poor* but his application the following year for £300 to reprint *Shiner* was quickly turned down.

The committee received in 1948/9 seven applications for assistance towards reprints, and approved a total of £300 for two: *Children of the Poor* and £100 to Reeds for another regional history, Arthur Gray's account of the Katikati settlement, *An Ulster Plantation*. In 1950/51 £57 was granted to Paul's Book Arcade for a reprint of O.T.J. Alpers's *Cheerful Yesterdays*, the only application of six for reprints assisted that year.

* * *

Direct grants to writers in the early years were either big, bold and controversial or small, tentative and unnoticed. Not much thought had been put into specific types of assistance and the committee reacted here, as elsewhere, on an ad hoc basis.

The largest and most controversial decision of the first year was a grant of £375 to Antony Alpers, son of O.T.J., to assist him in gathering material for a biography of Katherine Mansfield. Alpers had worked as a journalist in the early 1940s in Wellington, where he came to know Heenan. He left for London in 1947 to pursue Mansfield material but when he learnt that the advisory committee would support critical studies of New Zealand literature, he applied for assistance and also wrote to Heenan. According to Heenan in reply, the advisory committee 'stepped itself out' in dealing with his application.[30] At its third meeting Ian Gordon (himself a

Mansfield specialist) was full of praise for Alpers's work—Gordon later said that he knew this was going to be *the* biography of Katherine Mansfield[31]—and proposed a grant of £300 sterling, subject to an interim report after six months and a full report after a year. The committee accepted the proposal, and when Heenan indicated that Alpers was in some need, the recommendation was approved by the trustees within a couple of weeks. Alpers was given a further £200 the following year and £150 in 1950/51.

Direct grants to writers, though earnestly desired by the literary community, were in practice far from easy to dispense. In 1948/9 a travel grant to the poet and critic Allen Curnow caused agitation among committee members and consternation in official circles.

The idea that the Literary Fund might send talented writers overseas to extend their horizons, much as one of Heenan's Special Funds was starting to do in assisting promising young musicians and artists, was being mooted in literary circles by the end of 1947. Fairburn was greatly in favour.[32] He thought the most deserving candidates were Curnow, whose recent *Book of New Zealand Verse 1923–45* was being acclaimed, and the 21-year-old poet James K. Baxter. Brasch agreed, though preferring older writers and advocating Curnow (then in his late thirties) or Holcroft, who was also in favour of the idea (though not for himself).

Glover began organising a round-robin letter to the advisory committee, to be signed by prominent writers and artists, promoting Curnow as 'one of our best-known poets and a critic of outstanding ability'.[33] Brasch, however, favoured talking to individual members privately, urging them to put it to the committee themselves: 'It will thus seem to be their own idea and they are more likely to give it full support.'[34] He had already talked to Ian Gordon, who undertook to sound out his fellow committee members. He got a positive response at the Wellington standing committee meeting on 27 January 1948, and Glover's letter went forward to the general committee meeting on 25 February, signed by himself and Holcroft and asking for a grant to enable Curnow to spend a year in England.

The committee reacted cautiously and requested further investigation. Gordon eventually withdrew his motion and agreed to consult the British Council about possible subsidies. This was the meeting that Heenan joined near the end, and chatting afterwards he found the members 'rather too keen to play on the Curnow business'. He did indicate, however, that he might be able to find £300 sterling in his Cultural Fund to assist. 'Everything depends on the [trustees'] reception of the recommendation.'[35]

On hearing directly from Curnow, a journalist on the *Press* and a colleague of Schroder's, the Wellington committee was in favour of the proposal. Ormond Wilson was especially enthusiastic. Schroder had calculated that the cost of Curnow's visit, including a living allowance, would be about £900 sterling, and thought there would be some contribution from the British Council as well as Heenan's £300.[36] The committee therefore recommended, 'in keeping with the objectives of the Fund', a travel grant of £625 (the equivalent of £500 sterling).[37]

For the first time, however, the trustees openly balked at an advisory committee recommendation. At issue was not only the sheer size of the grant, but the ultimate benefit to the nation. A copy of Curnow's eloquent but diffident letter had been sent with the recommendation, but Fraser doubted whether his project 'was sufficiently sound and clear to warrant support' and objected that 'there was no security for any definite literary return'.[38] Schroder spoke to the Prime Minister personally, pointing out that Fairburn and Holcroft had approved of it and that Curnow was a most deserving candidate: he was young, had much to gain from such literary experiences and would obviously go on writing. Schroder felt that Fraser had been 'thoroughly convinced' by his arguments,[39] and the grant was subsequently approved.

That was not the end of the matter, however. The £300 sterling from the Cultural Fund was now in doubt, with Heenan backing off. He was not in tune with Curnow's work and saw any further assistance as 'wrapping him up in cotton wool'.[40] There was also the feeling that Curnow had already 'done better than any other beneficiary of either the Literary Fund or the Special Funds', and that to give him any more would be unfair.[41] The clash was essentially between two views—the official and the visionary—of what the Literary Fund should be trying to achieve. In the case of Alpers a specific and presumably worthwhile outcome could be identified to justify the grant; but in Curnow's case, simply enlarging a writer's world seemed to the official mind too intangible a goal to justify such a large amount of state support, and one hard to defend politically if necessary (especially since the Special Funds were under attack in Parliament and the press at the time).

After 'long botheration', Schroder had got the British Council to pay for Curnow's fares, and had persuaded his *Press* proprietors to chip in £75. Curnow went to England as planned, but on arrival in April 1949 he had just £120 to carry him through the next year. The British Council had only £50 left in its annual budget for the entire Commonwealth, but still slipped him £30, chiefly to attend the Shakespeare season at Stratford-upon-Avon. Its staff also suggested that he make a personal approach to Fraser, briefly in London for the Commonwealth Prime Ministers' Conference. Curnow managed to see Fraser and outlined a programme that could be carried out only if his resources were increased. Fraser thought £120 'totally inadequate' and expressed 'horror' that Curnow should be expected 'to eke out his grant from the ink-pot'. He said he would take up the matter with Internal Affairs on his return.[42] A Cultural Fund grant of £250 was eventually approved in July. Heenan wrote rather pointedly to Curnow: 'We were all delighted that you will have opportunity, free of any real worries about the means of living, to pursue your studies, shall I call them, in England . . .'[43]

Nevertheless, Curnow was forced to work on the *News Chronicle* from June to October. Yet he did become familiar with significant figures on the English poetry scene—notably Dylan Thomas, Louis MacNeice and John Lehmann—and, through his broadcasts, with the literary-journalistic ethos of the BBC's Third Programme. In the United States he made long-standing literary friendships and connections. He also saw a great deal of theatre. According to his biographer, Terry Sturm, Curnow's 'whole perspective on "the world" was deeply affected by his encounter with the big city, cosmopolitan cultures of London and New York, and his personal sense of identity was also deeply affected by his visits to ancestral Norfolk and Cornwall'. Sturm considers that probably about ten poems came immediately out of the trip, but 'in a broader sense his *Poems 1949–1957* is thoroughly imbued with the experience of travelling overseas'. The vision of Schroder and other members of the advisory committee was indeed fulfilled: Curnow's trip, according to Sturm, marked 'the beginning of that long engagement with the international culture which is so central to his major later achievement'.[44]

* * *

If assistance to a poet towards future achievement was challenged, the committee had so far done little to assist promising writers of fiction, as Heenan had noted. However a modest grant of £100 to David Ballantyne to continue work on his trilogy of novels led to the bitterest public attack on the Literary Fund yet.[45] When the 23-year-old journalist asked in October 1947 for a grant so that he could concentrate exclusively on his fiction, if only for a few months, he had already written the first two volumes which the committee wanted to see before deciding.

Lawlor's administrative incompetence led to a full six months' delay between application and reader's report,[46] but new member Professor von Zedlitz reported favourably, and a grant of £100 was recommended. However, when the text, which had now been accepted by an American publisher as *The Cunninghams*, was read by Lawlor, a devout Catholic, he was shocked to the core and did his best to scupper the grant. He certainly delayed it further, thus infuriating Ballantyne, who had resigned from his job to write the last novel of the sequence. This was not the last time that sexual content would cause problems to the committee, but von Zedlitz and Scholefield in the chair handled it wisely and eventually Ballantyne received his cheque.[47] Lectured by Lawlor, he had agreed to put 'nothing pornographic' in the new novel, but he took his revenge.

Ballantyne finally gave vent to his frustration and humiliation in an article that his American publisher had suggested he write for the *New York Times*. It appeared in the *New York Times Book Review* of 12 June 1949 under the heading 'New Zealand Letter', and devoted the first half to a sarcastic critique of the Literary Fund. He then briefly recounted his own experience with the committee, noting that he was the only fiction writer to have received a grant to date. His bitterness is clear:

> This is not the place to argue the matter of State patronage of literature, but one or two queries are pertinent. What sort of literature is it that must not be what the committee calls 'pornographic' (no definition of the word supplied by the committee)? What sort of literature is it that must not displease an extremely vocal sectarian element on the committee? Why should a writer have to submit his work for inspection by a committee of people whose qualifications for authority are for the most part political in nature?[48]

Scholefield had the article circulated to members, but there is no record in the minutes of any discussion of it. Gillespie replied personally to Ballantyne[49] and Scholefield publicly defended his committee and its decisions. Ballantyne's comments were 'wildly inaccurate', he said in a press statement, concluding:

> The Advisory Committee is not concerned with what a man writes; its main interest is to see some promise that he can or will be able to write, and to ensure that anything published with the aid of the fund shall be presented in good literary and typographical style. Also it endeavours to see that reasonable royalties are paid to the authors concerned.[50]

Wellington's *Evening Post* summed up the competing forces at work on the committee in a thoughtful editorial on literary patronage a few days later:

> . . . the task of the advisory committee appointed to administer the fund is both delicate and difficult. It must be obvious that it is impossible to satisfy everybody, whether in the role of writer or that of watchdog of the public interest.[51]

Internal Affairs, stung by the publicity, put out a press statement which offered only a summary of the committee's activities and a list of grants made, ending with a rather muted expression of confidence by the minister—'the New Zealand Literary Fund is making an effective contribution towards a New Zealand literature'– and a veiled attack on Ballantyne's article.[52]

Predictably, more condemnatory letters followed in the press, many from writers whose work had been rejected by the committee or who had failed to obtain a publisher's recommendation. The main complaints were the speculative grants to Alpers and Curnow, and the lack of assistance for new fiction—the only new novel that had been supported by the committee in its first two years was Whitworth's *Otago Interval*. An anonymous correspondent to Labour's own daily, the *Southern Cross*, did not mince words:

> No amount of self-congratulation by the advisory committee . . . can conceal the fact that most of the long list of publications made possible by the use of public money is absolutely valueless when considered as literature. . . .
>
> And worst of all, one writer has been paid heavily to go overseas and write a book about a real writer and one who has already been more than adequately covered.
>
> The intention of the fund was worthy, but the practice has proved faulty. Books which would never earn their own keep, are now turned out to keep publishers solvent at the State expense.[53]

Landfall also questioned the committee's decisions and concluded perceptively:

> . . . if successive governments are to maintain the Fund, the Committee must win a reputation for good judgment, and be able to point to a growing list of valuable books which might not have been published without it, and to serious writers

> whose work has benefited. Otherwise it will be axed at the first sign of a 'recession'; and not without reason.[54]

From the perspective of a later age the grants to Alpers, Curnow and Ballantyne seem entirely justified and among the most far-sighted and courageous of the committee's early decisions. The £625 given to Curnow was by far the largest grant made in the early years, though it was exceeded by the total of £725 given to Alpers. No grant of this size was made for many years.[55] However, the committee now showed some nervousness. In 1949/50 it granted £300 to the poet and memoirist D'Arcy Cresswell, fencing it with conditions, though no work eventually emerged. A further 'maintenance' grant of £100 the same year was given to a successful Reeds author, Peter Newton, whose *Wayleggo* (1947), his unsophisticated reminiscences of high-country mustering, had already been reprinted three times. The committee simply checked he was not throwing in his day job.

The two new maintenance grants made in 1950/51 (in addition to the third grant to Alpers) have a similar ad hoc quality. One was £200 to Ruth Park to complete *One-A-Pecker, Two-A-Pecker*, today considered one of the most accomplished historical novels set on the New Zealand goldfields.[56] Park, a New Zealander married to an Australian, was living and writing in Sydney, where she had published two successful novels. The other major grant was to G.R. (Bob) Gilbert, whose name is little known today, although he had a certain reputation in the 1940s as one of the more promising writers of the 'Sargeson school'. The committee was presumably relying on this in approving immediately a grant of £300, to be paid in weekly, fortnightly or monthly instalments as he preferred.[57] He continued to write prolifically but his later work remains unpublished.

By contrast, Maurice Duggan, today ranked with Mansfield and Sargeson as one of New Zealand's greatest exponents of short fiction,[58] had applied shortly afterwards for a grant to further his literary work. He did not get one, although he had already published ten short stories, including the 'startlingly original' 'Six Place Names and a Girl', which appeared in *Landfall* in March 1949 and drew many admirers, including the young Janet Frame.[59] Duggan, now in England, was greatly irritated by the unprofessional and confusing manner in which Lawlor handled his application and Sargeson complained to the committee.

For a committee that wanted to support promising creative writing, Duggan's case ought to have presented an ideal opportunity. Why was it not taken up? It is not clear from the record whether Gordon's report (no copy of which appears to have survived) recommended rejection or whether, as Sargeson thought, Lawlor failed to present his case properly.

* * *

The growing number of applications seeking help for literary journals, or 'little magazines', and annuals by 1951 forced the committee to devise a policy for subsidising periodicals, since that too had not formed part of its original aims. Ormond Wilson had asked James Bertram in September 1947 whether the new literary quarterly *Landfall* would be interested in a Literary Fund subsidy, but its editor, Charles Brasch, was concerned that state aid might compromise his editorial freedom. He preferred to let the magazine try to stand on its own feet first. If it later got into difficulties, such help could be welcome.[60]

Early in 1951 Wilson reported to the committee that

he had heard *Landfall* needed financial help. While a formal application might be made later, he suggested that the chairman and secretary be given the power to act in the meantime. The committee agreed to this and, seeing a new way to support creative writing, authorised a grant of £100 to be used for the payment of contributors. After the application was received, a further £100 was granted towards publishing costs. Commenting on this, the independent monthly *National Review* (itself then in its final year) cogently summed up the public perception of the Literary Fund by this time, for once without the polemic of an aggrieved participant:

> Although the State Literary Fund has, in the opinion of most unbiased observers, been put to controversial uses in its time, there will be—or should be—universal approval of its recent decision to make a grant to 'Landfall' . . . This money . . . although a small sum in itself, will make its effect felt over a fairly broad area—a result which commends itself in comparison with large grants to individuals.[61]

Teacher Frank Combs in mid-1949 wrote to the government proposing that it should publish a national literary periodical itself. After hearing reports from Gillespie and Gordon, the committee agreed that it was 'a bad thing' for the state to be directly involved in publishing such a journal, but that, if a group of people submitted a concrete proposal, a grant might be possible.[62] At the same meeting, Wilson produced an application for a grant from the organising committee of *Hilltop*, a new journal put out by the Literary Society of Victoria University College under the editorship of J.M. Thomson. The organisers wanted £100 to assist the magazine and its contributors, who included such up-and-coming literary figures as David Ballantyne, James K.

Baxter, Alistair Campbell, Louis Johnson, W.H. Oliver and Kendrick Smithyman. The general committee was initially in favour of the grant, but the Wellington committee deferred a decision until it had seen whether later issues of the magazine justified assistance. *Hilltop* died after the third issue.

More successful was an application for a subsidy to publish the *Yearbook of the Arts in New Zealand.* Established in 1945, this was the successor to the quarterly *Art in New Zealand*, founded in 1928 by the enterprising Harry H. Tombs. The *Yearbook* included some poetry under the associate editorship of Fairburn, and early in 1950 Tombs applied to the advisory committee for an annual grant of £250. They agreed to the subsidy sought, provided that it was used for editorial costs and contributors' fees, and that the retail price for the journal be not more than 30 shillings. Tombs later asked whether the subsidy could be increased to £350; it could not, but he was given that amount the following year—which proved, however, to be the *Yearbook*'s last.

Reeds did their best to ensure that their proposal for a *Poetry Yearbook*, an idea from the 27-year-old Louis Johnson, would receive sufficient sponsorship from the fund to make it viable. They first approached the advisory committee in February 1951 to seek approval in principle, and later supplied some sample poems and other details. Because of the continuing difficulties with Reeds, the advisory committee set up a special subcommittee to deal with the proposal, and authorised a preliminary grant of £50 for publishing costs and £100 for contributors, provided the retail price was within reach of the average buyer. In due course the grant to contributors was increased to £150, of which the editor would receive £50, and Ian Gordon would advise the publishers on the allocation of remuneration to contributors. The first *Poetry Yearbook* appeared in 1951, and the next year a new advisory committee increased the overall grant to £225 to meet increased production costs, although Ian Gordon was asked to keep an eye on Louis Johnson's editing, which was being criticised as lacking critical standards in the selection.[63] Reeds gave the *Yearbook* away after its third year, but Johnson persuaded Pegasus to take it over. Pegasus published it, always with the aid of a substantial Literary Fund grant, until 1964.

It was, however, the applications for assistance from little magazines, whose editorial standards and staying power were harder to assess, that galvanised the advisory committee into setting out a general policy for all periodicals. The Auckland-based monthly review *Here & Now* applied for a subsidy but was turned down at the end of 1950; so, in April 1951, was *Arachne*, the successor to *Hilltop*. By now the committee could see both a trend developing and a need for procedures to deal with it. A periodicals subcommittee (Gordon, Wilson and Holcroft) was set up to produce a statement setting out the basis on which all such applications would be considered.

In its preamble, the statement recognised that such assistance was necessarily indiscriminate, as the advisory committee could not interfere with the work of an editor, to whom it in a sense delegated the 'responsibility which it must normally take on itself'. To protect the committee from a deluge of applications, the preamble noted that it was not the function of a state fund to subsidise 'every literary group which springs into existence' nor to 'underwrite every literary venture, however worthy'. The committee wanted to encourage periodicals that provided scope for good writing, however, and recognised that no such journal would pay its way, so that Literary Fund assistance might be crucial in securing 'some degree of permanence for a journal of merit'. The criteria to be used in assessing applications were:

1. That the periodical has consistently published good writing.
2. That it has continued independently of State subsidy to prove that it has a function and a place in the New Zealand literary field.
3. That its editorial policy is stable enough to suggest that its standards will be maintained.
4. That its contributors include a representative section of New Zealand writers and do not merely belong to a small coterie.
5. That its financial losses are neither, through bad management or extravagant methods, unnecessarily large, nor yet so small that private resources could reasonably be expected to continue to meet them.
6. That a part at least of any grant from the Literary Fund be expended in payments, or increased payments, to contributors.
7. That while grants can be recommended for one year only, subsidies to periodicals should as a matter of policy be made only to those journals which the Committee expects will merit an annual grant over a period of years.[64]

These careful criteria effectively ruled out student magazines and ruled in only established or wider-ranging periodicals with some other source of financial backing, such as *Landfall* and the *Poetry Yearbook*.

* * *

The committee had begun to venture from time to time into literary matters beyond applications for grants. In a rare instance of an official intervention and possibly to mollify Lawlor over the support of Curnow, Fraser indicated that he wished the committee to consider publishing in an attractive format a collected edition of the poems of Eileen Duggan.[65] Lawlor made discreet enquiries and discovered that Duggan's work was 'tied up in agreements' with her publishers, Allen & Unwin in London, who subsequently did produce a mature selection, *More Poems* (1951). In later publicity the committee congratulated itself on taking an 'active interest in promoting publication for New Zealand authors outside of the Dominion'.[66]

The committee made recommendations on other literary matters. When the Caxton Press needed a new building with the growth of its printing and publishing business by the late 1940s, it found that building permits were very hard to obtain after the war. With the aid of both Heenan, who had an interest in typography, and the advisory committee, the building permit was finally approved by a Cabinet subcommittee. Heenan attributed this to the 'very strong recommendation' from the committee.[67]

Requests for assistance from organisations rather than individuals were also appearing, and the committee had no processes for dealing with them. A last-minute application to assist the Canterbury Centennial Writers' Conference in May 1951 was quickly granted £75. However, the committee had a long spat with the New Zealand Journalists' Association over sponsorship of a new literary award; they awarded £25 but argued interminably about the conditions of the award. In the end the journalists gave up and returned the grant.

Another project was first suggested by the author O.E. Middleton, who asked about the problem of small payments to New Zealand writers for creative work.[68] In referring the letter to PEN, members suggested that a pamphlet to advise New Zealand writers on all aspects of their work could be produced by the writers' organisation with the aid of a Literary Fund subsidy and distributed free. After the usual hassles with Reeds over cost and embarrassment over the poor quality of the text (tidied up by members of the committee), the handbook appeared at the end of 1952 and quickly sold out.

* * *

Not surprisingly, the decisions of the newly established committee were the subject of intense scrutiny by the literary community and the general public. When the first announcement was finally made in February 1948 and the grant to Alpers headed the list, it was widely criticised, as was the absence of any grants to creative writers. The weekly newspaper *Truth*, then a force in the land, wrote: 'It would have been more to the point if the committee helped the young writers of 1948 to achieve recognition by producing original work of their own composition.'[69] Several correspondents to the *Dominion* complained along the same lines.[70] The most forthright critic was John A. Lee in his *Fortnightly*, which, under the headline 'Literary Fund Aids Undertakers and Tombstone Makers', noted that the fund was supporting the biography of a 'deceased authoress' and the letters of 'dead pioneers, statesmen, etc.'. Lee asked: 'Would this committee turn down a Henry Lawson during his lifetime and publish an edition de luxe of his work after a quarter of a century? Anything so living as a creative book about New Zealand will have to run the gauntlet of the tombstone makers. The Literary Committee has got off to a DEADLY start.'[71] However, Heenan told the committee at the end of its first annual general meeting in April 1948 that he wanted it to continue to expand its work and that, even if it overspent the allocation, the annual grant could probably be increased, adding that he would 'like to see the committee showing encouragement to younger writers whose books had not yet been published'.[72]

Attempts to meet this need were to be a constant theme in the Fund's history. In February 1951 for example, an article headed 'Fiction and the Literary Fund' appeared in the Auckland-based but nationally distributed *Weekly News*.[73] It was written under the pen-name 'Analyst', which 'conceals the identity of a well-known and industrious New Zealand short story writer', presumably Frank Sargeson. The article attacked the Literary Fund both for its lack of support for publishing new fiction and for its support for publishing 'little local histories and specialised works on the Maoris', which the writer considered would have been published in any case; the fund was therefore not so much subsidising publishers, he said, as making them a 'straight-out gift'.

> This is a farcical state of affairs. The shaping of our literary future is being left to the working of commercial motives. A publisher would have to be a mighty altruist to ignore the fact that whereas a local factual work has no outside competition, a work of fiction has to compete, more or less, with the creative genius of all the world. To persuade him further the State Fund now subsidises him for preferring the safe type of book. . . .

Arguing that 'the creative fiction writer is the one most worthy of encouragement', 'Analyst' drew on his own experience in trying to get his stories published:

> One publisher to whom I submitted a batch of published stories declared himself 'highly impressed,' but that was not sufficient to make him consider publication with the help of any subsidy the Literary Fund was able to provide.

The article suggested that the Literary Fund 'earmark a portion of its annual £2000 endowment to enter the publishing field itself, issuing a new local novel once in two years', to be chosen by a competition organised by the fund. Scholefield replied blandly, mentioning the publication grant given in 1948/9 to Jess Whitworth's novel, *Otago Interval*, and saying that the committee was always glad to receive suggestions, particularly to assist creative writers.[74]

An attempt to promote the work of the advisory committee was made in response to the criticisms by 'Analyst', and timed to appear when many of New Zealand's writers and literary critics would be assembling in Christchurch for the May 1951 Writers' Conference, organised by Canterbury University College as a belated part of the province's centennial celebrations. It was a journalistically questionable article in the *New Zealand Listener*, of which Holcroft was editor and supposedly independent. Although unsigned, the article was suggested and written by Holcroft himself, and was intended to serve as both a complete record of the fund's activities and a guide for applicants.[75] The first half gave an extensive and detailed account, dense with statistics taken from the committee's annual reports. The second half purported to be the record of answers given by the Minister of Internal Affairs to questions from the *Listener*, whereas in fact the questions had been prepared by Holcroft and the answers by Scholefield, Gordon and Lawlor; the minister's only contribution was to approve the final article. In essence a justification of the committee's operations to date, it was not the impartial account that its presentation implied.[76]

If the advisory committee thought that criticism of its activities at the writers' conference had thus been forestalled, it was mistaken. Scholefield attended as the committee's chairman, even though he was unlikely to be in office much longer; Gillespie also attended. Lawlor was there too, but not as the committee's secretary; he was a late ring-in and chose to talk about 'the little reviews'. The conference was held during the waterfront dispute of 1951, which became a showdown between the farmer-dominated National Government and the militant trade unions, and early in his address Lawlor expressed support for both the political suppression of the left-wing journal *Tomorrow* in 1940 and the violent actions of the police in suppressing a street protest by watersiders in Wellington the previous week.[77] To an audience that was generally liberal, this was incendiary stuff.

The anger it provoked was minor compared with the outbursts that greeted his remarks about the little reviews, especially *Landfall*, which had just been given a grant of £200. Lawlor claimed that '*Landfall* has little or no regard for spiritual values or interest in home or family life', at which 'a number of the younger writers laughed in open derision'. A further prong of his attack was *Landfall*'s 'exclusiveness': 'I have more than a suspicion that because of literary snobbishness or literary cliqueism, or both, the contributors' columns of *Landfall* are open only to a privileged few'. Moreover, because of its influence, Lawlor seemed to imply that the magazine should reconsider its 'modernist' views:

> We are reaping a whirlwind of trouble from the disordered writing of the days we live in. A literary clique is endeavouring to corner the market of the printed word, and they are getting away with it. A public with a comic-strip mind is unable to see the shallowness of the unliterary jargon flourished before it by the new school . . . airing their jangled 'isms' and pitiful polemics. A favoured few find their way into the clique of new writers and so the trouble grows.[78]

At the conclusion of his address, 'half a dozen young New Zealand writers were on their feet with flashing eyes and barbed tongues,' Lawlor wrote. 'One referred to the lecture as "a disgusting attack on the younger writers".' Scholefield was shocked to find that, because Lawlor dealt with all public inquiries to the advisory committee, he represented its public face, and that younger writers suspected the entire committee held such reactionary views.[79] He therefore suggested to the organisers that they devote a special session to the Literary Fund.

This was conducted by Scholefield (74, and about to vacate the chair) and Gillespie (68), hardly a picture of youthful dynamism or empathy with younger writers. After some soothing remarks to suggest the careful attention the committee gave to the interests of writers, trouble began when Scholefield invited suggestions for other ways to use the Literary Fund for their benefit. 'This provoked a rather outspoken attack on the committee,' he later reported. Dunedin novelist C.R. Allen put it more explicitly when he wrote that 'wild young poets flew at the throats' of the hapless Scholefield and Gillespie.[80] Their leader was poet Louis Johnson, who declared that young writers were not able to gain access to the committee or to have their cases put fairly before it, obviously referring to Lawlor. The chairman later found out that this referred to a single instance, the refusal to give Maurice Duggan a maintenance grant.[81]

Johnson argued that at least one young writer should sit on the advisory committee, and moved that the active writers present should meet to form an informal body to function as a writers' guild, for the avowed purposes of seeking the appointment of liaison officers to sit on the committee, as the PEN nominees did. A clear division was thus made between older and younger writers, a division confirmed by the close vote, 17 to 15.[82] However in later discussions the younger writers were persuaded that membership of PEN might be more effective, as it would make the organisation more representative and active.[83] Reporting to Duggan on the conference, Sargeson said that the idea of a writers' union was abandoned 'in favour of all going into PEN en bloc in order to outvote the stuffies and put the liaison between PEN and the SLF on a better footing . . .' Sargeson also gleefully claimed that Lawlor had been 'shaken right to his bottom, and Scholefield had such a revelation that I hear he is resigning his chairmanship . . .'.[84] This gave rise to the enduring myth that Scholefield resigned because of the strong criticism of the Literary Fund he faced at the conference.[85] The record shows that he in fact resigned because the minister had endorsed his appointment as editor of the Richmond–Atkinson letters, and that he was following through on his own previously expressed wish.[86]

Some older writers expressed unease during the session on the Literary Fund about the implications of accepting help from the state. However the Australian critic and novelist Vance Palmer, who chaired the Commonwealth Literary Fund's advisory committee, pointed out the difficulties the Australian fund, in contrast to the New Zealand one, had had with political members of the advisory committee; with both the government and the opposition officially represented, at times they had reached a deadlock about grants. He also noted that the Australian fund granted literary scholarships of £400 a year, and expected the recipients to work fulltime on their projects for that year. This prompted the suggestion (not to be taken up by the Literary Fund for another 30 years) that, instead of making direct grants to publishers, the committee could offer them guarantees against loss, thus freeing up funds for

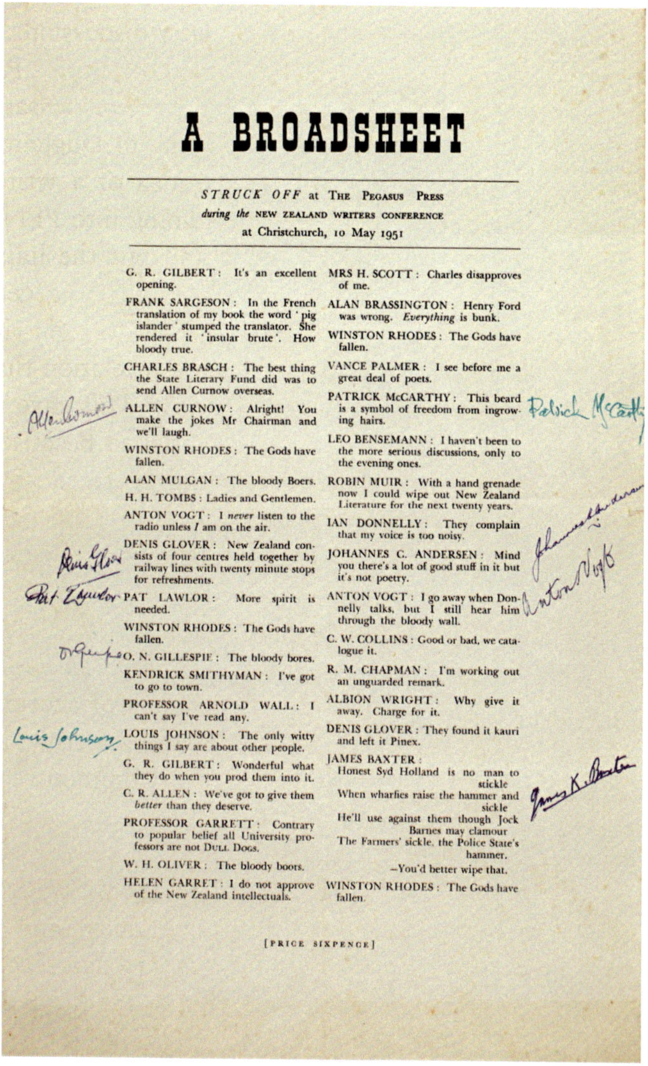

A BROADSHEET

STRUCK OFF at The Pegasus Press
during the NEW ZEALAND WRITERS CONFERENCE
at Christchurch, 10 May 1951

G. R. GILBERT: It's an excellent opening.

FRANK SARGESON: In the French translation of my book the word 'pig islander' stumped the translator. She rendered it 'insular brute'. How bloody true.

CHARLES BRASCH: The best thing the State Literary Fund did was to send Allen Curnow overseas.

ALLEN CURNOW: Alright! You make the jokes Mr Chairman and we'll laugh.

WINSTON RHODES: The Gods have fallen.

ALAN MULGAN: The bloody Boers.

H. H. TOMBS: Ladies and Gentlemen.

ANTON VOGT: I *never* listen to the radio unless *I* am on the air.

DENIS GLOVER: New Zealand consists of four centres held together by railway lines with twenty minute stops for refreshments.

PAT LAWLOR: More spirit is needed.

WINSTON RHODES: The Gods have fallen.

O. N. GILLESPIE: The bloody bores.

KENDRICK SMITHYMAN: I've got to go to town.

PROFESSOR ARNOLD WALL: I can't say I've read any.

LOUIS JOHNSON: The only witty things I say are about other people.

G. R. GILBERT: Wonderful what they do when you prod them into it.

C. R. ALLEN: We've got to give them *better* than they deserve.

PROFESSOR GARRETT: Contrary to popular belief all University professors are not Dull Dogs.

W. H. OLIVER: The bloody boors.

HELEN GARRET: I do not approve of the New Zealand intellectuals.

MRS H. SCOTT: Charles disapproves of me.

ALAN BRASSINGTON: Henry Ford was wrong. *Everything* is bunk.

WINSTON RHODES: The Gods have fallen.

VANCE PALMER: I see before me a great deal of poets.

PATRICK McCARTHY: This beard is a symbol of freedom from ingrowing hairs.

LEO BENSEMANN: I haven't been to the more serious discussions, only to the evening ones.

ROBIN MUIR: With a hand grenade now I could wipe out New Zealand Literature for the next twenty years.

IAN DONNELLY: They complain that my voice is too noisy.

JOHANNES C. ANDERSEN: Mind you there's a lot of good stuff in it but it's not poetry.

ANTON VOGT: I go away when Donnelly talks, but I still hear him through the bloody wall.

C. W. COLLINS: Good or bad, we catalogue it.

R. M. CHAPMAN: I'm working out an unguarded remark.

ALBION WRIGHT: Why give it away. Charge for it.

DENIS GLOVER: They found it kauri and left it Pinex.

JAMES BAXTER:
Honest Syd Holland is no man to stickle
When wharfies raise the hammer and sickle
He'll use against them though Jock Barnes may clamour
The Farmers' sickle, the Police State's hammer.
—You'd better wipe that.

WINSTON RHODES: The Gods have fallen.

[PRICE SIXPENCE]

A broadsheet 'struck off at the Pegasus Press during the New Zealand Writers Conference at Christchurch, 10 May 1951'. Each participant on the list is distinguished by a witty comment; some have signed.

Patrick Lawlor Collection, ATL, f-80-063-2-1

such scholarships. Scholefield pointed out that two grants (presumably to Alpers and Curnow) had already been made to writers, and for larger sums, but the conference eagerly passed a second resolution calling for the establishment of one or more annual scholarships in letters and asking the government to provide extra money for them.[87]

One outcome of the conference was a reconsideration of an earlier suggestion that there should be some 'automatic and regular review of our membership'[88] and Ormond Wilson then proposed a term of three years.[89] Ian Gordon as the new chairman raised the matter with the Minister of Internal Affairs. Another sequel was an extraordinary attack on the Literary Fund in the weekly newspaper *Truth*. An editorial headed 'Pampered Literary Pets' argued that, 'before State paternalism reached its present heights', writers who had something worthwhile to say 'came up the hard way—and their literary work was accordingly strengthened by experience and struggle. Nowadays, they want a cash guarantee before they start work. Apparently they have no confidence either in themselves or their message.' The editorial homed in, predictably, on the grants to Alpers and Curnow and, less predictably, on the £200 granted to publish Sheila Crawford's *Sheep and Sheepmen of Canterbury*, asking why 'the sheepmen of Canterbury cannot be approached to subsidise sheep farming publicity instead of making it a charge on the public purse?' The grant to D'Arcy Cresswell also drew fire. After arguing along Fairburn's lines—'When writers are dependent on the State for sustenance there is an indirect pressure on them to interpret life in terms acceptable to whatever Government is in power at the time', the editorial concluded:

> The entire set-up of subsidising writers is wrong except in rare cases of extreme hardship, particularly where a man

> or woman displays exceptional promise and is incapable of performing any other work because of physical limitations.
>
> . . . Continuing the ill-conceived practice of petting and pampering writers is, in actual fact, turning them into State servants in disguise.[90]

It is hard to know what prompted such an attack. Was it the attitude of entitlement, that the literary community had a right to state support and could dictate its terms, so strongly expressed by the younger writers at the Christchurch conference? Was it a response to the New Zealand Journalists' Association's unhappy experience with its award? Whatever its motivation, *Truth* claimed the following week that many people had expressed support for its views. The paper then gave a lot of space to one 'inquirer', who implied that there was something fishy in Scholefield's appointment as editor of the Richmond–Atkinson letters and in the payment of fees to members of the committee for readers' reports. In both cases there was a strong suggestion of scandal in the unethical use of taxpayer funds by insiders. There was also the claim that an author, interviewed by the committee about the criticisms made by an outside reviewer, found 'to his astonishment' that not one member of the committee had read his manuscript and that they were discussing not his work but the opinions of the reviewer, whose name was not revealed.[91]

Ian Gordon took an imperious approach in his correction, approved by the Minister and published in *Truth* the following week. He set out a brief version of the events leading to Scholefield's appointment as editor of the Richmond–Atkinson letters, stressing the independence of the special committee that recommended his appointment and ignoring the lack of public advertising of the position or its terms. He also pointed out that committee members received no payment for their work and read dozens of manuscripts without fee. He then explained how the system of commissioning detailed written reports worked, and said that for these a total of £125 had been paid to non-committee members and £92 to members in the five years of the fund's existence, making an average of £2 a year to each member. This average figure was misleading: the committee had in fact been reviewing manuscripts for less than four years, and the figure included the non-participant Ngaio Marsh in the head count. And in one year alone one committee member (Holcroft in 1950/51, his first year on the committee) had written five reports for a total of £15 15s, a sixth of the entire sum paid to members.

Gordon was on even shakier ground in claiming that the allegation about the interviewed author was 'hearsay evidence [that] has never been regarded as having any validity' and had 'no basis of fact. Every manuscript submitted is carefully scrutinised by at least one member of the committee.'[92] There is only one mention in the relevant minutes that an author was interviewed by the committee, and that was the journalist Frank Simpson. Gordon had looked at his *Chatham Exiles* manuscript when it first arrived and passed it on to Holcroft (then still a freelance writer and not a committee member) for a detailed report. When the Wellington committee discussed this manuscript with Simpson, Gordon was not present, and this may have given rise to both *Truth*'s allegation and the vehemence of Gordon's denial (which *Truth* described as 'varbiage [sic].'[93] However, there are many instances where the minutes provide no indication that any member of the committee had 'carefully scrutinised' a manuscript before it was rejected.

* * *

After a spate of letters to the editor followed it was time for the government to act. Arthur Harper (now styled Secretary of Internal Affairs) briefed his Minister on the 'sharp criticisms' of the advisory committee's 'principles and methods', and suggested that he take up the committee's own recommendations for change of personnel. They agreed that all current members would be retired at the end of that month, August 1951.[94] Before deciding on who should continue and who should be replaced (and by whom) for a fixed three-year term, the government needed to know whom PEN would recommend. The writers' organisation had been undergoing its own upheavals soon after the writers' conference, and 'the stuffies' only just managed to hang on at the annual general meeting, at which John Reece Cole, Charles Brasch, Rex Fairburn and Allen Curnow were all elected to the executive for the first time. Harper took discreet soundings from Gordon, whom the government wanted to continue as chairman and would appoint as its own representative if PEN did not. The three PEN nominees were again Gordon and Holcroft—and, in a lost opportunity to introduce younger blood, the 70-year-old Alan Mulgan.

With the PEN nominees settled, Bodkin asked his colleague Ron Algie, the Minister of Education and the nearest thing to an intellectual in the National Cabinet, for advice on whom the government should appoint. Obviously, the two openly Labour appointees, Mary Mackenzie and Ormond Wilson, would go, and Pei Te Hurinui Jones had long ago ceased to attend meetings. John Schroder was felt to be 'sound', but there was still a question mark over Gillespie; in the end both were reappointed. Sir Joseph Heenan died suddenly in October, before his reappointment could be decided. Lawlor continued as secretary.

The new National appointees were generally of a more conservative stripe, and none was a professional writer. They were Matthew Oram, Speaker of the House of Representatives; John Moffett, formerly literary editor and by then editor of the *Otago Daily Times* and author of a book on the artist Russell Clark; and (showing Algie's influence) four associated with education, three of them from Auckland: E.M. Blaiklock, Professor of Classics at Auckland University College, newspaper columnist 'Grammaticus' and later known as a writer on Christian ethics; A.E. Caddick, headmaster of Christchurch Boys' High School, with a particular interest in sport; Cecil Hull, recently retired as classics mistress at Auckland Girls' Grammar School and a book reviewer for 1YA; and Agnes Loudon, long-serving (1930–47) headmistress of Epsom Girls' Grammar School. The National Government decided to continue Labour's policy of including a representative of Maori, but its choice here was surprising: Bodkin did not take up Algie's suggestion of James Henare of Nga Puhi, National's Northern Maori candidate in 1946, and instead appointed Charles Bennett of Ngati Whakaue and Ngati Pikiao, briefly commander of the Maori Battalion and later President of the Labour Party; at the time of his appointment he was assistant-controller of welfare in the Department of Maori Affairs and, at 38, the youngest member of the committee by several years. The appointments were to take effect on 1 December 1951, and the existing advisory committee continued in the interim. The new committee comprised an unwieldy 12 members plus the secretary, but Miss Hull died unexpectedly before she could take up office and was not replaced.

* * *

In the first four years of its existence, the Literary Fund dispensed 49 grants. Only eight went to authors to assist them in their writing; three of these were for Alpers, who in total received £725. Eleven small sums were also awarded to authors, mostly for typing costs. Four went to writers' organisations but the remaining 23 grants assisted publication costs, including reprints.

Expenditure in the 1947/8 year was understandably modest (eight grants, £940, or around $74,000 in 2015). The next year the committee was bold, paying out 15 grants worth £1586 2s 6d (two of these though were carry-overs from the previous year). However, 1949 was election year, and by contrast, the decisions in 1949/50 were more cautious. At the final meeting for the year, in February 1950, Lawlor was anxious that there was still £340 unexpended from the annual grant. In total the committee managed to spend £1786 5s, of which new grants made up only £1251 5s, the balance of £535 having been committed the previous year.

The first National Government, which took office in November 1949, was no friend of the arts. Moreover, it had been elected on a platform of reducing and eventually abolishing government subsidies. Many writers feared it would do away with the Literary Fund altogether. In mid-January 1950, Arthur Harper briefed the new trustees—the Prime Minister, S.G. Holland; the Minister of Internal Affairs, W.A. Bodkin; and the Associate Minister of Finance, C.M. Bowden—on their role. Bodkin was regarded as a conscientious administrator[95] and invited Scholefield as chairman and Professor Gordon to a meeting with him and Bowden to discuss the working of the fund and proposals for the future. The ministers asked in detail about the various grants made and indicated 'general approval' of the committee's policies.[96] Holland had little interest in the Literary Fund, and soon delegated responsibility for it to his Minister of Internal Affairs, who became in effect the sole trustee.[97]

Scholefield, who had been Parliamentary Librarian for more than 20 years and knew the ways of politicians, was a diligent and wily chairman, and followed up with a comprehensive letter to Bodkin. He offered reassurance ('All of the recommendations of the Advisory Committee have been approved, and the total amount expended each year has not exceeded the sum granted') and positive assertion ('No single application has been turned down where there was any promise of literary success'), along with discussion of matters requiring attention, implying perhaps that the previous government had been derelict in failing to deal with them.[98]

So the Literary Fund had survived—although not quite intact. In line with the new government's desire to achieve cost savings throughout the public service, Bodkin cut the annual grant for 1950/51 from £2000 to £1500 (from around $129,000 to around $96,700 in 2015 prices), and later queried the additional amount of £200 charged to the Cultural Fund for readers' fees, members' travel expenses and the secretary's honorarium and expenses. The cut caused a small crisis when the year proved to be a peak in the number of applications and the committee ran out of money at the end of 1950. Internal Affairs was able to draw on a special reserve fund of £1715, however, held in a suspense account originally set up from the unused portion of the first year's grant and established at the request of Peter Fraser, who cannily foresaw that a need to supplement the annual funding might arise in the future.[99] Thus emboldened, the committee managed to spend more than

£2500 on new grants in 1950/51—the highest amount yet.

Reviewing the Literary Fund's first three years in *Landfall* at the end of 1950, Charles Brasch relented a little on his harsh criticism of 12 months before. He still found the list of grants 'disappointing':

> too many of them seem open to question on grounds other than actual differences of taste and judgment and risks which have turned out badly, and it is not surprising that some have caused concern. To have a book sponsored by the Fund has not yet become a recognition of achievement and a sign of literary distinction.

However, he now recognised that the problem lay in the kinds of books being submitted to the committee: 'if better books had been offering, some of these questionable ones, as border-line cases, might not have been subsidised. . . . there have been no rumours of the Committee turning down any good work submitted to it'.[100]

Both Brasch and 'Analyst' had put their fingers on a central problem for the advisory committee: its primary emphasis on assisting promising writers towards publication, mainly through grants in aid of publication but also through occasional grants for creative projects, had not produced applications of the kinds or quality it had expected, and had created other problems. The number of applications had been increasing steadily, peaking at 98 in 1950/51—members had to meet eight times during the year to get through all their business. Only 13 of these applications were successful. There were 58 for publication subsidies (four granted), six for reprints (one granted) and 34 for other forms of assistance (eight granted).[101] And many of these applications lay outside the committee's declared focus, so that it was still dealing with them ad hoc and its efforts were diffuse. It is little wonder that the advisory committee appeared to be drifting on the tide of applications it received, rather than setting out to attract the kinds of applications it wanted to support. Reacting rather than planning meant that the committee took the best part of a decade to settle into a widely accepted modus operandi.

3

IGNORANT NON-ENTITIES?: 1952–1955

Aged 43 when first elected to the chair in mid-1951, Professor Ian Gordon was by 25 years the youngest of the three chairmen of the Literary Fund Advisory Committee to date. A Scot from Edinburgh, Gordon had been appointed head of the department of English at Victoria University College in 1936 and was widely respected in local literary circles for his scholarship, his energy and his enlightened editing of the four issues of *New Zealand New Writing* produced by the Progressive Publishing Society in 1942–45, a project he initiated in emulation of John Lehmann's *Penguin New Writing*.[1] Under his brisk chairmanship, the advisory committee began to focus more on literature and creative writing, especially poetry, relegating historical works to second place in its aims and disposing quickly of applications clearly beyond its scope. Gordon also launched a campaign to explain and promote the Literary Fund's work. He soon had to deal with an expanded committee that was riven by cross-currents, however. As the number of applications declined sharply, the advisory committee was too big for its tasks, and for the first time political views began to colour its deliberations. The new chairman, an inveterate card player, needed considerable finesse to handle his potentially fractious new team. Possibly because of this, he tended to act more unilaterally than Scholefield; he assumed decision-making powers for many applications and often negotiated directly with departmental officials, only informing his committee afterwards. Gordon's skill in handling all these matters led to his continuing role as a government-appointed independent chairman as well as to a reduction in the size of the advisory committee, to a stable and secure structure, and to a period of relative tranquillity for the Literary Fund.

Professor Ian Gordon, 1959. Professor Gordon was chair of the Literary Fund Advisory Committee from 1951 to 1974.
Dominion Post Collection, ATL, EP/1959/1840

The many distractions of 1951 meant that, out of its restored budget of £2000 ($117,000 in 2015) for 1951/52, the outgoing committee had spent only £500. Apart from subsidising the *Poetry Yearbook*, its only innovative publishing decision had been to grant £100 to Pegasus Press to initiate a modestly priced series called 'Pegasus New Zealand Poets', following on the fledgling publisher's success with its elegantly produced first book, Alistair Campbell's first collection, *Mine Eyes Dazzle*, in 1950. A revised and cheaper edition of Campbell's book would be No. 1 in the series. Pegasus received £25 each for another four books by young poets: Hubert Witheford's *The Falcon Mask*, Pat Wilson's *The Bright Sea*, Louis Johnson's *Roughshod Among the Lilies* and Keith Sinclair's *Songs for a Summer.*

The new committee, at its first meeting in February 1952, could therefore afford to be bold. After re-electing Gordon to the chair, it managed to spend another £925, bringing the total expenditure for the financial year up to £1425 ($81,000 in 2015). Caxton Press was granted a subsidy of £350 to publish a posthumous selection of Robin Hyde's poems, *Houses by the Sea*, edited by her literary executor, Gloria Rawlinson. John Schroder was the driving force behind this subsidy. He had been a mentor and guide to Hyde in her burgeoning career as a poet, novelist and journalist from his early days on the Christchurch *Sun*, where her poems first crossed his desk in 1927.[2] After Hyde's suicide in London in 1939, Schroder also advised Rawlinson on the preparation of the poems. Rawlinson, after an initial submission to the new New Zealand University Press, took them to Denis Glover at Caxton.[3] Glover's relationship with Caxton was disintegrating through his 'drink-driven mismanagement'[4] and, increasingly failing to deliver, he was finding all kinds of excuses to explain delays. Now he complained about

Rawlinson's introduction and the inclusion of some of Hyde's letters with the poems. Negotiations with Glover proved protracted and difficult, and both he and Rawlinson approached the Literary Fund for help in mid-1951. The advisory committee agreed to subsidise an edition of 500 copies, later increased to 1000, provided the printing and financial details could be sorted out. A firm proposal came from Glover in time for the first meeting of the new committee, and Schroder used his position as an old hand to achieve the highest-equal publication subsidy yet granted. Glover left Caxton soon after, but the book still appeared at the end of 1952.

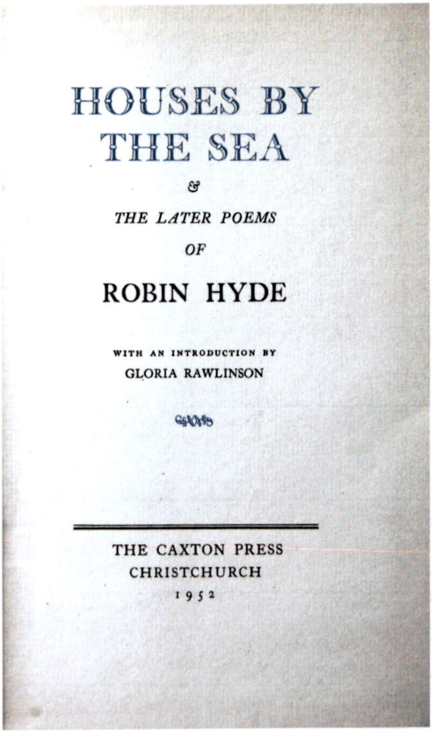

Title page of *Houses by the Sea*, subsidised by the Literary Fund, 1952.
Jock Phillips photograph

At that first meeting, a late application for a travel grant was granted equally quickly. John Reece Cole, an assistant in the National Library Service and lecturer in fiction at the New Zealand Library School, had been nominated by the Department of Internal Affairs for a fellowship to attend the 1952 International Arts Congress in the United States. Another 'son of Sargeson', he had published a well-received collection of short stories, *It Was So Late*, in 1949, had often contemplated applying to the advisory committee for a writing maintenance grant and had cultivated some of its Wellington members, especially Ian Gordon. When he applied for up to £170 to extend his American visit into a three-month study tour, the committee immediately granted him £200. Cole later reported enthusiastically on his experiences in the United States, but published no more fiction.[5]

Cole was instrumental in having a writing maintenance grant for Maurice Duggan finally approved after that first meeting. Still in England, Duggan had written about 70 pages of a novel and, desperately short of money and egged on by Sargeson, he applied to the committee in January 1952 for a grant of £276 (or £5 10s a week for 52 weeks) to complete it. Dan Davin, then negotiating with Duggan to include one of his stories in the *New Zealand Short Stories* volume he was editing in the Oxford World Classics series, wrote to Gordon in support. Sargeson also offered to write, but Cole asked him to keep out of it, and used his own influence with Gordon.[6] Presumably mindful of the consequences of the earlier rejection of Duggan, the advisory committee formed a special subcommittee (Gordon, Alan Mulgan and John Moffett), with the power to act quickly if necessary, to appraise his new manuscript. Duggan joked to Davin that getting a grant out of the Literary Fund was 'rather like getting oneself elected to the French Academy'.[7] However the three readers agreed and the weekly grant was quickly approved by the trustee. Eventually Duggan, seriously ill, used the money for fares to return to New Zealand; the novel was never completed but parts did reappear in short stories.

The first sign of division between committee members also came at that first meeting in 1952. The guidelines for grants to periodicals had been confirmed by the outgoing committee in November 1951, which noted that the only magazine then eligible for assistance was *Landfall.* When Brasch applied at the beginning of 1952 for £300 (£200 instead of £100 for production costs, and £100 for contributors) for *Landfall* for the year, however, the new committee asked whether he had considered increasing the price, and the fees paid to contributors. Brasch replied that he had considered increasing the price but that the first result would be a loss of circulation. Itemising the contributors' payments for the previous two issues, he showed how the Literary Fund subsidy had enabled him to double the rates paid.[8] This reasonable response provoked the first division between committee members recorded in the minutes. John Moffett and Matthew Oram wanted to refuse the grant altogether. Monte Holcroft and Agnes Loudon wished the full application to be granted. Oram, seconded by Moffett, then moved that the amount of the grant be reduced from £300 to £200, half of which was to be paid to the contributors of *literary* articles. This was carried on the casting vote of the chairman.[9]

The emphasis on literary articles is the key to understanding this unprecedented division. Along with literary work, *Landfall* published occasional political commentaries which included observations on the current

National Government, of which Oram, though nominally independent as Speaker, was part. Moffett too was generally seen in Dunedin as a conservative, and there may also have been ill feeling between him and Charles Brasch (who later wrote privately about the 'catastrophic decline' in the *Otago Daily Times* under Moffett's editorship).[10] Brasch wrote to the committee saying that he would 'operate as fairly as I can' the conditions attached to the £100 grant for payments to contributors,[11] but, when he applied again for a grant of £300 for *Landfall* at the start of 1953, Moffett again moved to block it because the journal 'was showing political bias'.[12] A reduced grant of £200 was given, £50 for production costs and £150 for payments to *literary* contributors. A testy correspondence with Brasch followed.

Charles Brasch, c.1955.
J.R. Cole Collection, ATL, F-19117-1/4

Moffett continued his campaign against *Landfall*. He opposed Brasch's application later in 1953 for a further £50 to meet rising production costs, but it was granted anyway. The journal's position was becoming acute: Brasch included a questionnaire seeking suggestions for making economies in the December 1953 issue, and reduced the size of the magazine from 80 to 64 pages. However when he applied for annual grants of £300 for 1954 and 1955, the committee granted only £250. Moffett's appointment to the advisory committee was not renewed in 1955, and in subsequent years *Landfall* was granted the full £300 (later £400) subsidy Brasch sought.

Possibly spurred on by the announcement of the first annual grant to *Landfall* in 1951, Noel Hoggard applied later that year for assistance with his occasional literary magazine, *Arena*.[13] Hoggard, 'a man without literary talent and with little literary judgement, but with a passion for being in the literary swim',[14] had published *Arena* (originally called *Letters*) since 1943. His application went to the periodicals subcommittee and appears to have lapsed there. *Arena* was regarded with affection by some in the literary community, as many young writers first published there. A petition—the first ever to the Literary Fund—from 'numerous writers' in November 1953 asked for financial assistance with both editing and printing to keep the venture going.[15] The petition was referred to Schroder and Holcroft (Gordon was overseas) with power to act up to £100. They recommended a grant of £50 and, when Hoggard asked for a renewal for 1955, increased it to £75. A new committee granted him £100 for 1956, partly to help him replace his ageing printing press, but that was the last subsidy; *Arena* continued nevertheless until 1975.

Another grant which became an annual subsidy was

initiated by the outgoing committee. PEN in its early days had set up two annual awards for the best writing published in the previous year: the Jessie Mackay Memorial Award for poetry (established in 1940) and the Hubert Church Memorial Award for prose (established in 1945 partly from a memorial bequest by Church's widow). The only annual awards for achievement by writers in New Zealand, they carried more prestige than financial reward, as each prize was only a few pounds and fluctuated each year. Discussions with PEN in 1951 led to a proposal to set a fixed sum of £25 for each award, with the Literary Fund making up the shortfall. As its very last recommendation, the outgoing committee approved the subsidy for the two awards.

The matter came before the new committee at its second meeting, when PEN sought subsidies of £17 16s for the Jessie Mackay Award and £17 15s for the Hubert Church Award. Lawlor had told PEN in confidence that the subsidy had been approved but then Internal Affairs had queried it, being 'a little doubtful about the principle of such a grant'. The new committee accepted the earlier recommendation, and Gordon agreed to discuss it with Internal Affairs. He later reported that the 'difficulties' had been 'adjusted' and ministerial approval given.[16] The next year PEN applied for subsidies of £17 15s for the Hubert Church Award and £22 15s for the Jessie Mackay Award, and asked 'if the committee would mind' if it gave a second prize for the Jessie Mackay Award out of its own funds. Both proposals were accepted, though only the first went to the Minister for approval.[17]

The first subsidy for the Hubert Church Award had a unique twist. The award was won by Frank Sargeson for his memoir 'Up onto the Roof and Down Again', published in *Landfall* in three issues over 1950–51 (the judges were Monte Holcroft and Jim Bertram). Because of the 'difficulties' in confirming the subsidy, there was a delay in paying out the £25 prize money. Sargeson wrote to Lawlor in August asking 'what on earth' was holding up the payment, which PEN had told him about in April. He added: 'I'm sure we both want to avoid Trouble if we can.'[18] Lawlor responded angrily promising payment and offering 'a few quid in the interim'.[19] Sargeson replied that he did not want a loan, just the payment due: 'An author in New Zealand doesn't require these amounts as pocket or pin money—they're what he depends on to get by with, & continue with his work. I don't relish shoes that leak, or pullovers that are more holes than pullovers.'[20]

Sargeson's name was to feature before the new committee in other ways. Helen Shaw, a long-time admirer of the writer, had initiated and edited a collection of nine critical essays on his work, *The Puritan and the Waif*, with contributions by Cresswell, Davin, Baxter, Duggan and others, including herself. Though an unprecedented venture for New Zealand writing, the contributions, according to Sargeson's biographer, Michael King, were not of a high standard (Duggan later described his own piece as 'inflated nonsense'[21]). The advisory committee found the same: when Caxton applied for a publication subsidy of £100 in August 1952, it was quickly declined. On Gordon's second thoughts, Holcroft was asked to read it. However, his judicious report praising four of the essays but pointing out the 'cloudy and repetitious' nature of the others, along with the inadequate editing, concluded it should not be supported.[22] Caxton did not proceed and Shaw eventually produced the manuscript in a 'rather tatty' cyclostyled edition of 50 copies.[23]

The following year the committee also rejected a Caxton proposal for a much more ambitious Sargeson project: a large single-volume collection of all his fiction to date, and later the suggestion of the first of a two-volume edition of Sargeson's works. Thinking that the committee had rejected the application out of hand, Sargeson called in to see Gordon on his way through Wellington, and had a 'very stormy session' with him about this and the rejection of the Shaw symposium. Sargeson reported:

> Gordon himself is not so bad, the trouble is mainly Lawlor plus the bunch of ratbags which is the committee. Nobody could be more stupid than Lawlor, and nobody more ignorant and nonentical than these people.[24]

Sargeson also organised a campaign to persuade the Literary Fund to assist O.E. Middleton, whose stories had been turned down earlier. He had later sent three chapters of a novel for consideration without making a formal application. A story was included in Davin's Oxford World Classics anthology of *New Zealand Short Stories* and a small book of his stories was published by Noel Hoggard's backyard Handcraft Press early in 1954. In May that year he applied for a grant to 'pursue literary undertakings' in Paris. The committee decided against this application, but was willing to consider a more specific project.[25] Sargeson got busy, drafting a petition to the committee which described Middleton as 'a gifted young writer who has already achieved considerable literary distinction' and pointing out that he suffered from deteriorating eyesight. The petition asked the committee 'to afford Mr Middleton every assistance . . . to enable him to develop his literary gift while his eyesight remains'.[26] Although there was some criticism that the petition confused 'personal and literary grounds',[27] Sargeson, aided by Brasch, collected 50 signatures from leading writers and scholars.[28] After a lengthy discussion, the committee agreed that the chairman should interview Middleton and be empowered to recommend a grant of up to £200, and that the petition be sent on to the Minister. Gordon was 'favourably impressed' by Middleton and, since the Department of External Affairs was willing to help the writer travel to France, recommended a grant of £200 to enable him to continue writing in the meantime.[29] Middleton later wrote to the committee saying that he would use the money scrupulously for its intended purpose. Probably the most consistently productive of the 'sons of Sargeson', he went on to publish four more collections of short stories and two novellas.[30]

Also in 1954 the committee made a writing maintenance grant of £200 to Joyce West, now known mainly as an accomplished writer for children, whose idyllic picture of rural life on the East Coast first appeared in *Drover's Road*, published by Dent in London in 1953. (She also collaborated with Mary Scott on murder-mystery romances for adults.) West applied for assistance to complete the writing of a new book, and aided by the strong support of her two friends, Mary Scott and Airini Woodhouse, the grant of £200 was quickly approved.[31] Surviving records do not indicate what West's literary project was, but her next book, *The Year of the Shining Cuckoo*, a 'vivid celebration of almost-bygone Northland isolation' that is generally regarded as her best work, did not appear until 1961. It was published by Paul's Book Arcade in New Zealand and then in London and New York and reprinted in New Zealand in 1985. West went on to publish four more children's books, most published overseas as well as in New Zealand.

The use of the money granted for writing projects was a particular concern in the case of Eve Langley (Clark), who, along with Temple Sutherland, was given a maintenance grant in November 1953. Langley had published short stories and poetry in Australian and New Zealand magazines, and an acclaimed novel, *The Pea-Pickers*, written in a distinctive prose-poetry style, in Australia in 1942. After a spell in Auckland Mental Hospital in the 1940s she resumed a period of prolific writing.[32] Gloria Rawlinson applied for assistance on her behalf and, sympathetic to Langley's position, the committee agreed to grant her £300. Professor Blaiklock agreed to supervise payment and to monitor Langley's progress for the committee. Langley's second novel, *White Topee*, written in the same style, was published in Australia in 1954 to a more muted reception. The following year she reported to the committee that she had completed another novel and was working on two more, but none was published.

The only other grant to a writer in this period was to the poet Hubert Witheford, whose second collection, *The Falcon Mask*, had been subsidised in the Pegasus New Zealand Poets series. Witheford, who with Louis Johnson and James K. Baxter was a member of the 'Wellington group' of the early 1950s, had a romantic, even mystical, view of the poet as priest and performer.[33] In May 1953, finding the New Zealand of the time inimical to the artist, he applied for a grant to complete a 'literary project' on a visit to England later in the year. Severely practical, the committee agreed to £100 provided Gordon and Schroder were 'satisfied with the applicant's financial arrangements for the journey'.[34] In the event, Witheford remained in England for almost all his life and privately published two major poetry collections there. He maintained some literary links with New Zealand, publishing the collection *A Native, Perhaps Beautiful* with Caxton in 1967 with the aid of a Literary Fund subsidy of £100, but the benefit of the writing grant for New Zealand literature must otherwise be regarded as slender.

Denis Glover applied in August 1953 for a grant of £100 to complete a 'long sequence of poems' about Banks Peninsula.[35] Although his celebrated *Arawata Bill* sequence, written at fever-pitch earlier that year, had just been published (the first edition sold out in a fortnight), Glover's application was perfunctory and unconvincing, and the committee declined it. Lawlor was asked to write a sympathetic letter. 'Towards Banks Peninsula', an eight-part elegy to Glover's old seafaring friend Mick Stimpson, appeared in his collection *Since Then*, published by his own Mermaid Press in 1957, and was extended and published with other poems about the peninsula in *Towards Banks Peninsula* (Pegasus) in 1979. Two applications from Louis Johnson for £50, one to complete a novel and the other to assist him and Alistair Campbell on a verse project, were similarly declined.

* * *

By far the bulk of the applications were still for publication subsidies. In 1952/53, for instance, the overall number of applications considered had dropped to 61 (from a peak of 98 in 1950/51), of which 42 were for publication (including nine from Reeds and four from Pegasus) and three from writers seeking assistance. Ten grants totalling £1658 10s (about $91,300 in 2015) were made: six for publication (totalling £835; two to Reeds), two to *Landfall* (totalling £400), the £276 writer's grant to Maurice Duggan and £40 10s for PEN's Jessie Mackay and Hubert Church awards, plus two further publication subsidies totalling £107 carried forward from the previous year.[36]

By 1954/55, the overall number of applications had

declined to 36, of which 29 were for publication (five from Pegasus and only one from Reeds), four were from writers seeking financial assistance and three for literary magazines or annuals. It is a reflection of the advisory committee's priorities by this time that, in recommending ten grants totalling £1825 (about $93,000 in 2015), it gave nearly half (£825) to periodicals *Landfall*, *Arena* and the *New Zealand Poetry Yearbook*. There were only three publication subsidies totalling £475, two grants to writers (Joyce West and O.E. Middleton) totalling £400, and special grants of £50 to PEN and £75 to Reeds to prepare and publish the revised edition of the *New Zealand Writers' Handbook* (the latter was subsequently refunded when the project was abandoned).[37]

The shift in priorities away from publication subsidies may have been deliberate. In July 1953 Schroder produced a searching paper, 'The Place of Publication Subsidies in the Committee's Policy'.[38] He pointed out that in its six years of existence the committee had recommended nearly 40 publication subsidies (for new books and reprints) totalling nearly £5700; other kinds of grants—support to literary periodicals and annuals (£1800), travel and maintenance grants to writers (£2975), for typing of manuscripts (£250) and prizes (£160)—totalled £5185, nearly as much. With the publication subsidies, the committee had been able to 'moderate retail prices' (the main object), 'induce publishers to print larger issues, exercise some influence on technical standards, and ensure fair royalty payments to authors'.

Schroder doubted whether reducing the retail price by a few shillings had much effect on sales, making it possible to sell out a print run of 2000 when only 1500 copies could have been sold at the higher price. He concluded

> not that we should abandon the subsidy device, but that we should use it less and govern our use of it
> 1. by making sure, whenever we can, that publication depends on subsidy, and subsidising, usually, only to obtain it;
> 2. by making more than we have done of the secondary or related objects, especially when publication does not depend on subsidy.

It followed, he continued, possibly with the Curnow grant in mind, that 'we should search widely and persistently for more various means of fulfilling our function'. He was not advocating a 'surrender to generous impulse or any inconsiderate haste, say, in making grants to enable writers to advance a literary project'. But once the committee had decided that a particular project 'promises to advance us and takes a fair place beside other projects, then we must . . . learn not to distrust it and ourselves because . . . it is new, or does not embody a plan to write a specific book. The method that will in the long run produce least is the method of tight, safe bargains: so much money down, so many words in print and between covers.' Consideration of the paper was twice deferred until Gordon was overseas, when members discussed it briefly and decided that 'the circulation of the paper had already produced results'.[39]

Some of the publication subsidies in this period were for significant sums, though not as large as the £350 to Caxton for *Houses by the Sea*. Eric McCormick had earlier been granted £100 towards the cost of copying source material for his book *The Expatriate*, a study of the artist Frances Hodgkins, and in November 1953 the New Zealand University Press was granted a subsidy of £250 to publish it. Whitcombe & Tombs were granted three subsidies of £200 each.[40] One was for L.J. Wild's *Life of Sir James G. Wilson of Bulls* on the recommendation of Schroder, who found it 'a book of great value', provided the print run was not less than 1000 copies.[41] The subsidy for Randal Burdon's *King Dick* was to enable a reduction in the retail price to 17s 6d. *Rouseabout Jane* by 'Jane Dare' (actually N.B. Warry), about a young Englishwoman who had come out to New Zealand and taken a job as a land girl, was subsidised on the recommendation of Caddick. Warry wanted the book published anonymously, but Gordon vetoed this as being against the committee's policy. Reeds were granted a subsidy of £200 for Nellie F.H. McLeod's biography of Jessie Mackay, *A Voice on the Wind*, after a 'very helpful' report by A.B. Cochran suggesting considerable revision, and £150 for G.E. Dewar's anecdotal history of the Chaslands district of South Otago, after a favourable report by Alan Mulgan.

Subsidies for reprints included £150 to Whitcombe & Tombs for John Logan Campbell's *Poenamo: Sketches of the Early Days in New Zealand* (first published in 1888), with an introduction by Joan Stevens; the subsidy required a print run of 2000 and a reduction in the retail price from 15s to 12s 6d. The publishers were asked to keep the type for 12 months, and a second printing soon became necessary. Pegasus was granted £200 to reprint Thomas Brunner's *The Great Journey*, an account of his epic expedition from Nelson to South Westland in 1846–48. The publisher had originally asked for £125, and noted that the higher subsidy would enable it to sell a two-guinea book for one guinea.

There was only one subsidy for fiction in this period. Helen Wilson's second novel, *Land of My Children*, which had earlier been turned down by Reeds, received a mixed reader's report from David Hall, who described it as a 'long and rambling novel which, despite some bright passages, never really lives'.[42] Nevertheless, the committee seems to have been determined to support fiction, and Paul's Book Arcade was granted £200; the costings required a subsidy of £186, and the extra £14 was to supplement the author's royalties. G.R. Gilbert had received a maintenance grant of £300 in 1950 to write fiction, and in 1954 Pegasus applied for a subsidy of £150 for a work of nonfiction, *Our Life in a Lighthouse*, a humorous account of Gilbert's experiences as a lighthouse keeper. The subsidy was declined but the book was published anyway in 1956 as *Love in a Lighthouse*.

An unusual form of subsidy was given in 1954 for C.E. Major's manuscript 'Seventy Years in New Zealand', a collection of reminiscences mainly about the author's early life in Wellington, Poverty Bay and Taranaki. While not finding this worthy of publication, the committee decided that its material was sufficiently valuable to justify a grant of £30 to enable five copies to be typed. Mulgan edited the text and Oram supervised the typing, and copies of the typescript were sent to libraries in each of the four main centres. The fifth copy was sent to the author just before he died.

Most of the smaller subsidies were for poetry. On Gordon's recommendation, Allen & Unwin in the United Kingdom were granted £75 to produce *The Sunlit Hour*, a collection of poems by Ruth Gilbert, the first time a subsidy had been granted to an overseas publisher. Pegasus was granted subsidies of £25 each to produce *Starveling Year* by Mary Stanley and *The Sound of the Morning* by John Caselberg, Numbers 6 and 7 in the Pegasus New Zealand Poets series. Having asked for £50 and £60 respectively, Caxton was granted £25 each towards the publication of *Unwilling Pilgrim* by Paul Henderson (Ruth France) and *She Was My Spring*, the last book by the veteran J.R. Hervey, and £25 (£60 asked for) for D'Arcy Cresswell's sequence *The Voyage of the Hurunui*. This last had been the subject of a dismissive report by Joan Stevens, and the committee made it clear that the grant was not to assist publication but to increase Cresswell's royalties; Caxton was asked not to include the customary acknowledgement to the Literary Fund. After various unsuccessful applications, the New Zealand Women Writers' Society was granted £25 to produce *Poems: An Anthology by New Zealand Women Writers*, edited by Alan R. Dunlop.

In 1954 Pegasus applied for a grant of £50 to publish Louis Johnson's *Poems in Black and White*. Holcroft's report was unenthusiastic: he felt that it 'might be better to let [the book] make its own way'.[43] Johnson revised the manuscript and in 1955 Pegasus asked again for a subsidy of £50; Johnson, by then secretary of PEN, also wrote to the committee giving 'his opinions regarding his work and thoughts relative to the rejection of the original MS'.[44] Ian Gordon then took the matter into his own hands; he obtained 'another opinion which was in accord with his own' and wrote to Johnson saying that a grant could not be recommended.[45]

* * *

The most tangible evidence of the Literary Fund's work was the books whose publication it had subsidised or which had been written by the authors it had assisted. The previous committee had wanted to recognise this by commissioning Leo Bensemann to create a design for reproduction inside the books it had assisted; during the design process the committee had finally settled on the official name of New Zealand Literary Fund. However, on objections from Internal Affairs, the device was shelved, and the standard form of acknowledgement remained (though overlooked several times by Reeds).

One requirement of the publication subsidy was that at least one copy of the book be sent to the fund, to be placed in a special collection in the Alexander Turnbull Library. In 1952, Internal Affairs asked the committee to assemble a second collection, to be put on display at the Government Buildings in Wellington. Ian Gordon, always keen to promote the fund, soon hit on the idea of using this display as an exhibition to tour the main centres. Lawlor approached Whitcombe & Tombs, who agreed to display the collection in their shops, as did Paul's Book Arcade in Hamilton. Members of the committee admired the displays in Wellington and Auckland. Encouraged, Gordon approached Internal Affairs about a similar display in New Zealand House in London during Coronation Year. Oram corresponded with the New Zealand High Commissioner, Sir Frederick Doidge, and Internal Affairs arranged to have the books transferred. A photograph of the committee was taken to assist the publicity.

At the same time, Whitcombe & Tombs and Pegasus applied for a grant of 100 guineas to cover the entry fee for participating in an exhibition of international book design being organised by the National Book League in London in 1953. Although considered beyond the scope of the committee's operations, this sowed another idea in Gordon's mind. He proposed that the Literary Fund exhibition be extended to take in other New Zealand books, and eventually more than 300 volumes were supplied—too many to display at New Zealand House. As he was by then on leave in London, he arranged for the exhibition to be transferred to the National Book League rooms, where it was so popular that it ran for seven weeks and obtained considerable publicity. A special catalogue was produced. The committee's annual report for 1954 modestly notes that

'The Committee has placed on record its appreciation of the splendid services given by Professor Gordon in connection with this Exhibition.'[46]

Gordon also used the news media to promote the fund's work. In an article published in various newspapers at the beginning of 1953—it featured on the editorial page of the *Dominion* under the heading 'Should Good Books Need Subsidising?'[47]—he argued:

> . . . if a writer is an Australian or a New Zealander, if his line is something less popular than the readily sold detective fiction, if he prefers to interpret his country without laboured explanations and simplifications for an overseas market, and above all, if he is a poet, then financial success is very much less assured. Even publication without hope of financial reward may be impossible.
>
> At this point, the literary funds in the two southern Dominions . . . can supply just the amount of pump-priming that is required. A few pounds judiciously awarded can insure a publisher against loss, and can make the difference between a bundle of typescript passing from hand to hand and a published volume of some importance.

After noting that there had been a 'minor boom' in New Zealand publications during the past few years and that local publishers had had 'quite a run of successes' without the benefit of state aid, Gordon claimed:

> Yet there remains a need for a literary fund. Over six years, the New Zealand Literary Fund has assisted in the publication of about 30 books, all of them above the level of mere competence, a few of them outstanding contributions to the writing of the country. Not all of the N.Z.L.F. books have pleased everybody. To do so would be impossible, and if possible would be unhealthy.

As a result, he concluded: 'The advisory committee asks only for good literary workmanship. It has no exclusive interest in any particular group of writers.'

Gordon's relentless optimism and enthusiasm contrast with Schroder's more realistic view, as expressed in his earlier paper. Schroder had been probably the most thoughtful and effective member of the committee, if a little inclined to ride hobby horses; he had an excellent grasp of its procedures but had twice declined nomination as chairman. It is little wonder that, when his appointment was not renewed in 1955, Schroder wrote to the Minister of Internal Affairs that this was 'a decision I have no reason to regret'.[48]

Despite his tussles with the advisory committee, even Charles Brasch took a generally favourable view of what it had achieved:

> It appears . . . that the Fund is doing its undoubtedly difficult work well. It cannot work wonders, but its help has made possible valuable publications, and no serious instances of injustice, of refusal to help authors and publishers, seem to be known. . . . It is in publishing books of that type [poetry and fiction] especially that the Fund's justification lies.

Picking up on several ideas that were in the air at that time, Brasch advocated the sponsorship of competitions—he was about to launch an annual competition for poetry, and later one for fiction—possibly by increasing the funding for the Jessie Mackay and Hubert Church awards; fellowships for writers, which 'should provide more stimulus to writers, and perhaps result in more good work being written'; and carrying over the unexpended portion of the committee's annual allocation, making it feasible to establish fellowships or to subsidise large projects.[49]

* * *

The terms of appointment of the current 11-member committee expired at the end of 1954, and early in 1955 both Internal Affairs officials and PEN began to consider a reconstituted committee. Gordon had made clear his dissatisfaction with the size of the committee and, with the number of applications declining and four members from outside Wellington, meetings had been reduced to four a year. Even so, administrative expenses were rising rapidly: from just under £150 in 1950/51 to £450 in 1954/55, an amount which, as Arthur Harper, pointed out to his new Minister, a now long-forgotten Bay of Islands farmer called S.W. Smith (Bodkin had retired at the 1954 election), 'bears a very high proportion to an item of £2000, not all of which has been spent over the last few years'.[50] Internal Affairs officials were in fact proposing a radical restructuring: halving the size of the committee to only two ministerial appointees (one to be a representative of the younger school of writers) in addition to the three PEN nominees, and providing the secretary from within Internal Affairs, as was done with the selection committees for music, drama and ballet. Lawlor's approach to the position had 'not been altogether satisfactory' and there would be considerable cost savings, as he was now paid an honorarium of £156 (it had been increased in 1950) plus expenses of about £50 a year, and the 'handicap of the lack of information about the deliberations of the Committee would be eliminated'.[51]

PEN was also pressing for a smaller committee, with secretary Louis Johnson arguing that 'the Committee as at present constituted is unwieldy . . . the work should be performed by a smaller group conversant with literary trends and needs in this country', and that a change of secretary 'could be effected with similar advantage'. He suggested that a younger writer, who was 'active in literary affairs' and whose literary work could benefit from the economic assistance of the honorarium, be appointed.[52] Johnson was in fact lining himself up for the position, and John Reece Cole was interested too. Johnson also gave as PEN's new nominees its president, O.N. Gillespie, Denis Glover and Ian Gordon.

Harper pondered on both proposals and produced his own, even more radical one. He advised Smith that the advisory committee should be reduced to four members plus the chairman, two to be nominated by PEN and three, including the chairman, to be appointed by the government. Ian Gordon, he felt, was 'eminently suited to the position' of chairman, possessing the 'confidence of the New Zealand literary world, and has done much for letters in New Zealand'. He should continue to be chairman but as a government appointment. The other government appointees would be Sir Matthew Oram and David Hall, a regular reader for the committee and resident fiction reviewer for the *Listener.* Bennett's contribution to the advisory committee had been negligible, and no Maori representative was mentioned. Harper left open the question of the secretary and his honorarium, but felt that the other administrative expenses (readers' fees, travelling expenses) should be borne by the department rather than charged to the Cultural Fund.[53]

The Minister in reply instructed that the committee be reduced to five members plus the chairman, two to be nominated by PEN (Gillespie and Denis Glover) and four, including the chairman, to be appointed by the government. Gordon was to be appointed chair, and the other three members would be Oram, Agnes Loudon and David Hall (the only new government member). Administrative expenses were to be transferred to the Internal Affairs vote, and a departmental official would provide secretarial services.[54]

Moffett and Blaiklock were clearly hurt at not being reappointed. Moffett interviewed the Minister, who 'confessed' that he had been 'ill-advised' about reconstituting the committee—the National Party wrote to him asking why there was no representative of fiction writing and suggesting Cedric Mentiplay, a journalist and writer of short stories[55]—and asked Moffett to recommend a new list when the matter came up again. Blaiklock also let it be known at every opportunity that he was prepared to serve again, 'in the light of events'.[56]

Lawlor, who had been ill, took it the worst. Nearly ten years later he wrote to Schroder that 'I was hurt when they dropped me, I felt that I had been submarined by the very people I had battled for.'[57] At the time he felt that 'subterranean forces were at work', and that a literary clique had been involved.[58] He wrote to Smith trusting that he would be given the opportunity of formally handing over his papers at the next committee meeting: 'I would then be able to take leave of the Committee in a manner due to my long term of office.'[59] The official replacing him, Andrew Sharp, visited him to discuss the handover, and reported:

> Mr Lawlor proved very cooperative and handed over all the papers on the spot, apart from those which related to the ms to be submitted to the forthcoming meeting.[60] . . . Mr Lawlor made no secret of the fact that he had been nettled by what he thought was the summary character of his dismissal, but had been considerably mollified by the Minister's further letter saying that he should be asked to hand over at the next meeting. . . . I think a tribute to his services in the Minister's forthcoming Press Statement will finally put his attitude in shape.[61]

The appointment of Sharp as secretary was in many ways an inspired choice. He had been a diplomat, serving in the New Zealand High Commissions in Canberra and Ottawa until ill health forced him to seek a quieter life in Internal Affairs. He was about to publish a major work, *Ancient Voyagers in the Pacific*, which, as Rachel Barrowman wrote, 'revolutionised the study of Maori origins by posing the theory of accidental migration (overturning that of the Great Fleet) which was to hold sway for the next two decades'.[62] He had been a Rhodes Scholar at St John's in Oxford when Charles Brasch was there; Brasch had found him 'likeable'. While applauding the departure of Lawlor, which would 'save a lot of time and muddle and unnecessary correspondence', Brasch was less impressed with Sharp when Glover took him to meet the new secretary shortly after his appointment: 'He has an accent of a rawness and crudity that would do credit to a Yahoo; and he struck me as having the blank bleak intelligence of an entirely neutral civil servant. But no doubt he will prove efficient on the Lit. Fund . . .'[63]

In Australia at this time, the conservative Prime Minister, Sir Robert Menzies, had assumed the chair of the Commonwealth Literary Fund, and was using his position to question and even reject applications from writers thought to be communist sympathisers.[64] This may have been behind Brasch's bemused comments in *Landfall* taking exception to Oram's reappointment:

> What place a politician has on the Literary Fund committee it would need a politician to explain. Does the Government fancy that through him it will be able to keep a group of wild men in check, and possibly restrain expenditure? But four of these six wild men were appointed by the Government anyway . . . . With no disrespect to Sir Matthew Oram, it may be suggested that he is wasting his time.[65]

4

STABILITY, WITH INTERRUPTIONS 1955–1964

Professor Gordon was energetic, enthusiastic and an experienced administrator; he was not a cloistered academic and he had an instinctive political sense, maintaining good relations with both writers and politicians. He kept a firm hold on proceedings. In 1957, for example, he proposed that after he had made an initial assessment of manuscripts submitted, those worthy of serious consideration should be read by himself, Hall and Glover, thus reducing reliance on outside readers and giving the committee a much firmer stake in decision-making.[1] Above all he seemed to have a different vision for the fund from those who had founded it with the principal aim of assisting the publication or republication of works of history and memoirs. It gradually became very clear that the new committee saw its purposes as more strictly literary, and that a primary focus was to be the encouragement of writers.

* * *

One question had clearly been on Gordon's mind for some time. In February 1955, before the new committee took office, he had raised the idea of a scholarship for writers. The paltry returns to writers in New Zealand and the absence of any regular and substantial assistance to them by the Literary Fund was already widely recognised. A writer's fellowship had been strenuously urged at the 1951 Writers' Conference; and in 1953 Charles Brasch proposed in a *Landfall* editorial 'fellowships for writers, on the lines of those offered by the Commonwealth Literary Fund in Australia and the Guggenheim Foundation in America'; in the same issue an 'Australian Letter' by Vance Palmer

Literary Fund Advisory Committee members inspecting New Zealand entries in the International Book Design Exhibition, May 1963. From left, Professor John Garrett, Professor Ian Gordon, Monte Holcroft, Hon. Leon Götz.
ANZ

explained how such fellowships were the core of state patronage of literature across the Tasman.[2] In mid-1955, PEN released a paper recommending a 'Katherine Mansfield Memorial Fellowship' of £500 a year for two years to an 'imaginative' writer to devote full time to writing or for overseas travel. Brasch leapt on this and returned to the attack in the September *Landfall*, urging the new committee to act.[3] They did. Wheels began turning and at their second meeting, in March 1956, a formal memo from the Secretary of Internal Affairs, Arthur Harper, was on the table.

Headed 'Literary Fellowship or Award', it indicated that the Minister, S.W. Smith, would like to see a proposal from the committee for either an award or a fellowship. Harper suggested £500 a year to be added to the annual appropriation. The committee heard from an official about awards in the other arts and a motion was carried recommending an annual award for 'work of outstanding literary merit' and an increase of the allocation to $2500 for 'more generous treatment . . . by direct financial assistance to writers in the form of bursaries, scholarships, travel awards . . .'.[4] At the September meeting the committee learnt that the Minister had approved an extra £500 from the Cultural Fund and they now recommended a Scholarship in Letters 'for the furtherance of New Zealand literature'. In addition, they resolved that a further £100 be made available for an annual Award for Achievement (which it later was). This dealt with any debate among the committee and offered both retrospective and prospective encouragement to writers. Five scholarship applicants were considered at the very next meeting; three were shortlisted and the first Scholarship in Letters awarded to scholar and writer Eric McCormick in early 1957, a choice approved by the ever-watchful Brasch.

The speed with which this all happened suggests the improved efficiency of a smaller committee and a commendable sensitivity to the literary lobby. In fact it marked a shift in the committee's attention towards understanding the difficult situation of writers in a small and isolated country and towards recognising their needs, especially those of novelists, for extended periods of time without financial stress. The fear that state aid might constrain and hobble creativity was slowly succeeded by the belief that it could provide, even temporarily, the necessary freedom for art. 'The aim of all patronage of the arts should be to allow the free play of imaginative energy', wrote Brasch in introducing the replies to a 1960 survey of New Zealand writers that vividly reveals the daily stress of their existence. In the same *Landfall* survey, Ian Cross argues that 'All the State Literary Fund should do—apart from subsidising *Landfall* of course—is buy writers the time to write.'[5]

The Scholarship in Letters, initially of £500, less than the average wage, was however for many years the most prestigious award made from the Fund (a limit of £250 was quickly set on all other grants to writers).[6] Over the next decade it was awarded with excellent judgement to a series of distinguished writers, almost all novelists and some very early in their careers: Maurice Shadbolt, Sylvia Ashton-Warner, Marilyn Duckworth, Maurice Gee, Noel Hilliard, Janet Frame, O.E. Middleton and Maurice Duggan. Marilyn Duckworth was awarded it for 1961 but only if the 'money would be put to good use' (not presumably on some feminine frivolity), but her reply that it would be spent on travel as background to her novel and on her family was considered satisfactory and she later won the scholarship a second time.[7] Sylvia Ashton-Warner tried very hard to refuse the 1959 Scholarship but eventually succumbed.[8] Janet Frame, in whom the committee took a fatherly interest, was encouraged to apply in 1963 and won the 1964 scholarship.[9] Sometimes runners-up were also assisted: Shadbolt in 1958 and Gee in 1960, for example.

From 1957 the two awards were financed from lottery funds but in 1961 the annual allocation was raised for the first time to £2600 to support them. After many comments that £500 was insufficient for the scholarship and an approach from PEN, it was increased in 1962 to £1000 (around $69,000 in 2015 wages) with the cost of the awards once more to be provided from lottery profits so that the total amount now available to the committee was £3700 annually.[10]

Denis Glover, at his final meeting as a member of the

Sketch by Denis Glover showing desperate writers eagerly pursuing a grant.
Courtesy Rupert Glover. Denis Glover Collection, ATL, C-078-006-2

committee, 9 June 1958, proposed that Janet Frame be given the first Award for Achievement for *Owls Do Cry*. He had already been an advocate for her travel grant and for a publishing subsidy: Rex Fairburn, writing to Glover in 1956, had remarked, 'My grope-vine tells me you are trying to Frame the S.L. Fund Committee', which was a pretty accurate rumour.[11] A decision on the 1957 Award was thus tactfully deferred but strongly recommended at the next meeting. Henceforth the Award for Achievement, generally given for a single work appearing the previous year but sometimes for a body of work, was another regular recognition of writers. While the judgement of committee members seems here a little more erratic, with some long-forgotten books on the list, this award also tended to single out works of fiction, with Ruth France's novel *The Race* and O.E. Middleton's short story collection *The Stone* other early recipients.

Twenty-three writers received smaller grants in this period to assist them with their writing. The sums were mostly modest—the largest was £320 to R.A.K. Mason—and their purposes included £100 for translating Maori poetry (Roger Oppenheim), £300 for a biography of composer Alfred Hill (J.M. Thomson), £75 for collecting early New Zealand songs (Rona Bailey). Seven assisted travel, so important for writers in a small faraway place, most notably Janet Frame's crucial trip to England and James K. Baxter's to India; Dan Davin was assisted to come and Anton Vogt to go; Maurice Gee was supported in England and Peter Bland in South East Asia. With the addition of the two awards, around 45 percent of total funding was now going to writers. By 1962, when the Scholarship was increased, significantly more was going to writers than to publishers or magazines, a trend which continued thereafter.

* * *

Publication subsidies were still a large item, however, on the committee table. In the 1961/62 year, for example, a total of £1023 (about $42,800 in 2015) was awarded to publishers for books ranging from Philip May's classic study of the West Coast gold rushes (Pegasus) to Bruce Mason's celebrated play *The End of the Golden Weather* (Price Milburn). An immediate effect of the appointment of Sharp was a much closer scrutiny of publisher applications. Specific information on print run, production costs, retail price and royalty was now required along with an estimate of the grant needed. At Sharp's first meeting there is reference to a formula provided by the Department on a 'maximum fair retail price in relation to a given subsidy',[12] and in a 1958 note revealingly headed 'Note on Formula for Preventing Milking of the Fund' he explains how after investigation of publisher practice in 1956, the Department and the committee agreed on a requirement that the retail price should not exceed three times the unit cost after the grant.[13] This formula was faithfully followed until 1967, though by 1962 Blackwood Paul was pleading for an increase in the markup.[14]

The author's royalty was another concern for the committee, with a standard requirement of 10 percent of the retail price established about the same time and retained throughout the history of the Fund. Denis Glover, with the suspicious mind of one who was a publisher himself, suggested that publishers be asked to provide royalty figures for subsidised books over a two-to-three-year period.[15]

Some authors despaired of their books ever appearing, although a subsidy had been paid to the publisher. Pilgrim Press (Bob Lowry) had been awarded £190 in September

1957 for *The Stone*; at the December 1958 meeting Holcroft reported Middleton's distress that the book had not been published in the time stipulated in the contract. Lowry was sent one stern letter and then another; and henceforth all publication grants were paid only on publication.[16] Kendrick Smithyman had even greater cause for complaint when a poetry collection for which Capricorn Press had been awarded £40 in June 1958, on the basis of a classic report by Denis Glover,[17] had still not appeared in 1961. Louis Johnson, a better poet than a publisher and trying to run Capricorn Press, the *New Zealand Poetry Yearbook* and the little magazine *Numbers* all at once, explained that Capricorn Press was heavily in debt. Finally the committee, in an act of true generosity, allowed him the £40 to wipe out his debts, and at the same meeting gave a further grant (£75) to Paul's Book Arcade, who finally published the book in 1962 under the title *Inheritance*.[18]

In these years Pegasus, run by Albion Wright (17 titles) and Paul's Book Arcade, run by Blackwood and Janet Paul (18 titles) received by far the most assistance from the Fund. Both small independent publishers founded at the end of the war, they used ancillary businesses (printing, bookselling) to support bold and imaginative publishing programmes with a strong literary bent. From 1962 to 1964 these two publishers were able to take the risk on eight new writers, including Amelia Batistich, Hone Tuwhare and C.K. Stead. The two long-established mainstream publishers, Reeds and Whitcombe and Tombs, were both occasionally (four and five times respectively) assisted and a variety of other small publishers, often associated with Bob Lowry, Louis Johnson or Denis Glover, also benefited. No publishing grant exceeded £350 though and most were for considerably less.

The flowering of fiction in the years from 1957 to 1961 was widely noticed: first novels by Ruth France, Noel Hilliard and M.K. Joseph, first (and second) novels by Frame, Ashton-Warner, Marilyn Duckworth, Barry Crump, three novels by Ian Cross, and Maurice Shadbolt's *The New Zealanders*, all appeared in these years. It has to be said that most of these books were first published overseas and the Literary Fund supported none of them except *Owls Do Cry* (though quickly assisting authors Crump and Ashton-Warner once their first books were successful) and declined Joseph's. In 1961 the committee distinguished itself by rejecting both an application from Pegasus for Janet Frame's *Faces in the Water* and one from Paul's Book Arcade for Bill Pearson's landmark novel *Coal Flat*, a decision that provoked outrage in some quarters.[19] While the Fund might have begun to offer time and money to novelists, it had so far made only a few hesitant stabs at encouraging publishers of new fiction. Its support of five reprints of novels, however, suggests that, to a committee now heavily peopled by academics, the idea of reinforcing an established tradition was more appealing than inventing a new one.

The publication of poetry was more sure of support with 22 books (including six issues of the *New Zealand Poetry Yearbook*), published by either Pegasus or Paul's Book Arcade, getting small grants. Among the poets were R.A.K. Mason, Kendrick Smithyman and M.K. Joseph but not Curnow or Baxter, whose publishers did not apply.

One example of how the Fund worked in practice can be seen in the early years of the poet Hone Tuwhare's career. From early 1958 he began publishing poems in magazines, encouraged by writer Noel Hilliard, who typed them up for him.[20] After a third poem in the *Listener* caught the eye of Janet Paul, now well established as a publisher with her husband Blackwood, she wondered if Hone Tuwhare might have enough poems for a book. Blackwood was 'fed up to the back teeth with bloody poets' but he reluctantly agreed to sign a letter to Tuwhare. After some months the young poet replied, saying 'if ever he had enough poems to put down on the kitchen floor to look at for himself, he'd send them to us'.[21] And he did, after some help from Hilliard and Bill Pearson.[22] The Pauls were delighted, accepted the book and applied for a Literary Fund grant to publish it under the title *No Ordinary Sun*. The manuscript was given for assessment to James K. Baxter at that time on the committee. His reader's report, handwritten, is a model of succinctness and clarity: addressed to Andrew Sharp, it reads 'Andy—I think these are good Jim Baxter'.[23] On such an authoritative opinion the committee recommended a grant of £40. But that was not the end of the story. Tuwhare wanted the book printed by the Auckland printer Bob Lowry at his private printing press on One Tree Hill; the Pauls agreed. Lowry began handsetting the book in elegant Caslon type; but when he was halfway through he rang Blackwood and said he had run out of lowercase 'e'; he would have to print half the book, then break up the type to do the second part. But before this happened, Lowry, sick and unhappy, committed suicide. The Pauls had to find someone else to finish the job. And this cost money. So back they went to the Literary Fund committee for another £15, which was granted. The book finally appeared in 1964 in an ambitious edition of 700 copies and sold out in ten days. The Fund continued to provide Tuwhare and his publishers with small grants throughout the 1970s.

At the third meeting of the slimmed-down committee, David Hall proposed a small insertion into the definitions of the categories of assistance from the Fund, aimed at reducing the flow of unsuitable manuscripts from writers of family histories or tedious memoirs, a suggestion quickly agreed to by the committee. The guidelines now read, 'By grants towards publishing costs . . . to enable the publication of writing *of literary merit* in such fields as creative literature, historical writing, reprints of New Zealand classics, and Maori literature'. The words 'of literary merit' would now eliminate many historical works and would encourage the publication of good writing in this field.[24] Thus, books of nonfiction subsidised from the Fund (15) tended to have literary subjects or literary credentials: Oxford University Press was given £250 to reprint Kippenberger's classic *Infantry Brigadier*; Hugh Price received £80 for publishing the New Zealand diary of Beatrice and Sidney Webb; Paul's Book Arcade got £100 for *Theatre in Danger*, an exchange of correspondence on theatre between Bruce Mason and John Pocock; Reeds £350 for John Pascoe's *Mr Explorer Douglas*; Whitcombe and Tombs £100 for *The Maorilander*, a study of writer William Satchell by Phillip Wilson, who had just won the second Scholarship in Letters. The numbers of applications too continued to fall, from 65 in 1954 to 29 in 1957. A further indication of the shift in focus towards more narrowly literary nonfiction was the decision in early 1963 to reject reprints of early memoirs 'in favour of new creative writing'.[25]

* * *

Published by Caxton and edited by Brasch, *Landfall* was by the mid-1950s well established and widely respected. It benefited from the surge of literary activity that followed the war, from the financial independence and the fine literary judgement of its editor and from his enlightened understanding that literature was connected to politics, history and the other arts. He brought the magazine out regularly, he paid his contributors, and his running editorial commentary on current events, including the activities of the Literary Fund Committee, was required reading. The magazine remained amazingly free of controversy, though one C.C. Chalmers complained to the Minister about the dreadful 'modern art' in the June 1961 issue. A judicious response explained that the Minister was guided by the advice of an expert committee but that he would pass on the complaint. Mr Chalmers, replying, thought National would lose the next election and regretted the demise of the Liberal Party. Unswayed by such views, the Fund awarded *Landfall* £300 annually from 1955, increasing this to £400 in 1961 after receiving an eloquent letter from Brasch detailing rising circulation but simultaneous rising deficits.[26]

The committee had quickly established that a grant to a literary magazine depended on the overall editorial quality, not on the specific contents of any one issue and that they did not therefore need to see any text in advance. They also insisted that no magazine should assume ongoing funding, and required a new application each year. Although *Landfall* was their prime exhibit, the committee did not completely ignore the other small magazines which sprang up occasionally, offering new writers their first chances of print. Noel Hoggard's *Arena* was modestly supported for three years (1955–8) though it continued to appear long after that. *Numbers*, a modest counterblast to *Landfall* and to the austere discrimination of Allen Curnow, soon to be embattled over the selection for his Penguin anthology of New Zealand verse, received an annual amount of £50 for three years with an increase to £100 in 1958/9. It had first appeared in July 1954 edited by Wellington poet Louis

Johnson, along with James K. Baxter and Charles Doyle, announcing itself as 'the voice of the contemporary artist in this society'. In spite of a slightly mocking *Listener* editorial on its first appearance by Monte Holcroft, who was then on the committee, it was generous and friendly to new young writers and J.C. Sturm and Maurice Shadbolt both had very early work published in it.

* * *

Unexpectedly, it was around this very small magazine that a serious debate threatening the integrity and independence of the Literary Fund arose. The ninth issue (February 1959) of *Numbers*, edited by Johnson alone, was presented as a special Wellington number; its editorial attacked the feeble advertising support the magazine had received and the philistine attitudes of the press, while pointing out the literary riches of the capital. No one, least of all the distinguished members of the Literary Fund Advisory Committee, was prepared for the outrage that greeted this issue: a nasty little note in the *Dominion* commented that in this state-funded journal three stories dealt with 'illicit love'; 'SALACIOUS TALES BY N.Z. AUTHORS' screamed an *Evening Post* news headline with a pointed over-caption, 'Helped By State Literary Fund', and the item notes that 'The basic theme of three [stories] are [sic] sex—the seduction of young women—and drinking hard liquor.' A heated correspondence and articles about possible prosecution followed. There was, however, measured support from *New Zealand Truth* and the *Otago Daily Times* and now Holcroft rode to the rescue in the *Listener*. After the flames had died, the next issue appeared in September 1959 with a note, 'Published without the aid of the New Zealand Literary Fund, with special acknowledgements to "The

Dominion" and "Evening Post"'; in a long editorial Johnson traversed the controversy in detail and ended up by saying the magazine would not be seeking further grants from the Literary Fund. It could not survive unassisted and that was its last issue.

The offending stories were by Marilyn Duckworth, then aged 23, Jacqueline Sturm (31) and Richard Packer (23). It is roughly true that they were all about seductions but Duckworth's is an idyllic interlude of young love, Sturm's is a more complex and subtle depiction of female ambivalence—

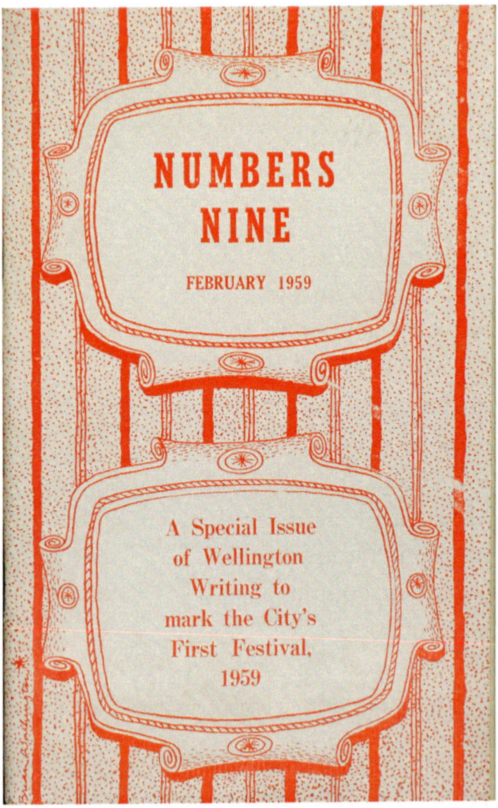

The elegant and inoffensive cover of a controversial issue.
J. C. Beaglehole Room, Victoria University of Wellington Library

assisted, it is true, by a lot of gin—and Packer's is a study of the effects on sexual behaviour of an ugly and violent home background. None is a great story, none is in the least explicit about sex, and none would cause anyone from a later age the slightest concern.

Tact or diplomacy were not Louis Johnson's strong points and he had annoyed the local press: there seems to have been visceral ill feeling between the press and the literary community. But these were the days of moral panic that followed the discovery of sexual activity among teenagers in the Hutt Valley, the resulting Mazengarb report and the widespread belief that it was all the fault of comics; in other words, that reading could lead to immorality.[27] A National-dominated press would not be above exploiting this atmosphere to embarrass a Literary Fund and its committee set up by Labour and now under a Labour Government.

Professor Gordon spoke to the press, saying that going on the past performance of the magazine the committee would not have expected anything like the last issue. He was in fact in a difficult position on several counts. Controversies of this kind could easily threaten the future of the Fund to which he was deeply committed; at the same time he did not want to alienate the literary community by submitting to state interference. Further, matters of 'indecency' in literature were still covered by the 1910 Indecent Publications Act (to which, after the Mazengarb report, a couple of hasty amendments were added). The inadequacies of the Act had been recognised for some time and a special literary committee set up to advise government on questions of literary merit. The chair of that committee was Professor Ian Gordon.

These events may have been in the mind of the new National Minister, the Hon. Leon Götz, two years later, when he asked the committee to consider restricting aid to periodicals to one 'pre-eminent in quality' (presumably *Landfall*).[28] Recognising that this would be the death of all the small magazines, where new untried writers might start out, the committee tactfully deferred a decision until a relevant application was received. Which it shortly was, from *Mate*, a journal edited from its second issue by the gifted young journalist Robin Dudding. Dudding had already applied successfully for funding in 1959 and 1960, declaring in his first letter, 'I am seeking vigour, purpose and entertainment in prose and poetry' and in respect of *Landfall*, 'I think there is a place for a magazine with less formal or a less humourless approach to writing'.[29] The committee was now able to give him £120 for three issues and to reply to the Minister 'that the periodical under consideration had proved itself, and that some competition between literary periodicals was desirable'.[30]

Another regular publication supported by the Fund during the 1950s and early 1960s was the *New Zealand Poetry Yearbook* edited by Louis Johnson with his usual energy and generosity and published by Pegasus. It was treated by the committee as a periodical and supported according to the Fund's periodical policy without mandatory reading of the copy. However, its open and inclusive approach led to strong criticisms of its quality, especially by Curnow, and the committee minutes reveal a growing nervousness about their continuing support. In 1954 Gordon asked to see manuscript or proofs before publication; in 1955 Johnson was told not to publish if he could not find enough good material; in 1957 Pegasus was asked to provide sales figures; in 1960 they were told the £300 granted was not to be regarded as a precedent and to produce the volume more cheaply if possible. In September 1961 the committee asked for copy, to be read by Gordon, Holcroft and Baxter; Johnson complained but complied. Some 'questionable phrases' in a poem by Peter Bland were 'revised' and the grant confirmed.[31] You could see this publication too was riding for a fall; and it seems clear that the Minister, mindful of the *Numbers* debacle, had leant on Gordon to see no further 'salacious' material was given support.[32]

Accordingly, at the meeting of 20 August 1963, when Baxter, Gordon and Holcroft reported favourably on the text of the next annual (no. 11), Gordon and Holcroft were empowered to recommend a grant of £300 to Pegasus 'subject to agreement of publisher to deletion of certain passages'. These turned out to be six poems, three by Baxter, two by Richard Packer (the author of one of the offending stories in *Numbers*, a poet and journalist and protégé of Johnson's) and one by Martyn Sanderson (later well known as an actor). At the November meeting letters from Pegasus, Louis Johnson and Baxter himself urged reconsideration of the condition. Baxter and Margaret Dalziel spoke in support but the rest of the committee resolved that the conditions be sustained and the poems removed.[33]

All hell broke loose. Professor Gordon made a press statement explaining that the poems were likely to give offence to the taxpayer. Albion Wright also spoke to the press; and so, rashly, did Baxter. *Truth* printed one of the Baxter poems. Louis Johnson angrily attacked the committee's 'editorial interference', its refusal to give an explanation for censoring the poems and its inconsistency in funding, for example, 'the current issue of *Landfall* in which the famous four-letter word of D.H. Lawrence's is used'.[34] Holcroft, too often inclined to use his editorial column in the services of the committee, defended its decision in an editorial called 'Freedom's Champion'.[35] Whereupon

Margaret Dalziel resigned. And for six weeks the *Listener* correspondence column exploded with fury as almost every writer in the country attacked Holcroft. He later called it 'the battle of Bowen St' and admitted he had been wrong, though from the best motive, a fear of endangering the future of the Fund.[36] Brasch too sounded forth, claiming that 'the incautious, muddled statements of no less than three of its members have made it a laughing-stock, and lost it the confidence of people who care about New Zealand letters'.[37]

Albion Wright of Pegasus, who was at that time first

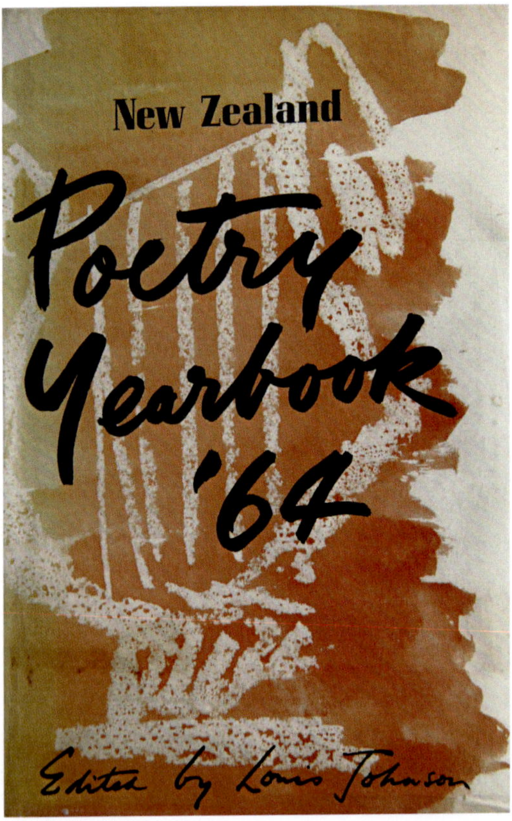

The last issue of the *New Zealand Poetry Yearbook*, a *cause célèbre* and not the finest moment of the Literary Fund Advisory Committee.
Jock Phillips photograph

President of the new New Zealand Book Publishers Association, refused to accept the condition. The eleventh, and last, *Poetry Yearbook* appeared with the poems and without the grant—and without payment of the contributors.[38] Baxter's last words on the subject can be found in an essay[39] and a poem:

> . . .
> Though I can't tell you what goes on
> In the holy hutch of Wellington
> Where Gordon, Garrett, Blaiklock, each
> Gang-shag the Liberty of Speech
> By saying my beatnik verses can't
> Be published with the usual grant,
> Yet I can tell you this at least
> Now that the wind is in the East:
> Three moa-grey professors in a row
> Most ably represent the status quo.
> I shall not breathe a word of the agenda
> Of that Committee of which I am a member:
> But let me praise with a high heart
> The burgeoning of Moral Art![40]

An article by Allen Curnow in the *New Zealand Herald* links this row to another debate going on at the same time, about the new Indecent Publications Act passed in October 1963.[41] The inadequacies of the 1910 Act had become obvious especially after the addition of the two hasty amendments in the wake of the Mazengarb report. When in 1960 Vladimir Nabokov's novel *Lolita* was found to be indecent under the Act and again in the Appeal Court, where the President, Mr Justice Gresson, dissented, it was time to rewrite the legislation.[42]

The new Act established an Indecent Publications Tribunal which alone would make decisions on indecency or otherwise. The members of the Tribunal were announced on Christmas Eve 1963 and one of them was Professor Gordon. He was thus in a peculiarly delicate position over that summer with the *Yearbook* row in full spate and writers deeply suspicious. Curnow's article was headed 'Signs point to growing pressures on liberty of N.Z. writers' and deplored Gordon's dual role, saying that 'too much pressure . . . tends to be concentrated in too few hands, far too well-known to each other in Wellington: . . . that is the main cause for disquiet in literary circles.'

Two publications were thus closed down, one because of pressure from a conservative and shallow press, the other because of an ill-judged attempt at censorship by the committee. In the background was the spectre of state interference into the freedom of writers which Fairburn and others had so feared when the Fund was first established. Writers and other artists were still, in the early 1960s, a small and poorly understood group treated with suspicion by the general public and regarded uneasily by politicians. Maybe, though, Gordon and the committee learned from all this because while he remained in the chair for another ten years, no further controversy of this kind arose and the decisions of the Indecent Publications Tribunal on which he was the leading literary expert were generally considered liberal. Nor was any attempt at political censorship made, as it was in the same period in Australia. During the long years of the Holyoake Government, which was not notably friendly to the arts, Gordon managed to steer the ship safely between political shoals and literary sharks with a certain canny skill.

* * *

The Fund continued for many years to help PEN with its two awards by topping up their available funds with small sums under £100; it also provided £200 for a writers' conference in 1959. Having in 1959 given £50 to the New Zealand Women Writers' Society for their bulletin, the committee, though refusing to promise an annual grant, was targeted throughout the 1960s. In 1961 they gave the society only £25, 'for general purposes', with one member dissenting. From 1966 this assistance ceased altogether.

From 1955 the committee was now reconstituted regularly every three years, but its character changed much more slowly. In 1957 Gillespie died and was replaced as a PEN representative by Holcroft who had served five years earlier. Professor Blaiklock was also reappointed at the end of 1957. Two new members with Labour allegiances joined the committee in September 1958: George Manning, the 71-year-old mayor of Christchurch, and historian Dr J.C. Beaglehole. The grumbles at the 1951 Writers' Conference about the greybeards of the Literary Fund committee seem not to have been heeded, as only one member of the committee (David Hall) was under 50 and there were no women. Weighty and wise, they were not likely to be bold or creative; Brasch described the selection of books subsidised between 1958 and 1961 as 'deadly safe'. In 1961 Professor J.C. Garrett from Canterbury University College and Dr Margaret Dalziel from the University of Otago replaced Manning and Hall along with James K. Baxter taking over from Beaglehole as the second PEN member; Gordon, Holcroft and Blaiklock, the 'three moa-grey professors', remained.[43] The young Bill Manhire reflected some years later:

> While a committee consisting of practising writers would be an obvious enough evil, the *Poetry Yearbook* controversy was

> perhaps an indication of the dangers inherent in a committee made up largely of committee-members. Some of those at the time certainly showed a very tenuous awareness of the public and poetic tastes which they insisted did exist.[44]

Gordon had been on the committee for 14 years and its chair for 10; Brasch thought he 'should be granted a long rest' (a respite in fact delayed another 12 years). He also suggested that no member should serve more than two three-year terms on end, with some staggering of appointments to ensure continuity. He repeated this call in 1964 in the wake of the *Yearbook* row, seeing the forthcoming expiry of the term of the current committee as an excellent opportunity to get rid of the long-serving members.[45]

Götz's successor as Minister for Internal Affairs, the Hon. David Seath, was also considering these matters with that controversy much in his mind. In his recommendations to Cabinet he specifically resisted disposing with Gordon in case government attitudes to his stand on the *Yearbook* should be misconstrued. He did, however, think that Blaiklock had been there long enough and should be replaced by another Auckland professor, J.C. Reid; and that Garrett, a relative newcomer and a useful one, should be reappointed. A Dunedin replacement for Margaret Dalziel could face embarrassment and an Invercargill journalist, F.W.G. Miller, was therefore suggested, to represent southern man and rectify the over-representation by 'University people'.[46]

The new PEN members proved tricky. The PEN president, Ruth Mackay (Gilbert), was a pro forma appointment but finding a second representative, preferably living in Wellington and unlikely to apply to the Fund, was difficult. Eventually Holcroft, who had already served for over 12 years and was very reluctant to stand again, accepted nomination as long as the vote was unanimous, which it was.[47] But both Brasch and Johnson protested to PEN; and Vincent O'Sullivan, a young academic, poet and editor of *Comment*, wrote acidly, 'a man who has . . . proved himself capable of personal animosity against particular writers in justification of his own committee vote, and evinced no compunction in employing editorial privileges in an independent journal to support a decision that indicated panic-measures—if one prefers to avoid saying crassness—is not the man best to serve literature'.[48]

On Christmas Eve 1962, the government announced the establishment of an organisation that would soon become the elephant in the advisory committee room. The Queen Elizabeth II Arts Council did not begin operation till August 1964, but at the February 1963 meeting of the committee Sharp explained that the Literary Fund would 'come under' the new body, whatever that meant.[49] While no merger would occur for many years, relations between the two funding organisations would vary from wary to uneasy to tense, and would be subject to lobbying and pressure from all quarters. The story of that relationship is a constant thread in the history of the Literary Fund from that date.

5

'A CIVILISED AND CIVILISING INSTITUTION' OR 'AN ESTABLISHMENT OF NEGLECT'? 1964–1974

Andrew Sharp had in 1966 been secretary of the committee for 11 years. His meticulous minutes and his courteous letters with the occasional wry comment are just hints that remain of the efficient and careful way in which he conducted his job.[1] During these years he was also on the National Commission to UNESCO and the Historic Places Trust and assistant to the Film Censor; at the same time he was deeply engaged in scholarly research and writing on early Pacific voyaging, publishing six books and numerous articles. His theories on how Polynesians first came to New Zealand are now discredited, but they attracted great interest at the time. In 1967 he left Internal Affairs to take up a Senior Research Fellowship at the University of Auckland.

His departure coincided with the twentieth anniversary of the founding of the Literary Fund. Fittingly, his final task was to write a history of the Fund.[2] A brief work, it simply gives an account of the establishment, the membership of committees, and any changes in policy and funding followed by a list of grants and awards given each year. It was a modest celebration, a signal that the Fund was now a stable and well-established institution (owing much to Sharp's quiet work behind the scenes), accepted widely by both writers and publishers. Publishers could speculate on new and talented writers with a little more confidence; writers could hope for some assistance in buying the time to write, especially precious to aspiring novelists. This was part of a wider understanding in government and the general public that the arts enriched the national life, explaining and entertaining, challenging and extending, and that the state had some obligation to encourage talent in the arts, both its production and its dissemination.

However, all was not rosy. Sharp's history was given a real bureaucratic runaround. Its distribution was discussed twice by the committee, then the new Secretary for Internal Affairs, Patrick O'Dea, told the committee in May 1967 that it would appear in the department's Annual Report, and in May 1968 that it would not. It eventually appeared, suitably updated, in booklet form in 1971, five years after its original composition. Its subject can hardly have been thought urgent or important.

It was not. The National Government was entrenched for the long haul and the arts were not top of its agenda. The Minister of Internal Affairs, David Seath, an accountant and formerly mayor of Taumarunui, a 'nervous man', according to Michael Bassett, 'easily frightened by Holyoake', showed little interest.[3] In a *Landfall* survey of literati who had been shown a draft of the Sharp history, almost all, though generally favourable, commented on the paltry size of the Fund: 'useful but too small' (Stead); 'meagre' compared with the Australian equivalent of

$147,000 (Sargeson); 'a piffling amount' (Albion Wright).[4]

In fact, the amount of money available to the fund in 1965 (£2600 from Vote and £1100 from lottery profits for the Scholarship and Award, in total around $141,300 in 2015) was less in real terms than the original sum with which the Fund began in 1947. With a downturn in the economy in 1966, the vote was then reduced to £2400 for 1967/8, rising briefly in 1968/9 to $5000. When this was unfortunately under-expended, it was further reduced by the kindly Minister of Finance, R.D. Muldoon, in the budget for 1969/70 to $4000. However, it became clear at the end of 1969 that with a greater number of grants and some carry-over from the under-expended previous year, expenditure was likely to be around $7100. The Minister thus agreed to a revised allocation of $6000 (around $94,200 in 2015) for 1969/70 and the same sum for the next year.[5] But it was all rather grudging.

In early 1967, just as the annual allocation was cut, a crisis arose over the Fund's most prestigious award, the Scholarship in Letters, funded from 1965 by the Queen Elizabeth II Arts Council from its lottery resources. It now refused to do this. Only after an impassioned plea from Gordon did the Minister agree to restore independent Lottery Board funding, which henceforth became an essential part of the resources available to the committee.[6] The grant was saved but not increased. The privately funded Robert Burns Fellowship at the University of Otago, the only other substantial grant for writers, had been from its inception in 1959 considerably more generous than the Scholarship in Letters: in 1970 the Burns Fellow, O.E. Middleton, was paid $4700, while Maurice Shadbolt received a miserly $2000 for the Scholarship, at a time when the average wage was about $2400 a year.[7]

Pressures on the Fund were growing as the literary and publishing sectors slowly became larger and more complex. A new generation, including James McNeish, C.K. Stead and Vincent O'Sullivan, was appearing and gradually the reading public was showing more interest in local writing. However, writers like Sargeson, Frame, Duckworth, Gee and Shadbolt still struggled to survive; Ian Cross gave up writing fiction altogether. Even though the committee had 'moved steadily towards the subsidisation of writers—rather than publishers—as its major activity',[8] the 'normal' amount available from the Fund to an individual writer at the end of the 1960s, apart from the Scholarship, was still $500, increased under pressure from the committee to $750 in 1970/1.[9] But such small sums were not going to relieve writers of the need to take other employment, especially if they planned longer projects.

Writers did now, however, regularly get a greater share of the annual allocation than any other group and the lion's share of that money went to novelists. This was a deliberate policy; as Gordon said, 'our greatest need is the opportunity to give full attention to literary production. This is especially true of the novel which suffers and dies under sporadic writing.'[10] Nine writers were specifically assisted to write novels in the years 1964–70 as against two poets and three playwrights; they included Graham Billing, Jean Watson, Vincent O'Sullivan, and Marilyn Duckworth. The Scholarship in Letters too was almost exclusively given to writers of fiction. The committee still contributed small sums, around $248, to PEN for their annual Hubert Church and Jessie Mackay awards. Even Sargeson now recognised the Fund as a 'civilised and civilising institution'.[11]

From 1965 the numbers of applications to the Fund were falling, a drop most marked among publishers and attributed by the committee to the constraints imposed by the threefold mark-up requirement. In early 1966 Blackwood and Janet Paul renewed in a more formal way their pleas for a revision of the 'threefold formula' and were referred to the New Zealand Book Publishers Association.[12] This was not an easy time for the Pauls, and in December, Sharp himself wrote to the association urging them to make 'representations'.[13] A year later, Ray Richards, at that time President of the New Zealand Book Publishers Association, replied with a cogent argument for increasing the mark-up to four times, pointing out that increased costs meant that retaining the old formula would inhibit publishers from producing the kind of books encouraged by the Advisory Committee.[14] The committee, anxious about the recent fall-off in publisher applications, moved immediately to raise the formula to four times for a year.[15] No effect was seen at first, but in 1969/70 eight grants were awarded to publishers (compared with two in 1968/9 and three in 1967/8) and the amount involved was that year, and probably for the last time, more than that awarded to writers.

Caxton, Pegasus and Blackwood and Janet Paul continued in this period to receive by far the most publishing assistance. But British publishers, chiefly established to bring in their own books, also began to dabble in local publishing. In the early 1960s Collins, for example, took on Professor J.C. Reid as a publishing adviser (he was also a member of the Literary Fund Advisory Committee, as Brasch disapprovingly noted) and in 1964–5 produced some oddly literary titles which were assisted by the Fund. After the death of Blackwood Paul in 1965, that firm was bought in 1967 by British firm Longmans and for a while, under the editorship of Phoebe Meikle, continued to publish novels and poetry. Oxford University Press too began to appear on the Literary Fund agenda in the early 1970s with works of poetry, and the University of Auckland Publications Committee (later Auckland University Press) became the first local university suppliant with Kendrick Smithyman's *Flying to Palmerston* (1968).[16]

The committee often showed how little they understood the conditions under which local publishers operated and their enthusiasm for fiction was not evident in grants awarded to publishers, with only two novels in ten years being supported. It was hardly surprising that publishers were reluctant to publish in this area and that novelists still published overseas. One novel they did support was a first novel by Samoan writer Albert Wendt, *Sons for the Return Home*, perceptively identified by Phoebe Meikle at Longman Paul and awarded $600 in 1973 in spite of the dissent of one committee member. C.K. Stead's celebrated novel, *Smith's Dream*, was turned down, apparently for political reasons, but Longman Paul proceeded anyway; they did not though with Norman Harvey's *One Magpie for Sorrow*, rejected on the grounds that it would stand on its own feet if the publisher increased the print run from 1250 copies. It appeared in 1967 with Whitcombe and Tombs and Robert Hale in London, winning the Literary Fund's Award for Achievement in 1968. The same thing happened in 1970 with Jean Watson's first novel, *Stand in the Rain*, which the committee, in a further display of naivety, thought would work unsubsidised if either the retail price or the print run (of 2500!) was increased. It is true that all three novels were finally successful but each was a significant risk, by a little-known first-time novelist—just the kind of enterprise, one would suppose, the Fund existed to encourage.

The committee did understand that publishers would not publish poetry, with its small print runs and limited market, without assistance and in 1964–74, 21 collections were supported. They included Vincent O'Sullivan's first two collections, Stead's first, Charles Doyle's anthology *Recent Poetry in New Zealand*, two collections by Kendrick Smithyman and, from 1971, *Poetry New Zealand*, Frank McKay's resurrection of the old *Poetry Yearbook*. Their approach to nonfiction was now more sparing and more focused on literary topics, such as Smithyman's *A Way of Saying* (Collins, 1965) and Brasch's *Present Company* (Blackwood and Janet Paul, 1966), though memoir and biography still featured. Sometimes publishers were close to despair: Dennis McEldowney at Auckland University Press recalls, 'It began to look as though, if two requests came before them at the same meeting, they would allow one and refuse the other. . . . Other publishers . . . also complained about erratic decisions which showed ignorance of publishing economics . . .'[17]

What all this adds up to is an institution running out of steam. It is not doing badly, but it coasts along without energy, invention or inspiration. It is comfortable but unchallenged either by government, the literary sector or its own members. '[H]owever well-meaning its members might be,' said one commentator at the Arts Conference 1970, 'it is a passive organisation.'[18] Sharp's successor was another civil servant, Harold White, who made little mark, his documentation of publishers' applications lacking the precision of Sharp's, and left after three years to become secretary and later director of the New Zealand Booksellers' Association. Perhaps provoked by the *Landfall* survey of September 1969, he did put up a number of modest policy proposals to the November meeting.[19] This tinkering around the edges, though, was overtaken by the much more urgent need to address overall funding.

A convention was by now established that members retired after two terms—six years—on the committee, though the position of the chair seemed inviolate. Helen Garrett replaced her husband on the committee in 1967, with Cabinet turning down a suggestion that Charles Brasch be appointed; Walter Scott, retired principal of Wellington Teachers Training College, replaced Holcroft for PEN. As the same conference commentator noted, 'The average age of Literary Fund Advisory Committee members is about 50 years'.[20]

But things were beginning to move. PEN was pushing for a public lending right for authors, to recompense them for library borrowings of their books, and the Arts Conference in April 1970 provided a forum for strong opinions on literature and the Literary Fund. Added to the criticisms of the passivity and elderly character of the committee were comments on the under-expenditure of 1968/9, the absence of publisher members and the inadequacy of current funding. Several remits, including one from Ralph Gooderidge of Oxford University Press, urged improved and streamlined assistance to publishers, and Keith Sinclair pushed for more fellowships for writers. The assumption behind much of this grumbling was that the Arts Council could do these things better. The conference finally resolved 'that a literature panel of the Arts Council be constituted and that the New Zealand State Literary Fund be abolished and that additional funds be provided by the Government for this purpose'.[21] (It also agreed to support the establishment of a public lending right system, more fellowships for writers and artists and the appointment of a parliamentary historian.) Though the Literary Fund committee noted this resolution at its next meeting, it took almost a year for the Arts Council to endorse it and for the Secretary of Internal

Affairs to return it to the committee for their views. By now of course they were on their mettle; they did not care to have their independence compromised and their funding possibly reduced. 'The Committee resolved that it should retain its existing status and that Professor Gordon should reply to this effect to the Minister of Internal Affairs.'[22] What had looked like a threat was perhaps a message that the Literary Fund Advisory Committee must be more active and imaginative if it was to survive.

By this time Mike Jarman had replaced Harold White as secretary. New committee members in 1971 were a youngish professor of English, Roly Frean, and an active president of PEN, Patricia Godsiff, along with a Dunedin journalist, D.G. (Gordon) Buchanan. Godsiff and Frean soon began stirring.

Godsiff suggested the establishment of an award for young writers (7 May 1971), an 'idea' that was regarded favourably, and after much coming and going it was set up in November 1972 as the PEN Young Writers Awards, financed by the Fund.[23] Godsiff also put up a paper (17 September 1971) on the question of funding reprints. The Fund had in recent years supported reprints of Philip Ross May's *The West Coast Gold Rushes*, Robin Hyde's *The Godwits Fly*, and Bill Pearson's *Coal Flat* but reprints were generally far cheaper to produce, and the money thus expended might more helpfully be used on new work. Accordingly, with a change in policy, the committee now 'decided that no grant would in future be recommended for a republication unless the Committee considered it of special merit', a policy that has remained in place ever since.

This appears to have encouraged Frean to raise a long overdue reconsideration of general policy and agreement that a 'more specific and coherent outline of Fund policy was required regarding applications for assistance'. The guidelines provided to applicants had not been reviewed for nearly 20 years, yet another sign of the way in which habit had begun to determine the actions of the committee. Newcomer Frean, a man of clear mind and high intelligence, expressed some uncertainty about the priorities being followed. He felt there was a lack of clarity about policy and purpose in regard to publishing and literary magazines. Well aware that the Arts Council still loomed in the background, he admitted to 'some impression that we were on the defensive as far as our autonomy was concerned'.[24] He was asked to draft a new version of the categories to be assisted.[25] His admirably succinct one-page document listed categories in order of priority, beginning still with publishing costs, followed by assistance to writers, then to magazines (which were not even mentioned in the previous guidelines). Interestingly, assistance for reprints was retained, favoured before assistance towards publication of 'historical, critical and other scholarly studies', presumably bearing in mind the series of reprints of early New Zealand novels currently coming out with at least two local publishers; it would, however, given the earlier decision, be used sparingly.[26] These suggested guidelines were adopted with minor alteration and made public in March the next year.[27]

Professor Frean and the Arts Conference were not the only ones who wanted to put a bomb under the Literary Fund Advisory Committee. At the same meeting at which his memo was presented, a delegation of three (Ian Cross, Ray Grover, Neva Clarke) from PEN made a formidable démarche, perhaps suggested by Godsiff, armed with a strongly worded paper written by Cross. It argued that not only was the fund inadequate compared with the resources given to the other arts but that its comparative position was likely to get worse if the committee did not act. They believed that PEN, the committee and anyone representing writers would be 'failing in their duty if they became just part of an establishment of neglect'. 'Accordingly P.E.N. is asking the Literary Fund to stop just passively rationing an inadequacy, and to become an advocate to Government in the interests of writers.' This clarion call was followed by suggestion of five different and quite reasonable ways in which increased funding could be used productively.[28] The committee demurred a little, murmuring about their statutory role. But they subsequently sprang into action with a special meeting (20 December), followed immediately (22 December) by a letter from Gordon to the Minister.

The timing was brilliant. Leaning heavily on the PEN paper he boldly asked for an increase from the current $6000 allocation to $22,000, to include $10,000 for basic

Professor Roly Frean joined the committee in 1971 and became its chair in 1976. Courtesy Nicola and Jessica Frean

expenditure and three fellowships of $4000 each. The Secretary for Internal Affairs, Pat O'Dea, allowed a summer break and a decent interval before he translated this request into the world of political reality and sent a memo to the Minister, dated 3 February 1972, endorsing the request but suggesting increases in the vote allocation in line with those recently given to the Arts Council, to $14,300 (for 1972/3), $15,730 (for 1973/4) and $17,146 (for 1974/5). But before this landed on the Minister's desk, Seath resigned, to be replaced by D.A. Highet, a very different personality notably sympathetic to the arts—and of course this was now an election year.

Highet signed a memo to Cabinet, which on 24 April 1972 approved allocations of $14,000 for 1972/73, $15,000 for 1973/4 and $17,000 for 1974/5, and provided for a review of funding before the end of the three-year period.[29] This was a handsome increase from the previous $6000: the Literary Fund now had for 1972/3 $17,200 (around $213,500 in 2015) at its disposal, with the $3200 from lottery funds for the Scholarship in Letters and the Award for Achievement. The committee now proposed a writer's bursary of $4000; adding an extra $1000 to the Scholarship to bring it up to $4000; and adding another $300 to the Award for Achievement, which would now amount to $500. The new Minister had also decided firmly against the merger with the Arts Council.[30] There must have been some satisfaction in PEN quarters. Once again PEN had pushed the committee into action. And the applications poured in. The December meeting was postponed till two days in February to cope with the large number.

Meanwhile things were going on out in the world. Frame and Sargeson and Gee and Shadbolt were writing novels; Allen Curnow exploded onto the scene after a long absence with *Trees, Effigies, Moving Objects* (1972); Baxter poured forth some of his greatest work before his untimely death in November 1972. Energy, irreverence, rebellion drove the talents of young writers against a background of the Vietnam War, the Campaign for Nuclear Disarmament, the Maori renaissance, the growth of feminism. Ian Wedde, Bill Manhire, Alan Brunton, Murray Edmond, David Mitchell, Jan Kemp, Rachel McAlpine were writing poems. Small magazines and small publishers proliferated, shining and fading with great speed.

Aspiring poets were often told by publishers to think of publishing in the magazines first. The magazines are where it begins, the first encounter with critical judgement, the first public exposure. Suddenly the magazines flourished: as Murray Edmond points out, 'Between 1969 and 1971 you could have sent your poems to *Arena*, *Edge*, *Experiment*, *Freed*, *Frontiers*, *Landfall*, *Mate*, *Orpheus*, *Otago Review*, *The Free Word*, *Tuatara* . . . or *The Universities' Arts Festival Yearbook* . . . . others such as *Cave, Lypsinc and New Argot* arrived shortly after.'[31] And this was not to mention student newspapers, the *Listener* or Australian literary journals. In 1969 Bill Manhire wondered 'whether the Fund pays enough attention (i.e. money) to the literary periodicals', pointing out that magazines were often the source of the books later supported by the Fund and arguing for 'an *earned* income' for contributors.[32] *Landfall* had of course been assisted for many years and by 1971 was getting $1000 a year. Robin Dudding had succeeded Charles Brasch as editor in 1966 and, though less inclined to weighty reflection, was more attuned to younger writers and highly skilled at identifying talent and originality. He had previously edited *Mate*, which also became a Fund regular, if a modest one;[33] and he went on in 1972 to edit

Islands. Many of the small magazines such as the famous *Freed* were iconoclastic by definition and would not have dreamt of coming anywhere near the Literary Fund. From the early 1970s, though, the committee did begin giving small amounts to magazines like *Cave*, *Argot*, and *Edge*, which welcomed experimental writing and published international writers alongside New Zealand ones.

The amount granted to magazines steadily rose over these years and by 1972 it exceeded that given to publishers. It was not without a fight though. A new magazine policy made it clear that a new small magazine must have produced at least one issue before it was considered and then only in its establishment phase.[34] Patricia Godsiff thought that *Edge* and *Cave* 'seem to me to be "trend" magazines representing clique interests and the expenditure of public money on them requires careful thought . . . . Too much for too few sums it up.'

She thought an application for publication assistance from Amphedesma Press, set up in London in 1970 by Bill Manhire and Kevin Cunningham, was 'in a similar category';[35] the application was declined.[36] The same sort of attitude probably explains the rejection of Arthur Baysting's important anthology *The Young New Zealand Poets* (Heinemann, 1973) and a bunch of four books of poetry (by Tuwhare, Murray Edmond, Denis List and Peter Olds) put up by Caveman Press.[37] But *Pipe Dreams in Ponsonby* by David Mitchell, that iconic 1972 collection, was supported (twice). And Frean suggested that a publisher should be appointed to the committee and also recommended granting the Award for Achievement for 1972 to Bob Gormack of Nag's Head Press.

The committee was beginning to hear noises outside its walls. The new Writer's Bursary was pinpointed for writers showing potential: its first recipients were jointly Ivan Bootham and Michael Henderson, and Ian Wedde won it in 1974. The establishment of the PEN Young Writer's Award was announced in November 1972 and first awarded the following year. Kerry A.L. Hulme had been beseeching the committee for some time and finally, in August 1973, was given $500. This provoked a grumpy letter asking who was this unknown and unproven writer being supported by the Literary Fund; Pam Hill, assisting Mike Jarman, wrote back politely saying that Ms Hulme had won the Te Awamutu Short Story competition and had one story published in the *Listener*.[38] (The committee, undeterred,

The 1970 edition of Hone Tuwhare's first and best-known collection, with cover designed by Para Matchitt.
Jock Phillips photograph

assisted her twice more before *the bone people* became an international sensation.)

By the end of 1973 most of the committee members were nearing the end of their term. A letter in the *Dominion* in October renewed old complaints about the longevity of the chairman and other members of the committee and the funding of established writers and magazines.[39] These matters were being considered by the new Labour Government, which had taken office in late 1972, and the November meeting was postponed till February 1974 as it made up its mind. Witi Ihimaera, then a humble journalist

The well-worn cover of an iconic collection published in 1972 by Stephen Chan's Association of Orientally Flavoured Syndics, with graphics by Pat Hanly. The Literary Fund contributed $500 to this publication, though this is not acknowledged in the book. Caveman Press reprinted it in 1975, again with a Literary Fund grant.
Jock Phillips photograph

in the Post Office hoping for some assistance with his writing, gave up in despair and Peter Olds, planning a novel, suspected a plot.[40]

No meeting happened in February, or in early March, but on 20 March 1974 the new Minister of Internal Affairs, Henry May, wrote to Professor Gordon noting his recent retirement from Victoria University and refusing to reappoint him to the chair of the Literary Fund Advisory Committee.[41]

6

A NEW ORDER 1974–1982

Six days after the Minister had dismissed Professor Gordon, the new chairman was writing to Mike Jarman asking to talk to him before the next committee meeting, finally scheduled for 4 April 1974. The Labour Government, led by Norman Kirk, had apparently listened to the widespread criticisms and had appointed C.K. Stead—42 years old, professor of English at the University of Auckland, novelist, poet and critic; articulate, outspoken and charming but often controversial. He agreed to take on the job because he so disapproved of the length of Professor Gordon's reign and because he strongly disagreed with some of the decisions the committee had made.[1] As a practising writer, living away from the capital, and a well-known opponent of New Zealand's involvement in the Vietnam War, he clearly expected, and was expected, to do things differently.

The years that followed were a tumultuous period of change, activity and expansion for the Literary Fund. The time was right. The Kirk Government was keen to make its mark. Henry May, the new Minister for Internal Affairs, had no particular interest in the arts or in literature but he was energetic and enthusiastic: appearing at a meeting in

May 1975, he impressed with his grasp of the role of the Literary Fund.[2] The Authors' Fund had been established in 1973. In the following year the government passed the Arts Council Act, which set up regional and community arts structures and channelled more resources into the arts area. By 1974 the Arts Council was getting $1.5 million from Vote (compared with $210,000 in 1971) and a further $260,000 (in total nearly $19 million in 2015) from the Lottery Board.

New young writers appeared and were read; small magazines proliferated. Big overseas publishers opened local branches with local lists and novelists began publishing here instead of offshore; smaller publishers committed to serious writing and new university presses appeared. New Zealand literature was now taught in schools and universities. Playmarket began assessing, developing and publishing playscripts in 1973 as professional theatre was established. The New Zealand Book Council was set up in 1972; and a monthly journal of the book trade, *New Zealand Bookworld*, appeared from 1973 (to 1981). The other new members of the committee, Roy Parsons, respected bookseller, Vincent O'Sullivan (for PEN), poet and scholar, and Trevor Reeves, independent publisher, were surely selected to reflect the greater diversity and complexity of the literary world. Reeves, of Caveman Press in Dunedin, recently established publisher, chiefly of poetry, had been at odds with the Literary Fund committee over its rejections of some of his books and probably came to the Minister's attention by his angry letters of complaint. One can guess that it was decided it might be wiser to have him inside the tent than out and, after Glover, he was the first publisher to sit on the committee. It was not a universally approved decision though, and some Dunedin writers set up a petition seeking his removal.

* * *

Stead's tenure was brief but active and confident. He immediately pressed for more funding. Just as swiftly, Henry May picked up the ball and ran with it straight to Cabinet, recommending an increase in the government allocation from $15,000 to $25,000 for 1974/5, $35,000 for 1975/6 and $45,000 for 1976/7. He stressed the popularity of literature and its 'value to our international image' and in two well-worn tactics, drew pointed comparisons with literature funding in Australia and with the funds now given to the other art forms.[3] By the August meeting the money was in the bag.

C.K. Stead, writer, scholar and chair of the Literary Fund Advisory Committee, 1974–76.
Robert Cross photograph

Responding to the difficult financial situation of Stead's good friend Frank Sargeson, the committee urged the Minister to act on making grants non-taxable, a vexed question which was not easily or swiftly solved. An adjustment was also made to the information required of publishers so that the drop in retail price made possible by a grant was clearly spelled out as an assurance that the reading public, rather than the profiteering publisher, benefited.[4] One or two decisions made by the previous committee were relitigated: the rejection of four books of poetry presented by Caveman Press, was reviewed, with books by Tuwhare and Peter Olds now receiving assistance; Lauris Edmond, previously spurned, was now assisted with editing Fairburn's letters. Among notable decisions were the Award for Achievement to John A. Lee ('particularly congratulated by Mr Highet', the *Dominion* noted[5]), a grant of $1000 to Patricia Grace to help her write her first novel, and the Scholarship in Letters, now increased from $4000 to $6000 for 1976, to novelist Maurice Gee to work on the book that became *Plumb.*

The previous committee had long been funding the well-respected journal *Landfall* on an annual basis, with $800 a year from 1960. This continued when Robin Dudding took over the editorship from Brasch in 1966. There was a hiatus when Dudding and Caxton got into strife, but after his departure in 1972, the grant was increased in the hope the journal would continue, which it did, though very uncertainly at first. Dudding, however, soon began a new journal, *Islands*, and the committee was quick to support him. Now with its increased allocation the committee was able in 1974 to give $3000 for that year to each magazine, while smaller magazines like *Mate* and *Edge*, with less consistent contents, were funded on an issue by issue basis.[6]

Cave was a new small magazine originally founded by Trevor Reeves, now on the advisory committee, but handed over after four issues to Dr Norman Simms of Hamilton. It was deliberately angular, not fitting the 'accepted editorial patterns of other New Zealand literary magazines' and including material in languages other than English as well as overseas submissions and reviews. Grants from the Fund were frequently less than requested. Not satisfied with their treatment by the Literary Fund Dr Simms, his co-editors and friends conducted a vigorous campaign for two years, contesting decisions and demanding annual funding. They bombarded their local MP, who bombarded the Minister, with letter after letter. They charged the committee with provincialism, conflicts of interest and general incompetence. Finally they wheeled up Lauris Edmond as their spokesperson to a meeting of the committee. The officials and successive Ministers, who had borne the brunt of the onslaught, had responded throughout with patience and courtesy; but they could perhaps have made plain earlier that the low standard of the material in *Cave*, as well as the limited selection of New Zealand writers, was the overriding influence in the advisory committee's decisions. The committee succeeded in getting this across to Lauris Edmond so that what could have been an unpleasant encounter cleared the air.[7] Though this dispute was named one of three current 'areas of concern' in the briefing to the new Minister in January 1976, in fact things calmed down thereafter.

Small magazines were perennially prickly, but alongside this wearisome debate was another much more positive development which was also prompted by the editor of a small magazine. Stephen Chan, much later Professor of International Relations at the School of Oriental and African

Studies in London, but then poet, publisher of *Pipe Dreams in Ponsonby* and editor of the student magazine *New Argot*, had interviewed Stead on his appointment and subsequently wrote to Henry May urging an increase in funding. Now he wrote again suggesting the establishment of book awards like the Canadian Governor-General's Awards, as both an incentive and an advertisement for New Zealand writing.[8] May was lukewarm in reply but the committee took up the idea with enthusiasm. They envisaged a possible expansion of the two existing PEN awards, the Jessie Mackay and the Hubert Church, which already received Literary Fund support. A flurry of discussions, formal and informal, followed, with PEN, with the Arts Council and with the newly established Book Council, whose president was Stead's colleague, history professor and writer Keith Sinclair. At times it was hard to know who was in control: one of the officials wrote, 'It appears that Carl baby is writing letters all over the place about this', while Karl baby was writing to Jarman, 'The other KS seems determined that the book awards should be his!'[9] However the Arts Council agreed to contribute to the awards and PEN and the Book Council agreed to nominate the judges and by September a full proposal was put up to the Minister. An October press statement announced that there would be three new literary awards, for fiction, poetry and nonfiction, each of $2000, with two judges in each category. PEN cleverly suggested that the two PEN awards, the Hubert Church and the Jessie Mackay, originally awarded for best books in prose and poetry, should now recognise best *first* books (as there were legal difficulties about adapting them to the new major awards).

The judges were selected, entries were called for and the first New Zealand Book Awards, for books published in

1975, were set to roll. There was, however, one casualty. The chair of the committee himself had a book of poetry, *Quesada*, published in that year and it would be eligible. The Department of Internal Affairs, touchy about charges of conflict of interest, took the view that while he was the chair no book of his could possibly win; Stead 'cared more about how my book fared than running the Lit Fund' and resigned. *Quesada* did win, though jointly with a book by Louis Johnson; and Stead bought two paintings by Colin McCahon with his $1000.[10]

Establishing the New Zealand Book Awards was the first major initiative by the Literary Fund for a long time, and the herald of many more in this decade. It was not only a means of recognising good writers and writing; it was above all designed to make them visible, to publicise and promote them before the public, with a lively award ceremony, speeches and notices in the press. The committee had not in the past paid much attention to promotion of literature but now, with the energetic assistance of the new secretary, Jim Booth, it began to be far more active, if somewhat lacking in experience.

A brochure was produced listing all the books entered in 1979 and 1980; in the same years an exhibition of the books was part of the award ceremony. There were of course criticisms of the awards and over the next few years tweaking occurred, with the addition in 1980 of a fourth award for book production (furiously opposed by some writers and PEN), prior announcement of a shortlist, and payment of the judges. However, gradually the Book Awards settled down and lasted until 1996, when they were amalgamated with the Montana Book Awards run by the book trade. They were recognised, sniffily by some, as rewarding literary merit first and foremost and acknowledging distinctions between writing in different genres, in contrast to the much more commercially oriented Wattie Book Award, with its big bang of a single winner and more skilled promotion.

* * *

The government changed and the chairman departed; but by great good fortune the impetus towards expansion, cooperation and visibility was maintained. The new chairman was Roly Frean, Professor of English at Massey University, who had been a force on the committee since

Pat Stuart, secretary of the LFAC, donating books entered in the 1980 New Zealand Book Awards to Aotea College.
Dominion Post Collection, ATL, EP/1980/3294

1971; and the well-known playwright Bruce Mason replaced O'Sullivan (who took up a Fulbright award at Yale) in early 1976 as one of the PEN members. The Labour Government was defeated in November 1975 but Allan Highet now took back his role as Minister of Internal Affairs and also became the first Minister for the Arts, a role he enjoyed and entered into with verve. It was widely thought that his second wife, the artist Shona McFarlane, encouraged him strongly in his quite exceptional efforts on behalf of the arts. As MP for Remuera, he had been involved in the annual Auckland arts festivals and perhaps represented a growing interest in arts among the Auckland well-to-do. He held the portfolio until 1984, throughout the term of the Muldoon Government, and left a lasting impression. He was sociable and took much pleasure in appearing at arts-related events. He was also the enthusiastic chair of the Lottery Board and was able to make up for any financial limitations in the government allocation by dipping into this ever-growing source of funds.[11]

Surprisingly though, the Department of Internal Affairs now took a hand in pushing the Literary Fund out into the world. The Secretary, recently dubbed Sir Patrick O'Dea as a tribute to his skills with royal tours, had set up a research unit; he had himself worked in this area early in his career but investigations by government departments on the impact of their work in the wider public were also a fashion of the day. A young research officer, Jock Vennell, who had some experience as a journalist and parliamentary press secretary and an interest in New Zealand literature, chose the Literary Fund as a topic of research among a list of possible areas; in August 1976 the committee heard for the first time that the Internal Affairs was looking into state aid to literature.[12]

Patronage and New Zealand Literature (1977), usually called the Vennell Report, appeared about 10 years after Sharp's booklet on the history of the Literary Fund and 30 years after the Fund's beginnings. Much more than a simple history, it was an attempt to find out in a systematic way what writers, publishers, editors and anyone else closely involved thought about the Fund. Vennell devised a nine-part questionnaire which he put before 54 people either in interviews or in writing. The questions were deliberately broad and covered the person's own experiences with the Fund, their views on the adequacy of funding, and on the most useful assistance, their ideas for expansion as well as opinions on suitable members of the committee and on a possible merger with the Arts Council.

Sylvia Ashton-Warner is congratulated by the Minister, Allan Highet, on winning the 1980 New Zealand Book Award for Fiction.
Sylvia Ashton-Warner Collection, PAColl-2522-1-04

All three sectors seemed to welcome the chance to have a say. There was universal agreement, which there would not have been in 1947, that state aid to literature was necessary. The responses were vigorous and opinionated, ranging from the moving and perceptive to the embittered and wildly impractical. Janet Frame wrote that 'without support from the Literary Fund I should have been unable to survive, let alone to write' and Maurice Gee claimed that a recent project 'would have taken four times as long' without financial help from the Fund; Kendrick Smithyman, Noel Hilliard and Frank Sargeson made similar comments. Hone Tuwhare, however, described his relations with the Fund as 'Not happy at all. It's been a struggle' and said he could not do much with 'a piddly grant of only $750'. He thought an annual allocation for the Fund of $250,000 would do the trick, though others punted more modestly for $100,000, the usual figure mentioned. Almost all writers agreed that the Fund's resources were inadequate. And almost all wanted more scholarships/fellowships and for longer periods.

The writers were often grudging about aid to publishers and publishers were often grudging about the Literary Fund. They repeated the claims that the committee did not understand publishers' costings, that delays in reaching decisions impeded the publication process, that awarding part of the amount requested was next to useless. Magazine publishers had gripes too. All respondents tended to argue for their own sector and were driven by their own specific difficulties with the Fund; comparisons between their own treatment and that of others abounded. The apparently halcyon situation in Australia was often mentioned.

The final report was thoughtful, clear, concise and bold. Its ideas revolutionised the purposes and practices of the Fund and dominated Literary Fund policy for the remainder of the Fund's life. Vennell's account of the responses was followed by a section ambitiously titled 'The Future', in which he argued strongly for a much greater involvement of the Fund in 'the country's writing and publishing community' and for much more active and aggressive promotion of literature. He suggested a number of specific ways both these objectives could be achieved, many derived from the comments he had received. His final sentence makes it very clear that in his view radical change was necessary:

> As a passive funding body with a small budget, the Literary Fund's contribution to literature in this country must inevitably be modest; as a lobbyist prepared to apply pressure where it can produce money to fertilise the roots of creative writing and promote a wider demand for New Zealand literature, the Fund has larger role to play.[13]

Vennell proposed expansion of programmes, especially for more fellowships for writers. An essential aspect of this proposal was extensive collaboration with other organisations, partly to secure further funding, partly to ensure other parts of the community had a stake in the health of the literary arts. This had happened on a minor scale with PEN for many years; the New Zealand Book Awards, jointly funded by the Queen Elizabeth II Arts Council, were a more recent cooperative venture. However, he now argued for private sponsorships, government corporation and university fellowships, joint programmes with the Book Council such as Writers-in-Schools, Arts Council funded regional fellowships, and a Maori writer-in-residence sponsored by the Maori Purposes Fund Board. He suggested also a writer's travel award to supplement the existing Katherine Mansfield Menton Fellowship, to be funded jointly with the Arts Council or the universities.

The new programmes would increase visibility and would require vigorous promotion and active input from the department and the committee to attract readers of local writing. The rumbling discontents of the respondents and the charges of elitism and isolation were a worry, and it was clear to Vennell that much better communication between the Fund and the literary community was necessary. Even before the report became public the Department issued the first *New Zealand Literary Fund Newsletter*, a modest typed leaflet intended to appear quarterly after each meeting; it did for a while but more sparingly in the 1980s, with its last number in July 1988.

The quality of the report was a first step—it was welcomed in the press, with an editorial by academic Roger Robinson in the *Listener*, for example, saying that it 'offers wide and wise recommendations for encouraging the literary arts through the interaction of state assistance and an ingenious diversity of independent patronage'.[14] But its embrace by the sitting committee was the next, and the committed energy of (now) executive officer Jim Booth and secretary Virginia Silva at the Department of Internal Affairs was crucial.

The committee was reconstituted at the beginning of 1977 with four new members: novelist David Ballantyne, Professor James Bertram from Victoria University of Wellington, publisher Elizabeth Caffin, and exciting young poet and fiction writer Ian Wedde. They discussed the Vennell Report at their very first meeting in March and asked Booth and Silva to prepare papers on private patronage, and on new ways of assisting publishers and magazines; in May the committee focused on publication policy.

Once the report was published in July, Frean, who was particularly skilled at planning and policy formulation, moved into action and called a special meeting to consider its recommendations. Awards for writers were the first priority: Booth was asked to approach a number of private firms suggesting sponsorship. A nonfiction award, a travel grant and a distinguished writers' award were all suggested for possible new sponsored programmes; the Historic Places Trust had also been approached about writers in residence in one of their houses. Questionnaires would be sent to magazine publishers.

Jim Booth was exceptionally able as well as amiable and by the end of the year he had landed sponsorships from three private companies—ICI, Quality Packers and Alex Harvey Industries. Two newsletters had already been sent out to the literary community and were widely welcomed; after discussion with Kate Fortune, director of the Book Council, the Literary Fund gave $600 towards the Writers in Schools scheme as a first step in an ongoing relationship; promising negotiations were underway with three universities about fellowships for writers. Virginia Silva had made a trip to the South Island to meet writers and publishers. And all the while the usual business of the Fund continued.

The ICI Writer's Bursary was designed for an emerging writer and would be worth $5000 annually, to be jointly funded by ICI and the Literary Fund. ICI were committed to one year, but hoped to be able to continue the bursary for five years. While this bursary would replace the existing bursary for promising writers, the committee would be willing to grant a second bursary of $4000 from the same shortlist. Applications were called for in March 1978, and 49 were received. Highet announced in July that the winner was playwright Michael Heath, with fiction writer Wendy

Simons getting the smaller writing bursary. ICI worked well with the Literary Fund and agreed to continue the bursary.[15] Writers who won it over the next decade included Russell Haley, David Hill, Anne de Roo and Elizabeth Knox.

One question in Jock Vennell's list asked whether the Fund should assist biography and history as well as poetry and fiction; most replies supported this as long as it was not given priority. Allen Curnow supported it without conditions, saying these 'are forms of literature'. Perhaps Alex Harvey Industries thought so too as they offered to jointly fund an annual award of $7000 for 'research towards the publication of literary, historical or critical works'.[16] Applications were called for in mid-year, but there was some delay before the first announcement. Out of 44 entrants the judges unanimously chose Michael King, who was planning a biography of former Labour prime minster Peter Fraser. Unfortunately this topic did not appeal to Alex Harvey Industries. Awkward negotiations ensued and eventually the bursary was given, in March 1979, to Margaret Scott, the Katherine Mansfield scholar. Somewhat miffed at this turn of events, the committee were happily able to persuade the Minister to find $7000 from lottery funds for Michael King. A similar difficulty, though of a rather different character, arose in 1980/81 when the judges wished to award the bursary to Stevan Eldred-Grigg to write a book entitled 'Chastising the Flesh', 'which will investigate sex, drugs and repression of pleasure in colonial New Zealand'.[17] This was too much for AHI and the award went once more to the second choice. Hardly surprisingly, it was not continued after the initial three-year term was up.[18] The adequate funding of serious and gifted writers of nonfiction who were not university teachers remained a problem, and still does.

The value of awards such as these was not only the freedom to write for an extended period without financial anxiety or interruption. They also represented recognition of talent and potential achievement by knowledgeable judges. They gave a writer permission to believe in herself and her work. In this sense the new bursary offered by Quality Packers, the Choysa Bursary for Children's Writers, may have been the most important. While some assistance had been given to writers and books for children, this dedicated award acknowledged the particular skills of the children's writer as equal to those of writers for adults and marked the emergence of a vibrant literature for children. Fifty-two writers applied for the bursary, worth $5000, jointly funded, by the beginning of August 1978. It was given to the writer-illustrator Lynley Dodd, who was then at the very beginning of a remarkable career frequently involving a dog. Many of the great New Zealand writers for children have won the Choysa Bursary: William Taylor, Sherryl Jordan, Tessa Duder, Joy Cowley, and Gaelyn Gordon.

Now the busy team at Internal Affairs turned their attention to the universities. In September 1977 the Minister wrote to the Vice Chancellors of the three universities in Christchurch, Wellington and Auckland, suggesting fellowships for writers similar to the long-established Robert Burns Fellowship at the University of Otago. Two years earlier Bill Manhire had set up at Victoria University of Wellington his influential creative writing course and it is perhaps no coincidence that that university was quick to respond positively. In late April 1978 the Vice Chancellor, Danny Taylor, agreed to set aside half a lecturer's salary, to be matched by the Literary Fund, and applications were called for a full-year fellowship in 1979. A selection panel including two members of the Literary Fund Advisory

Committee considered 20 applicants and awarded the first university writing fellowship to playwright Joseph Musaphia, who managed to write four plays during the year.

The new Vice Chancellor at Canterbury, Professor Bert Brownlie, had welcomed the approach even earlier but the Literary Fund, aware both of their limited funds and the strength of the Burns Fellowship, suggested the variant of a six-month fellowship at a total cost of $6000, to be equally shared. Here, too, conditions were agreed and the fellowship for 1979 was advertised. Nine writers applied and a selection panel, including two Advisory Committee members, decided on Michael Morrissey as the first fellow. After a couple of years with a disappointingly small number of applicants, the fellowship was increased to nine months for 1982. In 1985 it became a full-year arrangement as the Ursula Bethell Residency for Creative Writers.

The universities very quickly took over the writing fellowships as their own. After the University of Auckland had agreed to a six-month fellowship in late 1978, the Advisory Committee and officials were astonished to see a report in the *Listener* in June 1979 that the fellowship had been awarded, unbeknownst to them but presumably in expectation of some Literary Fund revenue, to Robin Dudding. However, after a stern letter to the Vice Chancellor, ruffled feathers were smoothed and the fellowship proceeded in 1980 (for 1981) with the Literary Fund Advisory Committee involved in setting the guidelines and selecting the fellow (Margaret Sutherland).

There were occasional disagreements about selection and difficulties about matching rises in university salaries, but the university fellowships were a successful and enduring commitment to writers. Their list of candidates is generally not large because a shift to the location is required but they have attracted many leading writers. Writers have enjoyed contact with students and with teaching staff as well as the amenities of the institution; and English departments in particular have greatly benefited from the creative talents in their midst. Relations with the Literary Fund were generally cordial and the fellowships sat comfortably in the university context. This was the best of the cooperative arrangements entered into at that time.

By mid-1978, that is, one year after the publication of the Vennell Report, three private sponsorships for writers and two university fellowships had been established: this amounted to a total of $36,000 (almost $218,000 in 2015) a year now available to writers, in addition to the existing Scholarship in Letters ($6000) and the writer's bursary ($4000). This was a massive achievement owing much to Jim Booth, assisted by Pam Hill and Virginia Silva, and followed by another very able official, Pat Stuart. It vastly increased opportunities for writers to work intensively on literary projects and it broadened the commitment to the patronage of literature to include other organisations outside government. A more complex and more sophisticated society had begun to value and appreciate works of the literary imagination.

* * *

All this required finance, as the new commitments were to be jointly funded. Highet managed to secure for 1978/9 a substantial increase in the allocation, from $53,000 to $75,000 (around $442,000 in 2015), an increase of over 40 percent; but this proved to be insufficient. It would cover the three new bursaries and a revised magazine policy but there remained the university residencies and the usual applications from writers and publishers, which had increased markedly with all the noise and fanfare. So towards the end of 1978 the Minister, in his capacity as Minister in charge of section 93 of the Gaming and Lotteries Act 1977, acceded to a request from Jarman (on behalf of the secretary) to produce another $20,000 plus the $7000 for Michael King.

Funding writers was a breeze compared with the many difficulties associated with those who selected, edited, printed and distributed their work. Magazines and publishers were often deeply committed to local writing but they had to face a market which was small and choosy; furthermore, the academics and writers of the committee and the devoted public servants of Department of Internal Affairs had little commercial or marketing experience. Vennell had noted 'a mixed and sometimes acrimonious reaction' on the question of aid to literary magazines[19] and Booth, in following up with magazine editors subsequently, concluded 'we have a serious problem in this area'.[20] Small magazines were proliferating, their costs were steadily rising and there was widespread resentment at the preferential treatment given to *Landfall* and *Islands*.

Accordingly, Frean in characteristically cerebral fashion prepared a paper for a special meeting in April 1978, proposing a standard formula to determine the assistance, on a per issue basis, to all magazines of an acceptable standard. It aimed to subsidise production costs, using a rather elaborate formula, assist the payment of contributors, and recognise editorial quality.[21] It intended to treat all magazines equally and, in order to give them some degree of stability, it introduced an element of predictability.

The Minister agreed to the new policy. However, this method of determining grants to magazines was a mixed success because when production costs rose, as they inevitably did, without any rise in print run or revenue, the grant fell; and at the beginning of 1980 most magazines were still struggling. A decision to buy 100 subscriptions to six journals for distribution to sympathetic institutions and individuals did not seem to help. In April 1981, Alistair Paterson, editor of *Climate* (previously *Mate*), claimed he could keep the magazine going no longer, asserting that the Literary Fund's 'present policy appears to be aimed at precisely such an end'.[22] Later that year the magazine policy was reviewed and publication and editorial subsidies were replaced by a simple 50 percent of revenue.[23]

Professor Frean had long been aware of some discontent among publishers. He moved swiftly to improve communication by asking Booth to initiate discussions with publishers and to contact the Book Publishers Association, 'with a view to their suggesting a long-term proposal which would be mutually beneficial given the Fund's limited resources and considering the advantages of planning a year in advance'.[24] A variety of suggestions had been made: a guarantee against loss scheme, block grants to reputable literary publishers, publishing projects initiated and funded by the Literary Fund, the introduction of a standard application form.[25]

The publishing sector had become increasingly diverse and numerous but at the same time fewer books were being published especially fiction. In 1977, in order to speak more effectively for the industry, its two organisations, the Book Publishers Representatives Association and the New Zealand Book Publishers Association, combined to form the Book Publishers Association of New Zealand (BPANZ), with Ray Richards, longtime Reeds publisher, as its director. He was succeeded two years later by Gerard

Reid in a fulltime and notably active role. It was thus an organisation keen to engage with government on behalf of its members. In November 1977 Booth heard from Ann Mallinson (ABP/Methuen), chair of the New Zealand Publishing Committee of the BPANZ, that they did not favour a guarantee against loss scheme but rather a simple grant of 50 percent of the production costs, supported by printing quotations and payable on publication.[26]

Unsurprisingly the committee leapt on this straightforward suggestion and floated it in the next issue of the newsletter (no. 4, March 1978). Some vociferous opinions were expressed, especially by small independent publishers who did not feel the BPANZ necessarily spoke for them. The officials, undeterred, then embarked on widespread discussions with approximately 20 publishers throughout the country who had applied to the Fund in the past.[27] Some favoured a guarantee against loss scheme, some a capital fund. But by September the Minister had agreed to a very broad policy to support literary works, to be judged according to literary merit and economic need. The policy stipulated that the publisher had first accepted the proposal so that acceptance should not be conditional on receiving a grant. A detailed standard application form would be used and would indicate such items as print run, retail price, royalty rate, production costs. To provide informed opinion on these matters it was proposed to appoint a publisher nominated by the BPANZ as an advisor to the committee, an idea that had been in the air for some time. Eventually, in 1980, Ann Mallinson took up this role, attending committee meetings and advising on all publishing applications, a remarkably selfless step since she and her husband David Rendel had only just set up their own independent publishing company, Mallinson Rendel.

In 1981 she became a full member of the committee and thenceforth there was always a BPANZ representative on the committee.

This could have unexpected benefits all round. Though Lynley Dodd had published two books in Britain, she struck difficulties in finding a publisher for the book she wrote on the Choysa Bursary, *The Smallest Turtle*, which disappointed Quality Packers. However, when Elizabeth Alley, now on the committee with Elizabeth Caffin's departure overseas, commented on this to Ann Mallinson, Ann rang Lynley in the lunchbreak. Mallinson Rendel thus published that book and every other Lynley Dodd book thereafter to huge success.[28]

In the end there were few major changes in how the Fund administered grants to publishers. The scheme was now

Publisher Ann Mallinson was the first publisher representative on the LFAC, 1980.
Courtesy Ann Mallinson

clearer and more businesslike though, and the extensive discussions with the BPANZ and with individual literary publishers had opened valuable lines of communication and could only be beneficial to the Internal Affairs staff and to the committee. Discussions throughout 1980, sparked off by a strong letter to the Minister from Gerard Reid urging government assistance to a fragile industry, covered the extension of the public lending right to publishers and the introduction of a book bounty scheme to assist local printers. These questions were all discussed by the Advisory Committee. At the end of the year the Minister replied to the BPANZ, rejecting both an extension of the PLR and an expansion of direct grants but raising the possibility of a separate fund from lottery profits, out of which a variety of forms of assistance such as loans or guarantees against loss could be made available. Eventually the publishers and the committee agreed on a guarantee against loss scheme with a particular focus on fiction, in addition to the existing direct grant assistance. However a substantial sum was needed to set this up, and it was not as yet forthcoming.

Publishing grants averaged 16 percent of the annual allocation, from \$5888 in 1974/5 to \$27,740 in 1982, and more than doubled in real terms. Far more books were supported with books of poetry by far the largest group assisted (84) along with 23 novels and 21 books of short stories. In those eight years though only 10 works of nonfiction were subsidised. Thirty-six publishers were helped, many of them small and short-lived; the real winners were Auckland University Press (20), John McIndoe (15), Caveman Press (12) and Pegasus (12).

In their discussions with publishers it became clear to Pat Stuart (now secretary of the committee) and her colleagues that the real problem for New Zealand publishers of fiction and poetry was the short print runs appropriate for the local market. Because this led to a high unit cost a grant did not enable the publisher to reduce the retail price, as the Advisory Committee had traditionally thought, but simply to sell a book at the price usual for the genre without losing money. What the Literary Fund therefore should consider was whether it could expand the market by assisting with promotional activities, especially for small publishers who did not employ their own marketing staff. This idea appealed to the Minister, who, in a speech in October to open a New Zealand Book Exhibition organised by the BPANZ at St Lukes, Auckland, argued vigorously for better promotion especially for fiction and poetry. The Literary Fund, he said, 'is prepared to support and initiate promotional proposals'.[29]

Publishers such as Patricia Chapman at Dunmore Press and Alan Loney at Hawk Press made a number of suggestions as to how the Literary Fund might help small publishers to market their books. Gary McCormick also fired off a set of wide-ranging ideas and he and Sam Hunt assisted a Literary Fund promotion and bookstall at the Nambassa festival at Waihi in January 1979.[30] But book promotion is a skilled and time-consuming task that depends on experience and contacts, and though the Internal Affairs staff put plenty of energy into some of these ideas, their successes were modest. For a time they produced a quarterly catalogue of new books called *Books*, but their chief efforts focused on the Book Awards. They also encouraged Air New Zealand to purchase copies each of *Islands*, *Landfall*, *Pacific Quarterly Moana* and *Climate* for their international flights on a one-year trial basis: 4000 copies were sold.[31] But the inevitable happened: someone complained to Air NZ about 'offensive material' and the deal was not renewed.

* * *

Professor Frean had provided much of the drive and intelligence behind the huge expansion of the Fund's activities in the 1970s. But now, along with Ian Wedde, James Bertram and Bruce Mason, he retired from the committee in late 1979 to be succeeded in the chair by Professor Ray Copland. A charming, witty and widely read man, Copland had taught English for many years at the University of Canterbury, where he was much loved and respected by his students. His knowledge of New Zealand literature was unparalleled. Other new members were librarian Kevin Cunningham, playwright Roger Hall and academic Frank McKay.

The pace of change did not let up. To celebrate the International Year of the Child in 1979 a telethon had raised $2.7 million to benefit children; a Literary Fund application for the establishment of a Children's Publication Fund was successful, with $20,000 available for 1981 specifically to assist the publication of books for children. A committee chaired by Roger Hall and including two experts in children's literature (Dorothy Butler and Alison Grant) chose eight books from the 24 manuscripts submitted by publishers to be awarded grants up to 50 percent of the production cost; they also made a special grant of $2000 to the children's magazine *Jabberwocky*. Among the eight titles were books by Lynley Dodd, William Taylor, Tessa Duder and Joy Cowley, all well-known writers for children but then very early in their careers. This initiative was a great boost for the publishers of books for children, Oxford University Press, Price Milburn, Whitcoulls and the newly established independent firm of Mallinson Rendel; but the money was a one-off windfall. Urgent pleas were made to Highet for the 1982 year and he managed to provide funding from lottery proceeds but could not promise this on an ongoing basis.[32] This fund thus fell into abeyance before being fully restored in 1985.

Hard on the heels of this development was yet another encouragement for the writing and publishing of books for children: the setting up of dedicated book awards. The idea had been tossed around for some time, but a meeting late in 1981 of Wendy Harrex, of Oxford University Press and the BPANZ, Michael Keith of School Publications, Pat Stuart and Chris Rutledge of Internal Affairs/Literary Fund got the ball rolling. When Daphne Brasell, then at the Government Printing Office, heard about it at the annual conference of the BPANZ, they offered to sponsor it.[33] The Literary Fund committee approved, the Department of Internal Affairs agreed to handle the administration and entries were called for in mid-1982. The first Children's Book of the Year was *The Silent One* by Joy Cowley, one of the books assisted in 1981 by the Children's Publication Fund. There were now three different institutions set up to support writers and publishers of New Zealand children's books. As Betty Gilderdale wrote, 'Such developments made possible at least the beginnings of a stable professional base for children's authors'.[34] And we can add the annual contribution to the Writers in Schools scheme, now a regular $3750 pa; and a special grant of $10,000 from lottery funds made in 1980 to Kidsarus for four children's picture books two of which would appear in te reo Maori as well as English, and all of which would be published in association with established publishers.[35]

One further sally into the business world, a small but effective one, was first suggested by Roger Hall. In October 1979 Pat Stuart was talking to IBM about a possible award for a writer of an electric typewriter, a dreamlike object for the hard-working owner of an old portable past its best. IBM agreed to donate a reconditioned Selectric golfball typewriter for 1980 and 1981 to a fulltime writer on the basis of need. The Advisory Committee selected suitable writers and the first recipient was the heroic Robin Dudding who, sporting shorts and a huge beard, received the machine from the IBM local manager. 'He didn't have an electric typewriter,' he told the *Auckland Star*, and 'people might even start to get their letters on time.'[36] The next year the committee chose Maurice Gee, who was widely admired as a writer and known to struggle financially, but when he heard of 'afternoon tea with the minister and the IBM manager' and had seen 'one of these things and they look pretty complicated to me', he changed his mind. The second machine went to Ian Wedde, another penurious talent. Four years later Ian wrote an almost moving letter recounting how much he had valued the typewriter: 'it's probably had a lot to do with the fact that I can now survive by freelance writing'. A long paragraph listed the many works it had typed; he finished, 'It has been worth its weight in gold—it's been my life-support system, quite literally'.[37]

By now the Queen Elizabeth II Arts Council was a well-established partner in the New Zealand Book Awards. Hamish Keith, its intelligent, lively and opinionated chair, suggested in his speech at the 1977 awards ceremony that 'it is time the Arts Council and the Literary Fund moved closer together' and as both institutions expanded under the supportive eye of Highet, overlaps, connections and blurring of lines happened more and more often.[38]

Occasionally the Arts Council funded writers or literary magazines or publishers; in 1974/5 it contributed to the Katherine Mansfield Menton Fellowship. Between 1974 and 1980 there were various discussions between the two bodies, and relations remained cordial, but the Literary Fund Advisory Committee remained hesitant about too close a relationship: a request by the Arts Council in 1980 to have an observer at Literary Fund Advisory Committee meetings was firmly rejected. However, when in late 1980 the poet Kendrick Smithyman was invited to the prestigious Harbourfront Festival in Toronto, no fund existed to help him get there. In a remarkably civilised negotiation with the Arts Council and its officers, agreement was easily reached that each organisation would put up $3000 to establish an Overseas Travel Fund for writers. Smithyman went to Canada and members of the Writers' Guild were able to go to Sydney for a conference.

A further proposal from the Arts Council was made in late 1981 by executive officer Ruth Harley for a jointly funded playwright's fellowship. This was quickly agreed to in December by the Advisory Committee. Each organisation would offer $2500 for a playwright, who would be working for six months in association with a local theatre to gain practical experience of production realities. Dean Parker, to work at the Mercury Theatre in Auckland, was the first fellow.

As we have seen, this was a period of massive expansion. The modest amount available to the committee for distribution from Vote and lottery funds in 1974/5 was $28,200; in 1981/2 the fund was $119,200, an increase of 160 percent in real terms (though the pace of growth had slowed down after 1978/9). And this does not include the external funding now being provided by private companies, universities and the Arts Council. Under Highet's guidance the proportion of funding coming from lottery sources gradually increased, reaching $31,200 in 1978/9, a third of the total.

By far the greater proportion of the new funding went to writers (in awards and fellowships). Much of the available funding was now committed each year, leaving a smaller proportion available for discretionary grants and assistance to publishers and magazines. (However, because the whole pot grew so did subsidies in those two sectors.) The number and total value of discretionary grants to writers fell from 1980 as the more generous fellowships and bursaries came on stream. All the Scholarships in Letters in these years were given to novelists, as were by far the greatest number of discretionary grants (18). The Scholarship (worth $9000 from 1980) tended to be awarded to well-established writers who did not otherwise make huge demands on the Fund (Gee, Hilliard, Du Fresne all got one other grant and Kidman two); this is also true of the writing bursary and the ICI. But for a writer of fiction whose talent was known there were now a number of ways to take a year off from normal employment to write a substantial work. And for a writer like Maurice Gee it was at last possible to survive on a combination of grants, royalties, writing for radio and television: the 1976 Scholarship in Letters had been the turning point.[39]

The cultural expansion of the late 1970s and early 1980s has often been noted. Theatres were born, the New Zealand Film Commission was established, local television features appeared, small presses and magazines flourished, Maori writers emerged. The population was growing, global trends were quickly apparent and widely influential. In one sense this energetic creativity pushed against the grain of the prevailing political climate, a National Government led by the much-derided Robert Muldoon. However some of it was encouraged and funded by that government, and credit must go to the persistent and dedicated Allan Highet. The

Literary Fund had grown in confidence and understanding as well as in resources: Pat Stuart rebuked Gerard Reid firmly for erroneously claiming in its newsletter that the BPANZ had suggested the appointment of a publishing advisor and the establishment of the Book Production Award. This may have implied, she said,

> that the Literary Fund Advisory Committee and the Minister for the Arts only act on new proposals and ideas which have been suggested by other organisations. This could not be further from the truth. The Advisory Committee has a tradition of initiating and carrying through new policies and ideas. The increases in its allocation in recent years has enabled it to become more involved in projects which are intended to improve its own performance and to ensure that its very limited funds are wisely spent.[40]

So there!

In May 1982 Roger Hall was replaced by Professor Terry Sturm, recently appointed to a chair in English at the University of Auckland, who in November became the next chairman of the committee.

7

LAST DAYS OF THE LITERARY FUND 1974–1982

Professor Sturm had done graduate studies in New Zealand literature at a time when this was not common and he was passionate about its health and its growth. With the New Zealand writer always at the centre of his attention as the chair, he went to great pains to listen to writers and to argue for their interests. Meetings were always long: he was very thorough and he allowed every voice to be heard. But his fair-mindedness meant he was highly respected by the bureaucrats as well as by the writers.

As it happened, Sturm was very quickly called upon to stand up for writers in a confrontation with government about the PEN representatives on the committee. Government appointed four of the six committee members directly but PEN, which had instigated the establishment of the Literary Fund long before, also nominated two writer representatives; its choices had hitherto been accepted without question. With the terms of Frank McKay and David Ballantyne coming to an end from August 1982, the PEN executive had in May sent out ballot papers to its membership to choose the next two; poet Louis Johnson and poet, novelist, critic, professor and former chair of the committee C.K. Stead, were thus selected. By mid-September though, PEN had not heard that these appointments had been confirmed and Shona McFarlane, Highet's wife, who was on the PEN executive, said there had been some comment about both nominees being male.[1]

There had indeed been a hitch. The newly elected National caucus had insisted on vetting nominations made by outside bodies and refused to accept these nominations; so did Cabinet, until Highet on a second attempt persuaded both bodies to agree to the appointments but for one year only instead of the usual three. Sturm immediately shot off a letter to the Minister asking for an explanation and a reconsideration.[2] Stead, writing to PEN, said 'I really don't care much whether I'm on the Lit Fund or not. But I care terribly about the way this govt. gets its own way by bullying.'[3]

Fiona Kidman, the current president of PEN, called on the Minister at his request. Her report of the meeting strongly suggests he was embarrassed—'he greatly regretted . . .'—as he explained he had met with opposition from both caucus and Cabinet and the one-year term was a compromise to gain agreement. The following year a slate of four names was to be put up. The reasons given for this unexpected deviation from past practice were the absence of a woman and the fact that Stead's appointment would mean there were two professors of English from the same university on the committee. Though Highet subsequently denied political considerations had been involved, Stead, and most other interested persons, thought that his conviction the previous year as an active protestor against the 1981 Springbok rugby tour was the real reason and that the Prime Minister, Robert Muldoon, was responsible for government hostility to the appointment.[4]

The Auckland papers made a big fuss, with two editorials in the *New Zealand Herald* and several articles in the *Auckland Star*, all critical of the government and suspicious of its motives. A strong letter was sent to the Minister by the Literary Fund Advisory Committee after their November meeting. Fiona Kidman made her views very clear in her annual report at the PEN AGM in April 1983: 'our recommendations . . . were met with stonewalling tactics by the Government who, for reasons which never became really apparent, were not prepared to accept the nominations. . . . Writers are better equipped to decide who should make decisions on literary matters on their behalf than are politicians.'[5] The Auckland and Dunedin branches agreed that the only names they would

Professor Terry Sturm, admired and gifted chair of the LFAC, 1982–88, and of the Literature Committee of the Queen Elizabeth II Arts Council, 1988–92.
Courtesy Linda Cassells

now put up were once more those of Stead and Johnson (who had been dissuaded from withdrawing). The matter was raised again in September 1983 by the *New Zealand Times*, which provoked a question in the House by Labour MP John Terris. Highet batted it back.

In the meantime, however, Sturm had proposed to the new PEN president, Tony Simpson, and to the Minister a possible solution: that the two nominees remain on the committee for the full three-year term but that a working party be established to look at the structure and operations of the committee including writer representation. This was duly done, with the Literary Fund, PEN and the Department of Internal Affairs all represented. Now Highet could deflect any questions by saying that the group was working on it and he was awaiting their deliberations.[6] Nothing of any significance came out of these discussions, but time passed and before too long a snap election had been called and the government changed. The new Minister, Peter Tapsell, quickly agreed to the two PEN representatives serving for their full term.[7]

In the circumstances Sturm was lucky to have an experienced committee to work with: Ray Copland and Ann Mallinson remained; so did Dunedin dentist Alan Roddick, who had replaced Kevin Cunningham in 1981. At the next reconstitution of the committee in 1985 Sturm continued in the chair and Louis Johnson was joined by Dale Williams, writer, editor, critic, as the other PEN member; Elizabeth Caffin, now at Collins Publishers and from August 1986 at Auckland University Press, followed Ann Mallinson as the BPANZ representative, while writer Keri Hulme and Massey University academic William Broughton were two other new members.

* * *

The drive for expansion, set off by the Vennell Report, had not halted and Sturm was keen to implement some earlier plans still unrealised or now abandoned. However, since 1978/9 increases in funding had been minimal, inflation was rife and while grants to writers were increasingly inadequate, the money available for one-off grants to both writers and publishers was also diminishing all the time. One particular difficulty was matching rises in university salaries so that the university writing fellows kept abreast of their colleagues. In late 1982 a finance subcommittee tabled a 19-page report, probably written by Sturm, which clearly demonstrated the financial crisis and which became the basis for a 'new policy' budget submission. It fell on deaf ears at Treasury, though, and the only increase for the 1983/4 year was a mere $13,000 inflation adjustment. A deputation of Sturm, Mallinson and Johnson to the Minister got no further and was advised to seek funds from the Lottery Board to reactivate the Children's Publication Fund (which they did without success), though later he came up with a special grant to allow an increase in the term of the Auckland University fellowship.[8] And at a lunch with the committee in November 1983, he raised the possibility of a special 'Arts and Letters' lottery.

The same process was repeated the next year with the New Policy submission showing a more aggressive tone in comparing the derisory increases since 1979/80 with those of the Consumer Price Index, taking issue with the Treasury's argument that private funding precluded the need for any more government assistance, and threatening the abolition of programmes. Its conclusion was that in real terms the cut in expenditure between 1979/80 and 1983/4 was over $65,000, bearing especially heavily on assistance to writers and to literary magazines. It now asked for $76,684 to match annual cost increases outside the control of the Literary Fund, to redress programmes eroded by inflation and now inadequately funded, and to fund essential new areas of development.

This time, to Sturm's relief, an extra $65,000 ($25,000 from vote and $40,000 from the Lottery Board, in total around $187,200 in 2015), an increase of almost half, was granted for 1984/5. The committee planned increases for all programmes, with the Scholarship in Letters going up to $16,000, the Writing Bursary and all other six-month bursaries to $8000, project grants to writers rising to a maximum of $4000. The Award for Achievement doubled to $1000, its first increase since 1973; it went in 1985 to a worthy winner, children's writer Margaret Mahy. More funds were set aside for magazines and for publishing grants; grants to PEN for the Best First Book awards and the Young Writers' Incentive Award Scheme were increased; an extra $1000 was granted to the Book Council's Writers in Schools scheme.

Even more satisfying, the new funding allowed the establishment of several new policies, an annual Travel Bursary of $5000, a fund to assist the establishment of literary magazines, and a much desired Non-Fiction Assistance Fund.

But this was not all. In November 1984 the committee heard that $122,500 would be available to the Fund from the special Arts and Letters lottery, a parting gift, as it were, from Highet, who had retired at the July election. Now at last the Children's Publication Fund could be re-established; and a Maori Publications Fund, a Guarantee against Loss scheme for fiction publishing, and an Australia/NZ Literary Exchange, recently proposed by the Literature Board of Australia, could be set up over a five-year period.

Pressure on funding continued though, in spite of regular increases from lottery revenue, which in 1986/7 reached $150,000 (around $317,000 in 2015), exceeding the Vote allocation for the first time. There was a constant struggle to keep the fixed commitments to writers abreast of inflation: the Scholarship in Letters went up to $20,000 in 1985/6 and to $24,000 in 1986/7, when a second Scholarship was offered to mark the fortieth anniversary of the founding of the Literary Fund; the Writing Bursary was increased to $10,000 in 1985/6 and the other six-month bursaries matched it the following year; the New Zealand Book Awards and the university fellowships were also increased. But this left little for anything else. By mid-1987 Sturm issued a press statement declaring that all programmes would have to be cut; an increase in Vote money of $24,000 was largely compensation for Goods and Services Tax (GST), just introduced, and was derisory compared with an extra $2.3 million committed to the Arts Council for 1987/8; and there was no increase in lottery funding. 'The New Zealand Literary Fund Advisory Committee's view was that government funding priorities for the arts revealed a deplorable lack of understanding of the needs of New Zealand writers and of the value of their contribution to New Zealand society.'[9] In the event, a small amount of money was carried over from the previous year and $16,000 unexpended from the Authors Fund was added.

Let us remember, though, that the initial government grant for the Literary Fund in 1946 was £2000; allowing for inflation that would have equated to $69,226 in 1986; the actual budget for 1986/7 was $292,000, four times as much. Even since 1976 the real increase had been impressive: the equivalent in 1986 of the $44,200 budget of 1976/7 would have been $147,667, three times as much.

These increases however cannot be seen in isolation. They reflected similar growth in other areas of arts patronage, both in New Zealand and in similar countries like Australia and Canada; and beside the funding given to other arts through the Arts Council, the amounts were minimal.

* * *

Compared with the very limited assistance to writers and publishers in the early days of the Fund, the range of programmes being offered by the Literary Fund was now extensive, with approximately 60 percent of revenue going to writers. The focus had moved steadily away from simple and passive general assistance towards more specialised and dedicated grants. The writing community had grown; it had become more varied and less isolated from the wider society, more confident of its local sources. The audience too had expanded, placing more value on its own writing and wanting to hear from voices previously undervalued or unheard, especially those of Maori and of women. There was increasing international interest in New Zealand writing. The media paid more attention, writers became celebrities especially after Keri Hulme won the Booker Prize in 1985. The Readers and Writers Week in Wellington in 1986 was the first of many literary festivals rapidly proliferating and eagerly followed. Publishers like Bert Hingley at Hodder & Stoughton or Brian Turner at John McIndoe began to take chances on literary fiction, with the best novelists now publishing in New Zealand rather than in Britain or the United States. Sturm noted that 'in 1986 and 1987 45 serious works of New Zealand fiction were published—all, except one, initially in New Zealand. Of those 45 books, approx two-thirds had been assisted by authors' grants, and approx one-fifth with publication subsidy.'[10] Writers, publishers, readers and educators all now had some dealings with the Literary Fund and opinions on what it should do and how it should do it.

Extended time to write was what every writer desired: 'Continuity is what I dream of,' said Ian Wedde, 'together with chances to stop sometimes for a read.'[11] Sturm was clear that the Literary Fund should 'aim to make reasonable, inflation-adjusted, subsistence grants to a smaller number of authors . . . rather than take the more "popular" course of making a larger number of small grants available' and the Scholarship in Letters for established writers remained its prestige grant.[12] Maurice Gee's novel *Prowlers* (1987) thanks the New Zealand Literary Fund for 'its generous encouragement and support' and in his next novel, *The Burning Boy* (1990), which won the 1991 New Zealand Book Award for Fiction, he mentions both the Scholarship in Letters and the Victoria University of Wellington Writer's Fellowship. In keeping with Sturm's efforts to give writers longer periods for ambitious projects the Literary Fund gave Gee the 1986 Scholarship and the following year the special fortieth anniversary one, allowing him a continuous period of 24 months to write free from financial anxiety. Fiona Kidman, who got the Scholarship in 1985, described the Scholarship in Letters as 'essential to the writing of this book', that is, *The Book of Secrets*, which won the New Zealand Book Award for Fiction in 1988. By 1988 there were for established writers two full-year Scholarships in Letters, three university fellowships and a six-month writing bursary. In addition it had become standard practice to offer project grants to shortlisted candidates for these awards.

Six-month bursaries specifically targeted new writers (ICI) and children's writers (Choysa), categories formerly ignored. Quality Packers, producers of Choysa tea, were enthusiastic sponsors and the bursary went from $5000 in 1979 to $10,000 in 1987 (though it should have been $13,786 to keep up with inflation) with Quality Packers offering an additional award for an illustrator of children's books from 1988 on and Sharron Barber, the wife of the CEO Alan Barber, serving on the selection committee. Writers were enthusiastic too, with over 40 applicants applying in 1984. The winner that year, William Taylor, remarked: 'I am now well known locally for buying only Choysa tea and advising everyone else of my acquaintance to do the same. And I drink a lot of tea.'[13] Quality Packers complained in late 1983 that no published books had yet resulted but there was often a time lag. Literary Fund secretary Susan Robertson quickly reported the success of bursars Anne de Roo, Lynley Dodd and Caroline Macdonald in the 1984 Children's Book of the Year awards and Tapsell was pleased to be able to mention in his awards ceremony speech of 1985 that publication was underway for projects completed by de Roo and Taylor.

The ICI bursary, which increased at the same rate, was also popular (usually 40 to 60 applicants, 67 in 1988); and ICI was particularly insistent it should be awarded to young writers without established reputations.[14] It was well run and demonstrated perceptive and far-sighted decisions, a tribute in no small way to Elizabeth Alley, who served on the selection committee from its inception. Its great coup was of course the award of not only the 1984 New Zealand Book Award for Fiction and the 1984 Pegasus Prize for Maori Literature but also the 1985 Booker Prize to Keri Hulme for *the bone people*. Hulme had been a persistent applicant for this bursary from 1978 when she wrote, 'I have the potential. I don't yet have the reputation (except maybe as an indefatigable hunter of grant monies)';[15] she finally won the bursary for 1982, and, as they say, the rest is history. She did not forget what she owed to this award and she prefaced a subsequent book of short stories with, 'Many of the stories gathered here would not have been written without the assistance of the 1982 ICI Writing Bursary. Patronage of literature in New Zealand, outside of governmental funding, is rare, and it is deeply and sincerely appreciated by those writers who receive it—especially this one.'[16] After a 10-year sponsorship ICI withdrew in 1989 and the committee set up a new bursary for emerging writers in memory of Louis Johnson, who had died suddenly in November 1988.

Life was not always easy with the three university fellowships, as the Literary Fund faced inflation-adjusted university salary scales which its budget did not provide for. However through painstaking negotiations, beseeching the Minister and juggling dollars, it was possible to increase the Auckland fellowship from six to nine months from 1984; and Canterbury, initially six months, became twelve months in 1985 with the Literary Fund contribution going from $3000 in 1978 to $12,000 in 1985. However, Victoria made unilateral decisions about payment to Fellows, which left the Literary Fund stranded. Eventually it was agreed to reduce the fellowship there to nine months, though with a room available for the full year. A fellowship at the University of Waikato was approved by the Advisory Committee in August 1985 but no funds were available until 1991 (Tessa Duder).

Though the numbers of applicants for the positions were small they were of high calibre and both parties benefited, as Russell Haley suggests:

> The Fellow's office at Auckland is like a nicely decorated monastic cell. There are no distractions. In the first term I

> wrote a complete novel and during the May break I decided it was poor stuff. But such is the financial and psychological security of the fellowship I was able to begin again and write another. *The Settlement* was finished in draft in October of my Fellowship year and it was accepted for publication by Hodder and Stoughton in the same month. . . . *The Settlement* will be my first published novel. . . . I sensed the complete support of the English Department staff. They'd help when I lost a word yet they made no demands on my time . . . [17]

The Travel Bursary recognised the importance of travel for writers from a small and isolated country and the first, in 1985, was given to Allen Curnow who over 30 years before had been sent abroad in a stroke of enlightenment by the fledgling committee. The Overseas Travel Fund, worth $15,000 by 1988, allowed several writers a year the widened perspective and refreshing insight into one's own land that travel brings. New Zealanders were now regularly seen and heard at the Habourfront Festival in Toronto and the Adelaide festival; and, along with Curnow, Bill Manhire and Lauris Edmond were present at the 1985 Cambridge Poetry Festival, where according to Manhire, their very successful public reading 'left the Canadian poets . . . looking/sounding thoroughly inept!'[18] The Australia/NZ Literary Exchange ($12,500 from the Arts & Letters lottery, $5,500 added June 1987 to allow visits in 1988 and 1990) took a little longer to set up, as targeted sponsors declined, but PEN agreed to take part in organising the exchange, selecting a Fellow and hosting an Australian writer.[19] Dunedin poet Cilla McQueen was chosen from a small field to go to Australia in 1987, followed by Australian writer Nick Hasluck crossing the Tasman in 1988 (he complained that his books were not in the bookshops, a perennial bilateral problem).

Nonfiction had long been an area of contention; identified as what it was not, it was difficult to define precisely and covered a wide range of material obviously of little interest to the Literary Fund. However, writers of serious nonfiction who valued their literary craft resented the priority given by the Fund for many years to 'creative' writing, that is, fiction, poetry and drama. In the *New Zealand Times* of 25 July 1982, for example, Michael King in his regular column wrote:

> Concern is growing in literary circles over the diminishing assistance for serious non-fiction writing. Neither the Arts Council nor the Literary Fund make money available for non-fiction projects as a matter of course. The only writers' scholarship offering such assistance, the AHI bursary, was last year withdrawn by its sponsors.

Though nonfiction was not explicitly mentioned in the new policy bids for 1983/4 or 1984/5, it does seem as if the concern indicated by King was noted; for a Non-Fiction Assistance Fund of $8000 was set up when the increased funding was received in 1984/5. The very brief announcement invited applications in the areas of literary history, criticism and scholarship, biography and autobiography, and historical projects of national (rather than local) interest, especially projects relating to the social and/or cultural development of New Zealand.

Applications from both writers and publishers were called for by November and were considered at the first meeting of 1985. Four writers (out of 11) were funded, one of them, Lynley Hood, receiving $6000, identified as the Non-Fiction Writing Bursary for 1985, to write a biography of Sylvia Ashton-Warner (successfully published in 1988 and winner of the Wattie Book Award in 1989).

The others were Jane Tolerton for her biography of Ettie Rout (winner of the New Zealand Book Award for Non-Fiction in 1993), Anne Kirker for her major book on New Zealand women artists (finalist in the Wattie Book Award in 1987) and Stevan Eldred-Grigg for a history of wealth in New Zealand and an oral history of two working-class women, later the novel *Oracles and Miracles* (runner-up in the Wattie Book Award 1988). In addition, Auckland University Press received $4000 to assist the publication of Raewyn Dalziel's biography of Julius Vogel. Although $8000 was budgeted, $23,000 was spent.

However, the concern in literary circles had not abated and Tony Simpson, writing in September 1984 as the president of PEN, queried the priority given to poetry, fiction and drama over nonfiction. He was not satisfied with Susan Robertson's reply, writing again sternly the following March asserting the PEN executive was 'gravely concerned' to hear their suspicions were correct and claiming that the Fund was deviating from the original intentions of its founders. Sturm thereupon wheeled in the big guns and sent a four-page letter which insisted that the policy was well-established, that pressure on funding necessitated choices, that, compared with fiction, nonfiction was now extensively published and supported, and finally that the new nonfiction funding had already had a significant effect and in the current year 1984/5 amounted to 25 percent of total writing and publishing projects.[20] Similar amounts were spent on nonfiction in the next three years with writers like Bruce Jesson, Dick Scott, James Belich, Ruth Dallas and both Tony Simpson and Michael King (who got $12,000 in 1987/8) receiving grants; and books like Erik Olssen's *Red Feds* (Oxford University Press), Peter Simpson's selection of Allen Curnow's critical writing, *Look Back Harder*

(Auckland University Press), and Bill Manhire's short study of Maurice Gee (also for Oxford University Press) were assisted.

This was a period in which growing numbers of serious, well researched and well-written books of history, on Maori and Pacific topics, of biography and memoir, were being published for a public increasingly interested in New Zealand's past and historic personalities. Many of these books, such as Claudia Orange's landmark book on the Treaty of Waitangi or Janet Frame's autobiography, were commercial successes and had no need of state patronage. Many of their authors, such as Keith Sinclair, Anne Salmond and Judith Binney, were university teachers whose writing was part of their job, and the guidelines expressly excluded projects otherwise eligible for university funding; but for others like King and Simpson, or Dick Scott and Stevan Eldred-Grigg, or Jane Tolerton and Julia Millen, financial assistance could make a book possible. (Nonfiction funding for writers far exceeded that given to assist publication.) In 1988 increased funding enabled the Fund to offer a full-year nonfiction bursary of $24,000. The first bursary was given to Carol Henderson for a biography of her father Gordon Tovey, 'whose contribution to art education, particularly in the field of Maori art, was extremely influential'.[21] In fact, in response to this letter from Sturm, the Maori and South Pacific Arts Council (MASPAC) contributed $12,000, so the remaining $12,000 went to Lauris Edmond to write her three-volume autobiography, later to become an iconic work for New Zealand women.[22]

All these awards, fellowships and bursaries were now the bulk of the 60 percent of Literary Fund money going to writers; the remainder was distributed in project grants, small sums up to a certain limit. In 1983/4 seven grants ranging from $500 to $3000 were awarded, amounting to $7250. In 1987/8 almost $100,000 went in 18 grants to creative writers and a further five to writers of nonfiction. There was no restriction on the type of author assisted and these grants could recognise and encourage a new talent or enable an established one to begin or complete or revise a project. Kate De Goldi recalls how important her first grant of $6000 was in allowing her to think she might become a writer.[23] Sometimes the committee used this pool to provide 'discretionary' grants to candidates shortlisted in the bursaries—in February 1988, for example, Maurice Shadbolt was awarded $10,000 for work and travel towards the novel that became *Monday's Warriors* (1990).

* * *

Patronage of this kind was always prospective, betting on the future, and though the committee was extremely conscientious as well as skilled in assessing the material provided, some mistakes and disappointments, particularly with unknown and untried authors, were inevitable. A 2005 research paper shows there was a far from perfect match between state funding and critical acclaim.[24] However, the book awards as an exercise in retrospective evaluation did provide a check on this; they also of course offered publicity to writers and publishers, a window for a New Zealand literature now moving into the cultural mainstream.

Fiction was usually the smallest category of books entered in the New Zealand Book Awards, followed closely by poetry, with book production and nonfiction by far the largest. The awards tended to go to established authors, such as Allen Curnow and Janet Frame, but Sue McCauley and Keri Hulme won the Fiction Award with first novels and Anne French's first collection, *All Cretans are Liars,* won the 1988 Poetry Award. The nonfiction choices were often controversial, the class being so amorphous. Comparisons with the Wattie Book Award were constantly made; however the winners in the Wattie and those in the New Zealand Book Awards were rarely identical, partly because the criteria were different.

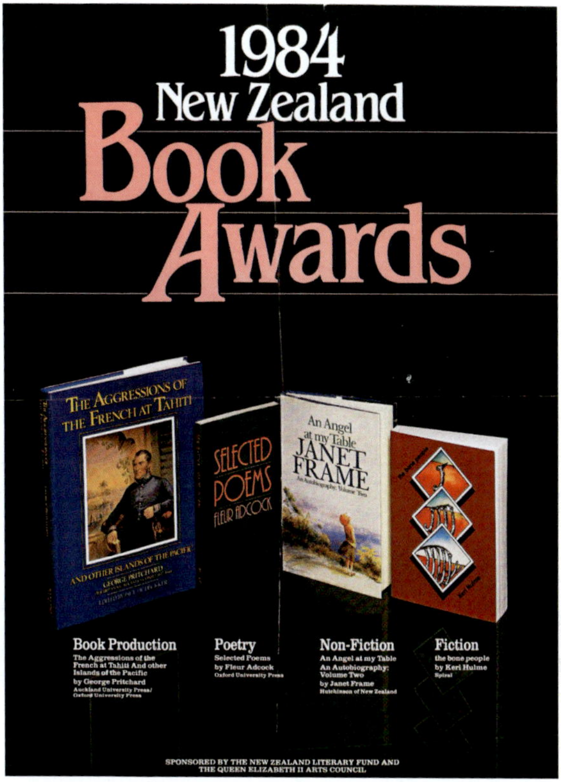

Poster showing the winners of the 1984 New Zealand Book Awards. The fiction winner was Keri Hulme's *the bone people*, twice subsidised by the Literary Fund, and the nonfiction winner the second volume of Janet Frame's autobiography, *An Angel at my Table*.
ATL, Eph-C-Book-AWARDS-1984-02. Courtesy Creative New Zealand

Over the years there was the usual minor tinkering with the guidelines, panics over breaches of confidentiality, crotchety commentary in the press and elsewhere. Gaining adequate publicity, a task for which even dedicated public servants had little time and no training, was always an issue. Recognising this, the Literary Fund Advisory Committee gratefully accepted an offer from the New Zealand Book Council in late 1986 to handle the book awards promotion for the next year. Kate Fortune was specially contracted to work on both adult and children's book awards and ran a well-organised and determined campaign. But Michael Gifkins, in his 'Bookmarks' column in the *Listener*, found much to complain about in the 1987 New Zealand Book Awards exercise: tied winners, the nomination of judges by PEN and the Book Council, the division of prize money, the lack of an overall winner and of the professional promotion ensured by having a company sponsor.[25]

The Advisory Committee thereupon did a thorough review and altered the guidelines to forbid tied results, hitherto an all too frequent outcome, and to clarify the definition of nonfiction. The judges would henceforth be chosen by the committee, rather than separately by PEN and the Book Council, and would be required to consult. A professional public relations firm, LOGOS, was hired for both the New Zealand Book Awards and the children's book awards for 1988.

The Children's Books of the Year Awards benefited from a dedicated sponsor in the Government Printing Office; they carried all the costs in the early years and handled much of the administrative and promotion work; they also suggested the inclusion of a nonfiction category first featuring in 1986, along with an increase in prize money. In 1987 Kate Fortune established a Young Readers' Week following on from the announcement of the awards. Booksellers, schools and children's librarians threw themselves into this, keen to contribute and assist in a general promotion of children's books.[26] Government Print withdrew in late 1988 after its privatisation but a new sponsor, AIM toothpaste, was quickly found and booksellers and publishers now put

Poster promoting the shortlist for the Children's Book of the Year in the Government Publishing Awards, 1982.
ATL, Eph-C-Book-AWARDS-1982-01. Courtesy Creative New Zealand

effort and energy into a wider annual celebration of books for children.

Sturm was always very careful to remain on good terms with PEN and to draw on its expertise, and clearly believed that the health of organisations representing writers and readers was a valid concern of the Advisory Committee. The Literary Fund continued to support PEN's two best first book awards, with prizes of $1000 each from 1984 and the Young Writers Incentive Award ($750). In 1987 PEN asked for more substantial assistance, for its gazette and for bringing out-of-town officeholders to meetings of its executive. A one-off grant of $2000 was given, but a further $10,000 was agreed to late in the year.

Funding for the New Zealand Book Council's popular Writers in Schools scheme gradually increased (from $3750 to $5750 in 1986/7). Committee members enjoyed the colourful reports diligently provided, with their accounts of Margaret Mahy delighting children in her famous wig, or pirate costume, or on one occasion a necklace of liquorice allsorts. As the Literary Fund money went to pay the writers, the committee was glad to increase the grant to $11,500 in 1988/9. The Fund also contributed $2500 to the Book Council for a public lecture series in 1985 and doubled it the next two years for an expanded programme.

* * *

New Zealand publishing was growing rapidly in the 1980s: writing in December 1986, Tony Reid claimed that between 1980 and 1984 the quantity of local books had risen by more than 60 percent and was now a third of the booksellers' turnover.[27] Literary Fund support for publishing continued at about the same level as before (an average of 18 percent of revenue in 1981–88, more generous than the Australian 10 percent) though it fell towards the end of the period. Individual grants were related to the production costs, up to a half but usually around one third. A few sterner conditions were now established: the book, which must have already been accepted by the publisher, should be submitted by him/her, it could not be in a limited edition (under 250 copies), nor normally by an author not resident in New Zealand, it must appear within two years and the requirement that author should be paid a 10 percent royalty was maintained.[28] At PEN's suggestion, the idea of subsidising the author royalty rather than the production cost was once again floated with publishers and once again rejected. An average of 27 books a year were funded but the individual grants rose as production costs rose; in 1986/7, $56,330 was dispensed to publishers compared with $29,960 in 1981/2. Thirty-seven publishers received grants between 1982 and 1988; most were small and temporary but the university presses (VUP, AUP, Otago and OUP) and John McIndoe remained the winners. Multi-national publishers like Penguin and Heinemann appeared sparingly. The history of poetry in New Zealand would have been very different without the Literary Fund as collections of poetry were far more frequently funded than any other genre, though grants for fiction, especially short stories, gradually rose.[29]

The guarantee against loss scheme for works of fiction set up late in 1984 did not find favour with publishers and was quickly canned, its funds going to the Children's Publication Fund now re-established and much in demand.[30] Along with the remnants of the IYC telethon fund and with a generous donation from Roger Hall there was at last enough to substantially assist the exciting developments in writing for children. Thirteen books for children from five publishers were assisted from 1985 to mid-1988 and two of them were chosen as the Children's Book of the Year, Barry Faville's *The Keeper* (1987) and Tessa Duder's *Alex* (1988), both published by Oxford University Press. The Maori Publication Fund, to assist writers and publications in te reo, also set up with $25,000 in late 1984, was the subject of discussion and exchange with the Maori Art Committee of MASPAC over several years and was finally operational in 1989.[31]

As if earlier attempts at book promotion were not sufficient warning, the committee embarked on a scheme to help small presses publicise their titles. In mid-1987 Dale Williams wrote a well-researched paper suggesting a six-monthly joint advertisement in the *Listener.* It took a while to get underway, but an advertisement duly appeared in June 1989. A month later Ann Mallinson for Mallinson Rendel, one of the publishers who had appeared in the advertisement, reported that book sales showed little impact; the scheme appears to have quietly died thereafter.[32]

* * *

Even though literary magazines were often considered the seedbed of great writing, they did not flourish in this period. For much of the decade the magazine budget was underspent. Caxton's *Landfall* continued solidly under a variety of editorial arrangements and was generously assisted, if frequently interrogated. *Islands*, though, staggered to a halt in 1981; a special grant of $5000 in November 1983 spurred Dudding to begin again and two issues appeared in 1984 and in 1985, and single issues in 1986 and 1987; all were well funded but the journal folded none the less.

Two new magazines, *Untold* and *Rambling Jack*, benefited from the establishment fund set up in late 1984 and subsequently received regular grants; but neither lasted long. Perhaps the real energy at this time was going into the postmodern journals such as *Parallax*, *And*, *Antic* and *Splash*, where the borders between criticism, theory and 'creative' writing, and between literature and art, were

The first issue of the South Island literary magazine, *Untold*, 1984, and the first issue of *Rambling Jack*, May 1986, published by Miracle Mart Receiving, and offering 'new poems & drawings'. The cover image is apparently 'A detail from "Rambling Jack at the Point Erin Baths overlooking Birkenhead" by Little Hat Jones' (who might be Gregory O'Brien).
Jock Phillips photographs

permeable. There was probably a measure of suspicion on both sides, but one-off grants went to *Parallax*, *And* and *Antic*. Again their lives were brief, either by accident or design. *Sport*, a new journal edited by Fergus Barrowman of Victoria University Press, appeared in 1988 and was funded from the beginning; it quickly established itself as a quality production, a reliable stayer and a valuable conduit for students of Bill Manhire's classes in creative writing.

The founders of *Sport*: Nigel Cox, Elizabeth Knox, Fergus Barrowman and Damien Wilkins, with the first issue, 1988.
Dominion Post Collection, ATL, EP/1988/3893

8

INTO THE ARTS COUNCIL 1984–1994

These were years of constant activity, reading, correspondence, decision-making, discussing, but all the while a dramatic change, 'the biggest change in the nature of the administration of literature since government patronage began in 1946', was unfolding.[1] Pushed by the writers' association PEN, the New Zealand Literary Fund Advisory Committee was the first organisation set up to deliver state assistance to the arts; with modest funding but dedicated committee members it had now lasted 40 years, steadily growing in influence and impact and enjoying the support and respect of writers and publishers. However, since the early days of the Arts Council, as we have seen, there had been voices that argued against the separate identity of the Literary Fund and urged that it become a part of the Arts Council structure. Hitherto this idea had been strongly opposed by writers and by the committee.[2] But at the AGM of PEN in 1982, a proposal was made that the Literary Fund move from the Department of Internal Affairs to the Queen Elizabeth II Arts Council. Tony Simpson undertook to prepare a report on the question for the next AGM and subsequently discussed it with the Minister and with Michael

Volkerling, Director of the Arts Council. In his carefully argued paper (26 April 1983), Simpson was generally in favour of the move but recommended a ballot be taken to decide whether PEN should continue its investigations into the possibility; the results of the ballot clearly supported this course of action.[3] The literary community, at least as represented by PEN, was no longer implacably opposed to the move.

Tony Simpson as president of PEN, Terry Sturm and Geoff Knox (Chief Executive Officer of the Arts Branch, Internal Affairs) comprised the review committee set up to deflect attention from the row about PEN representation. One of the items to be discussed was a possible merger between the Literary Fund and the Arts Council. Accordingly, Sturm raised it at the Advisory Committee meeting of May 1984: 'Michael Volkerling is going to be present at the Review Ctee meeting following ours in May—so I really need to have clear views and positions prepared for it'.[4] Sturm was not in favour of the merger, and the outcome of the discussion was clear:

> It was noted that writers had more direct influence with the Minister through the Department than they would have through the Arts Council. Furthermore, within the Council literature would have to compete with the other arts for funding. The Committee also believed that there was a greater diversity of representation on the Committee than there would be on an Arts Council panel and that the Council's permanent administrative staff were more involved in the allocation of Council funds than departmental staff were in Literary Fund decisions.[5]

These were prescient words.

But other forces were at work. With the expansion of programmes and the growing numbers of writers and publishers, the workload of the tiny departmental staff had become daunting. The newsletter, much appreciated in the sector, ceased completely between March 1984 and November 1986 and dwindled thereafter. In August 1984 the Secretary, Susan Robertson, had not been able to write the minutes of the previous meeting 'because the LF was critically under-staffed and . . . all work was substantially delayed'.[6] An extra staff member was promised. But even with this help, the new secretary, Gillian Martell, was soon struggling under the same load; the Secretary's report at her third meeting complains about being 'heavily taxed'.[7] Accordingly, a special two-day live-in meeting of the Advisory Committee was held at Burma Lodge, Wellington, in February 1986 with the aim of streamlining administrative arrangements and discussing current policy. There was widespread debate and strong criticism, some of it passed on from journalists and writers, of the current administration. The department was charged with inadequate publicity, pathetic efforts to increase funding, poor servicing of the committee. A new annual programme was proposed which, for example, set decisions on writers' grants at the August meeting, with publishers' grants at the May and November meetings.

A possible merger with the Arts Council was also canvassed and discussed with an invited group of writers and publishers.[8] This would of course have been one solution to the strains the administrative staff was experiencing. Also pushing in the same direction was the reformist drive of the new Labour Government elected in July 1984 and committed to restructuring the civil service. This meant reducing staff numbers and devolving many of the activities accumulated by the Department of Internal Affairs over the years. Labour Government policy also included the campaign spearheaded by Deputy Prime Minister Geoffrey Palmer to terminate as many quangos as possible. The Literary Fund Advisory Committee was clearly on the list (though when questioned in February 1986 the Department supported retaining it).[9] However, Peter Tapsell, the new Minister for Internal Affairs and Arts and Culture, soon had the Literary Fund in his sights and had already raised the issue in 1985. In a publication called *Arts 85: A Report on Progress*, published by the Arts Council in December 1985, the possibility, raised by the Minister, of bringing the Literary Fund and the Arts Council 'under common administration' is named as the first of a number of proposals for 'structural reform'.

Peter Tapsell, Minister for the Arts, 1984–87.
Parliamentary Collection, Parliamentary Service

Discussions in the committee, in the Department, with the Arts Council and with the Minister continued throughout 1986. The Advisory Committee began to formulate a set of conditions under which a transfer might occur. Sturm was adamant that such a move should only happen if it benefited the literary arts and insisted on extensive consultation with the literary community. The publishers were quick to express a view and their AGM in April passed a unanimous resolution in favour of the merger.[10] They particularly stressed the need for more efficient administration. A group of small publishers who were regular applicants to the Fund wrote a separate paper backing the move and also making a number of additional demands.[11] Opinion was gradually shifting.

In September Sturm wrote to a large number of writers, publishers and other interested persons reporting on the progress of the discussions and asking their views on a possible transfer. Replies were called for by 5 November, in time for a conference on the arts, Arts Forum 2000, which had been rather suddenly announced by the Minister in late August but which Sturm could see would be an excellent occasion to debate the matter and to reach some conclusions. Fifty-three replies were received and the forum too was well attended by the literary community with the Literature and Publishing Assembly a large, articulate and well-organised group of over a hundred participants chaired by Kate Fortune, now Director of the Booksellers Association, and convened by Sturm. Eccentricity, egotism and entertainment were all present, with Dun Mihaka vigorously selling his book *Whakapohane* at the back of the plenary session. According to Michael Gifkins, 'he fixed a noted member of the publishing fraternity with his very direct gaze and advised that the book did not even need intelligence to read it'.[12]

A lively session on the Literary Fund followed others on writing, publishing, and marketing. After 'considerable debate', in which strong opinions both for and against were expressed, the Literature and Publishing Assembly finally passed the following resolution:

> It is recommended that the Queen Elizabeth II Arts Council be restructured to embrace and take advantage of the presence of the literary arts within its terms of reference and responsibilities; and that the Literary Fund become a committee of the Council.[13]

At the Literature and Publishing Assembly of the Arts 2000 conference, November 1986. Rosemary Stagg, president Book Publishers Association of New Zealand, Professor Terry Sturm, Kate Fortune, director Booksellers Association of New Zealand. Alexander Turnbull presides above.
Peter Bush photograph

This way of expressing it was implicitly a criticism of the notion that appeared to be held by Internal Affairs and the Arts Council, that literature could just quietly slip into the Arts Council structure without any adjustment of philosophy or practice. Literature was a major force: 'Only the visual arts come anywhere near literature in the vigour of their local growth and in international perceptions of their quality . . .'[14] Literary people saw the Arts Council as very focused on the (expensive) performing arts and with little real understanding of the likely impact of the presence of literature. This resolution asserted its strength and its power.

In all the discussions both during the year and at the forum, a handful of issues were repeatedly stressed. They were funding, administration, the structure and practice of the committee, and access to the highest level of Arts Council policy. There was widespread agreement both in the written submissions and in the forum, from both individuals and organisations, that a number of assurances on these questions must be given for the literary community to accept such a major move.

Thus the resolution was followed by five provisos.

The first condition insisted that current funding be maintained or increased: the inadequacy of funding had long been a problem, especially when compared to that given to the other arts.

The second condition required the retention of the existing structure and current procedures. As we have seen, the convention that two members of the committee were selected by PEN was jealously guarded; the more recent arrangement whereby BPANZ chose a publisher member was also well established. The range of literary expertise usually including writers, publishers, academics had worked well and it was hoped that it would continue.

One of the advantages of the original committee structure was, as an advisory committee, its direct access to the Minister. There was considerable nervousness that in the proposed Arts Council structure the Literature Committee would be several layers removed from real political power. A third condition then demanded that the chair of the committee (and at least one other literary person) be a member of the Arts Council itself.

Particularly appealing to the existing committee and to Internal Affairs were the services that the Arts Council could offer. The administrative limitations of the Department had become increasingly frustrating and the thought of skilled and efficient administrative backup along with marketing capacities was alluring. This, fourth, condition thus required the provision of adequate administrative and promotional skills. (It should be said, though, that for all the attraction of this support, there was always the lurking fear of an overbearing bureaucracy which could in time take over more and more of the decision-making powers of the committee.)

The final condition made it very clear that unless assurances on these four matters were given the Advisory Committee would 'oppose changes to the status quo'. To have reached this point was a major achievement largely due to the skilful guidance and political skill of Terry Sturm. The literary community was fully informed and, amazingly, more or less united; it had argued from a position of strength and had not allowed itself to be rolled by either officials or politicians.

However, it very quickly emerged that all would not be plain sailing. Tapsell agreed to most of the conditions though only to retention, not to an increase, of funding. But he was adamantly opposed to the literary sector having specific representation on the Arts Council. While it was usual for each arts panel to be chaired by a member of the Council, that person was not specially qualified in that area nor seen as a lobbyist for that sector. To alter that arrangement now, the Minister thought, would be to establish an unfortunate precedent: 'unlimited sectarian groups would similarly demand representation on the Council, which would clearly make it unworkable'.[15] An impasse was reached; and the support of the Arts Council and its new chair, Ian Cochrane, for the views of the Literary Fund Advisory Committee did nothing to change Tapsell's mind.

Rather ironically, the quango hunt had in the meantime gathered apace. On 7 July 1987, unbeknownst to the committee, the Cabinet Policy Committee recommended that the Literary Fund Advisory Committee be terminated by 1 October and merged with the Arts Council. Urged on by a somewhat embarrassed Peter Boag (Secretary, Department of Internal Affairs), Tapsell moved swiftly and was granted a deferral of the decision on the grounds that negotiations were already underway, though how he hoped to solve the impasse is obscure.[16] Discussions continued and various solutions were floated.

But immediately after the election on 15 August, when Labour was returned, Michael Bassett took over the portfolios of both Internal Affairs and Arts and Culture. A historian with a keen interest in the arts, well known to Sturm, Bassett was strongly in favour of the merger and within six weeks had made some 'very constructive' proposals. He suggested that a person 'with an appropriate background in the literary arts' be appointed to the Arts Council as soon as a vacancy arose; and that in addition he would arrange to legislate an extra seat on the Arts Council

Michael Bassett, Minister for the Arts, 1987–90, who, with deft political skill, shepherded literature into the Queen Elizabeth II Arts Council.
Courtesy Michael Bassett

(from 13 to 14 members) which, though not specified, would acknowledge the new responsibility being assumed and which would in practice be filled by a literary person. He also suggested that a new award or programme be established to mark the transfer.

The deadlock was broken: the committee accepted this plan, as long as the other provisos were also fulfilled. Much toing and froing followed among all the parties to agree on detail, timing and personnel. But on 17 May 1988, at the ceremony to present the annual New Zealand Book Awards, Bassett was able to say:

> I am now delighted to formally announce that the Literary Fund will be transferring to the Arts Council in the next couple of months, as early as 1 July, and that the assurances that have been sought by the literary community will be met.[17]

Professor Sturm would become a member of the Arts Council, an appointment agreed by Cabinet that very morning; and an amendment to the Arts Council Act to provide an extra seat on the Council would be legislated for by mid-July. To mark the move, Bassett had some other goodies up his sleeve too. He had agreed with Sturm's suggestion of a permanent second Scholarship in Letters (of $24,000), which had been announced earlier and awarded to short-story writer and novelist Patricia Grace. He was also able to offer the Fund, or rather the Literature Committee, an extra $100,000 ($184,200 in 2015) from the Lottery Board for the 1988/9 year.

A formal document was signed two days later by Sturm, Boag and Cochrane and arrangements were put in place for all funds including those for administration to be passed over. Sturm would continue as the chair of the new Literature Committee, and three committee members (Broughton, Hulme, Caffin) agreed to stay on after their terms expired later that year to provide continuity; the two PEN members were replaced by Elizabeth Smither and Dick Scott for the first meeting at the Arts Council. Rosemary Wildblood, a writer then President of PEN, was appointed Programme Manager (Literature), a new position requiring a 'suitably qualified individual' with 'an understanding of the wider literary scene'. And the Lottery Board came up with yet another $100,000.[18] On 30 June a 'low-key official function', at which 'marriage metaphors multiplied', celebrated the merger. And on 1 July 1988 the Literary Fund and the Literary Fund Advisory Committee came to an end, after an honourable life.[19] On that date, state assistance to literature moved into a new phase in the wide embrace of the Queen Elizabeth II Arts Council.

* * *

How was it that when the literary community and the Literary Fund Advisory Committee had once been so strongly opposed, the actual transition in fact happened in such harmony? The very length of the negotiation process over several years probably allowed the participants to get used to the idea. Having initially been resistant, the Department changed its position, recognising that the Literary Fund had grown too big for it to handle efficiently among all its other responsibilities. Sturm's extraordinary patience and tactical skill were clearly important factors. Initially reluctant, he began to see that the transfer was inevitable; but he was determined that the literary community should participate fully in the decision.[20] By continuing and extensive consultation with writers and publishers and their organisations, by always stressing the national importance and international standing of New Zealand writing, by keeping on good terms with all parties, he played a vital role. His credibility was never in question and everyone knew that his one unwavering commitment was to the literary arts, as he called them, and to all those to whom they mattered.

Michael Bassett too came on the scene at the right moment, swiftly breaking the deadlock and arguing strongly on behalf of writers. He was fortunate that the introduction of Lotto the previous year had produced a welcome windfall for the arts, a generous proportion of which he sent in literature's direction, thus recognising the long penury of the Literary Fund and allaying the fears of some writers that this might continue or increase under the new regime. He made every effort to see that the Literature Committee started its life on as secure a financial basis as he could manage. While the merger fitted comfortably with government policy on state sector reform, it was not a cost-cutting exercise.

It should also be said that the Arts Council played its cards deftly and with tact. Always welcoming, they did not push or bully, were open to debate and to working out solutions. There is no question that the existing shared programmes, the Book Awards, the Playwrights' Award and the Overseas Travel Fund, had laid the groundwork for amicable cooperation.

Professor Sturm and the committee could no longer oppose the move once the Department was committed to it. If direct access to the Minister was sacrificed, there was something to be said for the 'arm's length' funding of the Arts Council; and its greater lobbying power might also be an advantage. Separate funding was retained for two years (1988/89 and 1989/90), and with the committee structure intact, the transition was gradual and there was little obvious change at first in the operations of the committee.

* * *

The established programmes remained and the usual processes of assessment by the committee continued. But the massive increases in funding that followed the merger offered opportunities: from $500,000 in 1988/89, income rose to $916,400 in 1989/90 (roughly $921,000 to $1,575,000 in 2015). The committee was able to expand most schemes in these two years, now offering four Scholarships in Letters (as well as a special 1990 two-year scholarship), two bursaries for new writers, two for children's writers, a nonfiction fellowship, and two travel bursaries. More funds went into promotion especially of small presses and into travel. Once the Literature Committee funding was fully integrated into that of the Arts Council in 1990/91, however, increases were much more modest, with additional income only for a few particular projects and to offset inflation; in 1993/4 there was actually a cut of 7 percent.

A writer's residency at the University of Waikato came on board in 1991 and one for a children's writer at Palmerston North Training College in 1992; a Massey University writer's fellowship began in 1993. There was greatly increased funding for international programmes, much of which came from already established sources in the Arts Council, and for PEN and the New Zealand Book Council, which received $47,000 in 1992/3 for its Writers in Schools programme, again assisted by an Arts Council Performers in Schools programme.

A paper written by Elizabeth Caffin before her departure at the end of 1989 analysed recent publishing subsidies, and recommended the establishment of annual block grants for publishers with strong track records of titles supported by the Literary Fund, a type of programme recently introduced in Australia. The new BPANZ member Wendy Harrex encouraged this, as did the association, and a block grant scheme began in 1991/2 using a special sum of $40,000. It reduced massive reading tasks by the committee and massive copying outlays by the publishers and was soon working well with six to eight publishers receiving block grants annually. Wendy Harrex also organised a successful subsidised independent publishers' catalogue, including initially books published in 1989 and not just books funded by the state; and later a catalogue of entries in the New Zealand Book Awards.

The role of the Literature Committee Programme Manager, Rosemary Wildblood, was not an easy one over these years. She was expected to take a much more active part in the formulation of policy than the Internal Affairs committee secretary. While the Literary Fund committee was nominally an advisory committee, in fact it had formulated policy without interference; now the programme manager was to take policy suggestions to the Council itself who formally decided on policy matters. The committee was seen mainly as an expert assessment body. It is probably true that the members of the committee did not fully understand the diminution of their role: at the beginning of 1989 four of the members had been on the Literary Fund Advisory Committee and had participated in the prolonged battle to retain many of its features. The membership gradually changed: Witi Ihimaera succeeded Keri Hulme in early 1990, Lawrence Jones succeeded William Broughton in 1991, Tony Simpson and Sue McCauley (quickly followed by Suzann Olsson) were the new PEN members in 1992, and Jane Connor followed Wendy Harrex at the end of that year. The new members though sensed the confidence of the committee; and indeed Professor Sturm, now on the Council and more aware of how the organisation worked, had to reprimand Tony Simpson for assuming in a report to PEN that the committee made policy. It soon became clear in the higher echelons of the Arts Council that the Literature Committee was not always operating in quite the same way as the other programme panels and was sometimes taking steps independently that should have been approved by the Council. A long-held and strongly worded criticism from PEN about assistance for nonfiction projects particularly attracted concern, as did the practice of the PEN members to report back to their organisation.[21] Rosemary Wildblood was caught in the middle and increasingly urged by her superiors to rein the committee in. It had more members, more meetings per year and longer terms of tenure than the panels of the other arts and was thus thought to cost more. Accordingly, she prepared in July 1992 a Council paper proposing a major restructure ('disestablishment' was the word used) of the committee, which included a division into nonfiction and general panels and the abolition of the PEN and BPANZ representation.

She took the draft to Auckland to show to Sturm, who was appalled and promptly resigned. His long commitment to New Zealand writers and his vigorous advocacy of their interests in many quarters was deeply affronted by a proposal to disenfranchise them without discussion or debate. Jenny Pattrick, now chair of the Arts Council, Peter Quin, the current director, and other senior figures were astonished and shocked at Sturm's reaction. They had thought his behaviour on the Council was exemplary, showing a dedication to the wider arts scene and a proper reluctance to act simply as a lobbyist for the literary sector. He felt that he would be unable to argue on behalf of writers if he remained on the Council and that his resignation would force the issue into the public arena. It did. A bitter row ensued, with PEN vociferous, Rosemary Wildblood and the Arts Council vilified, and Sturm receiving widespread support among writers.[22] Andrew Mason, previously literary editor of the *Listener*, was appointed to the vacancies on the Council and as chair of the Literature Committee to complete Sturm's term. The Arts Council backed down and the PEN and BPANZ representation remained, though with tighter rules about reporting back. The committee was reduced to five members, their terms to two years and their meetings to three instead of four a year.

This heated debate was conducted under the shadow of impending legislation which had been under discussion and in formulation for some time. The entire Arts Council structure was overthrown in 1994, with a new Act and a new name, Creative New Zealand; and the abolition of all previous panels and committees. The selection and administration of government assistance to literature from this point bore little resemblance to the historical processes of the Literary Fund Advisory Committee. Expert advice was now restricted to a disempowered selection panel subject to higher decision-making powers and without any input into policy at all. While the entry into the Arts Council had been positive and hopeful, the writers and publishers present at a meeting in Auckland in 1996 were angry and exasperated at the way things had turned out, at the shift of power away from practitioners into the hands of bureaucrats, at an obscure and mystifying assessment process and at the use of a language derived from management and showing none of the sensitivity to which writers were by nature alert. As Ian Wedde has said:

> CNZ grants have become progressively more bureaucratised; their outcome targets and descriptions often confuse the purpose of the grants, which is primarily to support the work of writers in a small cultural market; they tend to be focused on completion at the expense of development (i.e. on publication at the expense of research); on project deadlines at the expense of creative processes. Accountability is necessary, but over-regulation is likely to be counter-productive.[23]

9

DÉNOUEMENT

Here is Maurice Shadbolt writing in 1960: 'To survive as a writer anywhere is difficult; in New Zealand it's a nightmare—a paradise for amateurs but a nightmare for anyone who takes writing seriously enough to want to work at it full-time. . . .'[1] Writers are paid for their work chiefly by royalties on the sales of their books. A New Zealand writer who is committed first and foremost to financial success must pursue an international audience; the market in New Zealand is simply not large enough to sustain a writer consistently over a career. This is hard enough for a writer in popular genres but for one interested in experimental or challenging writing, the barriers are huge. Some writers, especially poets, were able to develop literary careers while holding down fulltime jobs. Many of New Zealand's best-known writers—Allen Curnow, Bill Manhire, Vincent O'Sullivan, C.K. Stead—were academics for large parts of their careers, and made few demands on the Literary Fund. Others eked out a living from other kinds of writing jobs: Fiona Kidman worked for radio, Maurice Gee for television, Maurice Shadbolt as a journalist; Elizabeth Smither worked as a librarian. But none of these jobs allowed the extended periods of time necessary for producing serious works of fiction and it is hardly surprising that the great New Zealand novel was for so long unwritten.

Private patronage of literature has been limited. From time to time private firms have supported awards and prizes.[2] But the Robert Burns Fellowship at the University of Otago and the Katherine Mansfield Fellowship at Menton were the only substantial privately funded grants that existed up to 1988. Private money contributed to the AHI Bursary, the ICI Bursary and the Choysa Bursary; later the Todd Foundation and the Louis Johnson estate supported bursaries too. But in the period from 1947 to 1988 the state, in a pattern familiar in other areas of New Zealand life, assumed by far the largest responsibility for encouraging writers. (This includes the university and training college residencies and the Authors' Fund as well as the Literary Fund.) The money available was always modest; the aspiring candidates always many.

The most striking testament to the effect of the Literary Fund comes from the writers themselves:

> Grants from the Literary Fund effectively produced my literary career. Most of the substantial work I wrote between 1974 and 1988 (for example *Dick Seddon's Great Dive*, *Symmes Hole*, *Survival Arts* and a first draft of *Chinese Opera*) could not have been produced without this assistance.
> —Ian Wedde

> I cannot imagine that I could have conducted my life as a writer without assistance from the Literary Fund. . . . A number of grants in the 1980s made a dramatic difference to my life and ability to carry on as a writer. When I got the Scholarship in Letters I remember clearing my desk to take a year's leave. And suddenly I knew I was never coming back. The faith shown in me, despite only a handful

> of books, convinced me that somehow I could go on.
> —Fiona Kidman

> Money from the Fund had two faces—an encouraging and enabling one (serious face) and a rewarding one, a kind of smile. I've had both, and can say, with complete honesty, that I would have written a lot less without that practical help and reward.
> —Maurice Gee[3]

These writers, and others, were assisted over a long period of time, through many different manifestations of the advisory committee. Maurice Gee received 13 grants of different kinds and amounts over 40 years, including the Scholarship in Letters four times, which made the *Plumb* trilogy possible. Likewise Maurice Shadbolt's New Zealand Wars trilogy was supported by two Scholarships in Letters and a smaller project grant. Fiona Kidman, who also received the Scholarship in Letters four times, had 10 grants in 20 years, mostly, as she says, in the 1980s; they included a Travel Bursary, the Victoria University of Wellington Writing Fellowship and the Award for Achievement (all in 1988). Ian Wedde had six grants over 12 years quite apart from at least nine grants to his publishers.

All these are now well-known and established writers. As they began to produce more work which was increasingly recognised, it was important to keep them going. The Scholarship in Letters gave each of them a lifeline, a year free to write, the time to research and form a novel. Later the university fellowships played the same role. You knew you would get a result and one worth having. Further, such assistance signalled to the writers and to the wider community that this was a real and serious profession, one to which you could commit your life and one which had the potential for powerful cultural and social impact. Within the limitations of its funding the Literary Fund did much to establish a writing profession in this country.

Criticisms were often made that the Literary Fund committee made safe and conservative choices of familiar names. But most of them were not well known when they were first assisted: Maurice Gee had not published a book, only stories in little magazines; the same is true of Patricia Grace. Ian Wedde had published two slim volumes of verse with small publishers; Elizabeth Smither one. These initial grants were punts.

Contrary to some opinion, the committee was from early on keen to encourage new writers, and the original Writing Bursary was specifically intended to support an emerging writer. Later the ICI Bursary, the Louis Johnson and the Todd Foundation grants did the same. Not all the young writers so assisted did in fact 'emerge'; some sank into oblivion. But that was inevitable when track records were limited and names unknown. Keri A.L. Hulme got $500 in 1973, a full decade before *the bone people* appeared; although, as we have seen, there was a complaint about thus funding an unknown, it turned out to be a risk worth taking. Elizabeth Smither recalls the euphoria on getting her first grant:

> The first grant I received from the Literary Fund Advisory Committee was for $4,000 in 1978. Accompanied by a formal letter it said my application for a larger grant had not succeeded but, like the runner up to a dux, the committee would like to offer me a small discretionary grant. *Proxime accessit* was more than fine by me; it set me dancing on the carpet. And though there were other and larger grants to come it still gives me happiness to think of that $4,000.[4]

Sometimes it was brave and imaginative publishers who took the first risk on new writers, coming to the Fund for assistance on projects with uncertain markets. Thus first books by Hone Tuwhare, Amelia Batistich, Lauris Edmond, Jenny Bornholdt, Elizabeth Knox, for example, were all assisted at publication and before their writers were given any grants at all. Publishers were by definition more proactive in seeking out new talent and provided a first assessment of quality that the advisory committee took note of: you did not embark on publishing a new and unknown writer unless you were convinced he or she was talented. A clue might be the writer's background in Bill Manhire's course; Jenny Bornholdt and Elizabeth Knox had been early students of Manhire's. Or it might be the appearance of the writer in a literary journal. Often the decision to fund publication of a first book was reinforced by awards for the PEN/NZSA Best First Book, also subsidised by the Fund: Robert Sullivan's *Jazz Waiata* and Anne French's *All Cretans are Liars*, for example, won the Jessie Mackay Best First Book of Poetry Award.

In general the awards set up and supported by the Literary Fund frequently matched earlier decisions, grants given to the writers or the publishers, though the judges were not the members of the committee. Up to 1988, 16 of the category winners in the New Zealand Book Awards had been subsidised at publication, five at the writing stage; and of course the writers won the prizes in both cases. In the independently funded Wattie Book Awards, running concurrently and more focused on market, seven subsidised writers were among the top three. The winners of the Children's Book of the Year from 1982 to 1988 were all, writers and/or publishers, assisted by the Literary Fund.

The Literary Fund thus worked with other organisations

and institutions towards the professionalisation of serious creative writing and towards a wider public recognition of New Zealand literary talent. If the Fund played a role in establishing a canon it did not do so alone. Publishers, writers' and publishers' associations, private sponsors were all associated with the Literary Fund in different ways in strengthening the literary arts and in developing an extensive and supportive infrastructure. By 1988, contemporary New Zealand literature was no longer a few isolated, alienated voices but an increasingly diverse, energetic and applauded group addressing a variety of readers.

While the short story and the poem have traditionally been the strengths of New Zealand literature, the flourishing of the novel from the late 1970s owed much to Literary Fund assistance. The provision, after the catalyst of the Vennell Report, of a number of substantial grants in aid to writers, predominantly given to novelists, allowed Gee, Shadbolt, Kidman, Grace, Duckworth to produce their best work. It thickened and enlarged the form; it recognised variety and diversity. The same generosity was not apparent in assisting the publication of novels, though, and the committee probably had too sanguine a belief in the commercial viability of works of fiction in a small market. Increasingly the larger publishers were forced to seek assistance for their fiction publishing.

Poets had at least from the 1930s spoken well in New Zealand, and would have gone on doing so without state assistance. However, poetry was widely understood to sell in limited quantities and almost all the serious poetry published in the 40 years of the Fund's existence was assisted at publication. Likewise literary magazines, where many writers first encountered an editor and thence an audience, could not survive without financial support.

Landfall, *Islands* and *Sport*, as well as the review journal *New Zealand Books* have thus had long and productive lives, while others less consistently rigorous and more intermittently funded, have foundered.

If the Schools Publication Branch of the Ministry of Education was the true seedbed of children's literature in New Zealand, the Literary Fund was the compost and the rain, initially with the Choysa Bursary and the Children's Publication Fund. Again the Fund combined with enterprising publishers and gifted writers, with dedicated booksellers and schoolteachers, to enrich the reading experience of children with local stories.

For literature does not exist in isolation. At first the Literary Fund Advisory Committee concentrated on cultivating its own garden; but increasingly it helped to place creative writing into a wider context. The writers' organisation PEN had been there at its beginning and their two fortunes remained entwined, with the PEN members ever watchful. The Literary Fund also assisted the Book Council with its outreach activities, most notably its Writers in Schools programme. It supported festivals, conferences and book exhibitions. It began sending writers abroad, not only to broaden their experience but to display their work. As the sector grew it was listened to, taken seriously, discussed.

The committee was constituted as an advisory committee to Ministers and in practice its decisions, on policy and on its execution, were rarely questioned. Initially the membership was a large and motley collection of 'bookmen', but by 1955 was settled at six. They generally included several academics from university English departments, at least two writers and from 1979 a publisher. They approached submissions from different angles but with considerable knowledge and expertise, so that decisions were reached by consensus with relatively few major disagreements. In the early years the committee was inclined to interfere in the presentation of literary works by making ill-informed suggestions to publishers; and it reached its lowest point in attempting to censor the *New Zealand Poetry Yearbook*. But in general the good sense of the members prevailed, their opinions clear from selection rather than sledgehammer. More carefully drafted guidelines for submissions, a specialty of Frean's, were a distinct advantage. So undoubtedly was the dedication of the members: the initial system of using outside readers was soon abandoned and all members read all submissions, a huge task four times a year.

Writers and publishers certainly complained from time to time at rejection, but such anger never reached a real groundswell among the literary community. For most of its time and among most writers the committee was respected. The role of the chair was vital, requiring good relations with the committee, the minister and the writing and publishing communities, both characteristically articulate and opinionated. From 1951 all the chairmen were university professors, but the committee was lucky in its chairs and both Gordon and Sturm were outstanding. Gordon presided over the gradual emergence of a stable, smoothly functioning body, while Sturm guided the Fund into the Arts Council with political skill and a real passion for New Zealand writing.

The officials from the Department of Internal Affairs who over the years serviced the committee were also frequently able, from Andrew Sharp who managed the committee with an almost invisible hand, to Jim Booth who masterminded the Vennell proposals, to Mike Jarman and Pat Stuart.

Thankfully the fears expressed in the early years by Fairburn and others that writers would feel obliged to pander to their political masters were not realised: occasionally politicians made mild suggestions, but indifference was their worst failing. That is, except for one event: the attempt in 1982–3 to interfere in the PEN nominations, an unwise move cleverly evaded by delaying tactics and a change of government. Government did have control of the purse strings and at times exercised this harshly; but an enlightened minister like Highet could exercise a powerful effect for improvement.

The Literary Fund was probably in the late 1940s an idea whose time had come, modelled as it was on the usual overseas precedents. It occurred at a time of renewal and revived cultural energy in company with other literary initiatives such as the founding of *Landfall* and *Te Ao Hou*, of Pegasus and Paul's Book Arcade and the New Zealand University Press as publishers, and of Parson's Bookshop, the appearance of Curnow's landmark anthology, *A Book of New Zealand Verse* and of Frank Sargeson's *That Summer and Other Stories*. Writers like Glover, McCormick, Smithyman and Keith Sinclair were returned from the war, talented and eager. Nevertheless, the inspired partnership of Peter Fraser as Prime Minister and Joseph Heenan at Internal Affairs was a great good fortune. They are its true architects.

The end of the Fund was an almost predictable consequence of the major state sector reforms carried out by the Fourth Labour Government from 1984 and of fashionable ideas such as the dangers of interest-group capture and the benefits of arms-length funding. Fortunately, for a time and thanks to Lotto, more funding was provided for literature during the transition, which certainly helped to soften resistance. However the loss of a funding agency particularly dedicated to writers and writing, under the clear guidance of a group of experts to whom these things mattered, was long regretted.

NOTES

ABBREVIATIONS

AM	Andrew Mason
ANZ	Archives New Zealand
ATL	Alexander Turnbull Library
AUP	Auckland University Press
CUP	Canterbury University Press
DIA	Department of Internal Affairs
EC	Elizabeth Caffin
LF	Literary Fund
LFAC	Literary Fund Advisory Committee
NZH	New Zealand Herald
OUP	Oxford University Press
VUP	Victoria University Press
QEII	Queen Elizabeth II Arts Council

1. AN IDEA TAKES ROOT: 1936–1947

1 'Notes of a Deputation', 27 November 1944, IA 1 86/1 pt 1, ANZ. The examples of 'New Zealand classics' given by the deputation included Samuel Butler's *Canterbury Settlement*, Frederick Maning's *Old New Zealand*, Jerningham Wakefield's *Adventure in New Zealand*, H. Guthrie-Smith's *Tutira*, Vincent Pyke's goldfields novel *The Story of Wild Will Enderby*, Pember Reeves's *The Long White Cloud*, the now-obscure *The Real and the True* by Lord Pembroke, Laing and Blackwell's *The Plants of New Zealand*, James Cowan's *The New Zealand Wars*, O.T.J. Alpers's *Cheerful Yesterdays* and Lindsay Buick's

The Treaty of Waitangi. The list had been reached at meetings of PEN members and, according to J.C. Beaglehole, several of these books were still in print, while the third edition of *Tutira* was with Blackwells in London awaiting publication at the end of the war, as the Under-Secretary for Internal Affairs, Joseph Heenan (who regarded it as 'New Zealand's greatest book'), pointed out at the meeting.

2 Frank Moorhouse, 'The Writer and the State: Patronage, National Security and Secrets', Frederick Watson Fellowship Paper, National Archives of Australia, 2005, pp.1–5.

3 Chris Hilliard, *The Bookmen's Dominion: Cultural Life in New Zealand, 1920–1950* (AUP: Auckland, 2006), p.44.

4 Heenan later in the meeting praised the 'patriotic attitude' of Reeds, who had published many worthwhile New Zealand books 'without thought of financial return'.

5 See William Renwick (ed.), *Creating a National Spirit: Celebrating New Zealand's Centennial* (VUP: Wellington, 2004).

6 Michael Bassett, *The Mother of All Departments: The History of the Department of Internal Affairs* (AUP: Auckland, 1997), p.115.

7 'Notes of a Deputation', 27 November 1944.

8 See Hilliard, *The Bookmen's Dominion.*

9 IA 1 86/4, ANZ.

10 The Canadian Governor-General's Awards for Literature, established by John Buchan in 1936, were given annually for fiction, poetry, general literature and historical literature. They were administered by the Canadian Authors' Association, who made the rules and selected the judges. In Estonia, before World War II, the government directly subsidised learned societies, literary organisations, literary research and publishers. The state literary fund, supported by revenue from alcohol, tobacco and entertainment taxes, and passport fees, gave periodic stipends, sickness allowances and honoraria to individual writers, and grants for specific work. There were occasional grants for overseas travel, and support for the journal published by the Estonian Society of Authors (see *PEN Gazette*, no. 5, January 1941, 11–12).

11 Beaglehole to Heenan, 15 September 1938, IA 1 126/8/33, ANZ.

12 'Recommendations from Centennial Historical Committee (Executive Members)', comprising G.H. Scholefield, J.C.

Beaglehole, A.D. McIntosh and E.H. McCormick, undated but filed 4 November 1937, IA 1 126/8/24, ANZ.

13 Wood to Heenan, 27 July 1938; Beaglehole to Heenan, 15 September 1938, both IA 1 126/8/24, ANZ.

14 Beaglehole to Heenan, 15 September 1938, IA 1 126/8/33, ANZ. The final comment refers to another candidate for assistance that Beaglehole had reviewed at about the same time, which appears to have been an early draft of Harold Miller's book, *Race Conflict in New Zealand, 1814–1865*, Blackwood and Janet Paul, Auckland, 1966.

15 Rachel Barrowman, *A Popular Vision: The Arts and the Left in New Zealand 1930–1950* (VUP: Wellington, 1991), pp.6–7.

16 Heenan to W. Downie Stewart, 16 February 1942, IA 1 126/8/50, ANZ.

17 Beaglehole to Heenan, 19 October 1944, IA 1 86/1 pt 1, ANZ.

18 Another was the commissioning by the Minister for Arts and Culture, Michael Bassett, of *Voices*, a verse sequence by C.K. Stead, to mark the 1990 sesquicentenary.

19 The third work of 'national importance' was Lord Listowel's 'Message to the Maori People', a 26-page pamphlet thanking Maori, on behalf of the British Government, for their contribution to the war effort.

20 Peter Fraser to Heenan, 15 August and 6 September 1940, IA 1 126/8/45, ANZ.

21 Beaglehole to Heenan, 17 April 1941, IA 1 126/8/45, ANZ.

22 IA 1 126/8/45, ANZ.

23 IA 1 126/8/56, ANZ.

24 IA 1 126/8/48, ANZ; Barrowman, *A Popular Vision*, p.6.

25 'Commonwealth Literary Fund', attachment to 'Notes of a Deputation', 27 November 1944.

26 David Colquhoun, entry on James Cowan, *Dictionary of New Zealand Biography, Volume 3, 1901–1920* (AUP/DIA: Wellington, 1996), pp.120–21.

27 PEN MS-Papers 73-161-1/03, Correspondence 1940–43, ATL; Mackay to G.H. Scholefield, 15 March 1937, Scholefield MS-Papers 212/C2B, ATL. See also Heather Roberts, entry on Jessie Mackay, *Dictionary of New Zealand Biography, Volume 2, 1870–1900* (Bridget Williams Books/DIA: Wellington, 1993), p.293.

28 Dennis McEldowney, 'Publishing, Patronage, Literary Magazines', in *The Oxford History of New Zealand Literature in English*, Terry Sturm (ed.), 2nd ed. (OUP: Auckland, 1998),

p.659. It probably helped that Duggan was a member of Fraser's network of informal advisers, and that she had written a collection entitled *New Zealand Poems*, 'In Honour of the Centennial of the Dominion of New Zealand'.

29 D'Arcy Cresswell, *Present Without Leave* (Cassell: London, 1939), pp.252–3.

30 The letter appears to have been intended for Heenan all along, as pre-arranged with Glover, who shared with Heenan an interest in printing; Sargeson described this scheme later as 'a thoroughly dirty piece of work really' (see Barrowman, *A Popular Vision*, p.7).

31 Michael King, *Frank Sargeson: A Life* (Viking, Auckland: 1995), p.279.

32 Dennis McEldowney, *Frank Sargeson in His Time* (John McIndoe: Dunedin, 1976), p.39.

33 Barrowman, *A Popular Vision*, p.8. Heenan went even further, however, when he discovered that Sargeson's bach had been condemned by a health inspector: he arranged for £1 a week of the new pension to be capitalised into a grant for a new house, and personally interviewed the managers of the State Advances Corporation and the Auckland Savings Bank, who had both declined Sargeson's application for a loan.

34 'Dr A.J. Harrop—Application for Grant. Views submitted by Dr J.C. Beaglehole', undated, filed 4 Nov. 1937, IA 1 126/8/24, ANZ.

35 M.H. Holcroft, *The Waiting Hills*, in *Discovered Isles* (Caxton Press: Christchurch, 1950), p.184.

36 Holcroft, *The Waiting Hills*, p.188.

37 Holcroft, *The Waiting Hills*. pp.180–1. Holcroft also provided his own list of 'classics', including *Tutira*, *The Long White Cloud*, *Adventure in New Zealand*, *Old New Zealand*, Robert McNab's *Historical Records*, J.B. Condliffe's *New Zealand in the Making* and *The Letters and Journals of Samuel Marsden*.

38 AM was unable to locate any minutes of PEN's early meetings, and had to rely on Lawlor's PEN correspondence files.

39 M.H. Holcroft, *The Way of a Writer* (Cape Catley: Whatamongo Bay, 1984), p.180.

40 'Aid for Authors in N.Z.', *Southland Times*, 29 November 1944; 'State Endowment of Literature', *Southland Times*, 30 November 1944 (the editorial is unsigned, but the style and arguments are vintage Holcroft). Denham's suggestion was couched in the form of notice of a question to Peter Fraser, in his

capacity as Minister of Education.

41 *Landfall*, vol. 1 no. 4 (December 1947), 245; *PEN Gazette*, no. 20 (April 1948), 1. The same argument, that PEN did not represent all writers, was used in the attempt to disband the Literature Committee in 1992.

42 M.C. Keane, editor of the Christchurch *Press* 1919–29, was celebrated as a writer of light topical verse, but PEN was presumably referring to his serious historical poems; his work is virtually unknown today.

43 *PEN Gazette*, no. 12 (November 1945), 1.

44 Heenan accepted PEN's invitation to join it in 1939. As PEN membership normally required a history of meritorious publication, and Heenan had published nothing but literary and sporting articles, particularly on horse racing, his was presumably regarded as an honorary membership for services to literature.

45 Heenan to W.B. Sutch, 10 April 1945, Heenan MS-Papers 1132-226, ATL. Quoted by Rachel Barrowman in 'Culture-organising: Joe Heenan and the beginnings of state patronage of the arts', *New Zealand Studies*, vol. 6 no. 2 (July 1996), 3.

46 Heenan, memorandum 'Deputation from P.E.N. re Literary Fund' for Minister of Internal Affairs, 22 November 1944, IA 1 86/1 pt 1, ANZ.

47 J.H.E. Schroder to Heenan, 3 July 1945; Heenan to Schroder, 13 July 1945; both Heenan MS-Papers 1132-206, ATL.

48 Barrowman, *A Popular Vision*, p.8.

49 Heenan, 'Note for file', 19 November 1945, IA 1 86/1 pt 1, ANZ.

50 James Elliott to Fraser, 21 November 1945, IA 1 86/1 pt 1, ANZ.

51 Elliott to Fraser, 23 April 1946, IA 1 86/1 pt 1, ANZ.

52 Michael Bassett and Michael King, *Tomorrow Comes the Song: A Life of Peter Fraser* (Penguin: Auckland, 2000), p.300.

53 Editorial, 'A Cultural Question', *Southern Cross*, 18 March 1946.

54 Heenan to Parry, 10 July 1946, IA 1 86/1 pt 1, ANZ.

55 Heenan to Parry, 16 August 1946, IA 1 86/1 pt 1, ANZ.

56 Heenan, 'Note for file', 30 November 1946, IA 1 86/1 pt 1, ANZ. The University of New Zealand was then setting up its own press, in which J.C. Beaglehole was a leading light, and the need for liaison between the press and the literary fund was discussed. It was agreed that some projects could receive help from both.

57 Heenan to Fraser and Parry, 'Surplus Art Union Profits—Creation of Special Funds', 3 May 1946, IA 57/1, ANZ.
58 Beaglehole to Heenan, 'Expenditure of Literary Fund', 29 April 1946, IA 57/1, ANZ. It is clear that Beaglehole is in fact referring to the Cultural Fund.
59 Heenan to Fraser and Parry, 'Surplus Art Union Profits—Creation of Special Funds', 3 May 1946.
60 'Note of Explanation', undated MS, Fairburn Collection, Auckland University Library, quoted in *Rex Fairburn: Walking on My Feet*, James and Helen McNeish (Collins: Auckland, 1983), p.160.
61 Fairburn to Sargeson, 21 November 1947, in *The Letters of A.R.D. Fairburn*, selected and edited by Lauris Edmond (OUP: Auckland, 1981), Letter 143.
62 Fairburn to Sargeson, 26 November 1947, in Edmond (ed.), *Letters*, Letter 146.
63 'Note on the State Literary Fund', A.R.D. Fairburn, *Collected Poems* (Pegasus: Christchurch, 1966), p.154.
64 'Lines composed in the Glover kitchen during a memorable visit, and printed by the Sumner Division of the Caxton Press 19 Nov 1947'. A copy survives in Lauris Edmond MS-Papers 4680-38, ATL.
65 See Edmond (ed.), Letters 142, 144, 146, 147, 170; McNeishes, pp.161–62; King, p.283; Denys Trussell, *Fairburn* (AUP/OUP: Auckland, 1984), p.218. Lauris Edmond, in her editing of the Fairburn letters, may have unwittingly perpetuated the confusion about the poem's target, for she seems not to have realised that the Cultural and General Arts Fund had already been established, and that this fund would have paid the pension Sargeson sought for Fairburn. She notes, for example, that Fairburn's mention of 'Joe Heenan's secret patronage' (Letter 142) referred to the Literary Fund, which makes nonsense of his reference in the next sentence to '[t]he *public* Fund' (Fairburn's emphasis). Fairburn also seems not to have known the name of the Cultural and General Arts Fund, as he does not use it in his correspondence, but refers often to the State Literary Fund by name.
66 Edmond (ed.), Letter 147.
67 E.H. McCormick, *An Absurd Ambition: Autobiographical Writings*, Dennis McEldowney, ed. (AUP: Auckland, 1996), p.138.
68 Holcroft, *The Waiting Hills*, p.189.

69 Holcroft, *The Waiting Hills*, p.190.
70 E.H. McCormick, 'The State as a Publisher of Books and Periodicals', *New Zealand Libraries*, vol. 9 no. 2 (March 1946), 31–32.
71 McCormick's and Plischke's books had in fact been published by the Department of Internal Affairs, Plischke's at the express request of Peter Fraser.
72 M. H. Holcroft, *Creative Problems in New Zealand* (Caxton: Christchurch, 1947), p.35.
73 Holcroft, *Creative Problems in New Zealand*, pp.30–31.
74 Holcroft, *Creative Problems in New Zealand*, p.31.
75 Fairburn to Sargeson, 26 November 1947, Edmond (ed.), Letter 146.
76 Fairburn to Brasch, 4 December 1947, Edmond (ed.), Letter 147. Lawlor was by then the secretary to the Literary Fund Advisory Committee, and Sir James Elliott its first chairman.
77 Lawlor to Heenan, 30 October 1936, IA 1 86/1/4, ANZ.
78 Heenan to Fraser, Nash and Parry, 17 December 1946, IA 1 86/1/4, ANZ.
79 K.G Jordan (Fraser's Private Secretary) to Heenan, 17 March 1947, IA 1 86/1/4, ANZ; Roger Robinson and Nelson Wattie (eds), *The Oxford Companion to New Zealand Literature* (OUP: Auckland, 1998), p.359.
80 Holcroft, *The Way of a Writer*, p.84.
81 Heenan to Jordan, 20 March 1947, IA 1 86/1/4, ANZ.
82 Heenan to Lawlor, 23 June 1947, IA 1 86/1/4, ANZ.
83 J.A. Lee to Parry, 29 August 1947, IA 1 86/1 pt 2, ANZ.
84 King, p.282. Unfortunately, Ormond Wilson's memoirs, *An Outsider Looks Back* (Port Nicholson Press: Wellington, 1980), makes no mention of his stint on the Literary Fund Advisory Committee.
85 Bassett and King, p.259; Keith Sinclair, *Walter Nash* (AUP/OUP: Auckland, 1976), p.86. Mary Mackenzie, who had an interest in repertory theatre, used to drive Nash to his various electorate engagements on weekends.
86 *Landfall*, vol. 1 no. 4 (December 1947), 244. Ngaio Marsh was the only 'practising writer' and in the event she did not attend a single Advisory Committee meeting.

2. A DELICATE AND DIFFICULT TASK: 1947–1951

1 Literary Fund Advisory Committee (LFAC) Minutes, 10 July

1947, IA 81/1, ANZ.

2 LFAC Minutes, 10 July 1947.

3 *Landfall*, vol. 1 no. 4 (December 1947), 'Notes', 241.

4 Chris Hilliard, *The Bookmen's Dominion: Cultural Life in New Zealand, 1920–1950* (AUP: Auckland, 2006), p.108. Ngaio Marsh was the only such writer and she never attended a meeting.

5 Report of Wellington subcommittee on rules of procedure, adopted 25 Feb. 1948, LFAC Minutes.

6 LFAC Minutes, 7 September 1949.

7 LFAC Minutes, 8 June 1949.

8 Bodkin to Scholefield, 26 April 1950, IA 1 86/1/4, ANZ.

9 Scholefield to Bodkin, 28 March 1950, IA 1 86/1/4, ANZ.

10 Since the PM had appointed Lawlor himself, Harper had to ask Fraser whether the committee could take action: handwritten note for meeting with PM, 12 May 1949, IA 1 86/1 Pt 1, ANZ. No reply is recorded.

11 LFAC Minutes, 25 February 1948.

12 Quoted by Frances Porter in entry on Guy Scholefield, *Dictionary of New Zealand Biography, Volume 4, 1920–1940* (AUP/DIA: Wellington, 1998), pp.459–61.

13 Harper to Bodkin, 26 April 1950, IA 1 86/1/4, ANZ.

14 PEN *Gazette*, no. 22 (October 1948).

15 *New Zealand Listener*, 11 May 1951, 7. *Landfall* noted in December 1950 that, since the Literary Fund had been established, novels or collections of short stories by Sargeson (*I Saw in My Dream*), Davin (*The Gorse Blooms Pale*, *For the Rest of Our Lives* and *Roads from Home*), James Courage (*The Fifth Child*, *Desire without Content*), Ballantyne and Erik de Mauny (*The Huntsman in His Career*) had been published overseas rather than in New Zealand.

16 LFAC Minutes, 14 June 1950; Holcroft's report is in MS-Papers 0314/2, ATL. When the book was published in a new edition by Price Milburn in 1972, all the prefatory material was dropped.

17 Anticipating that Tombs would accept the £100 grant, Lawlor had a cheque sent before receiving confirmation; as negotiations continued, he had to ask for the cheque to be returned to Internal Affairs.

18 See Harold Dowrick's highly critical letter in *Landfall*, vol. 4 no. 2 (June 1950), 175–76.

19 LFAC Minutes, Wellington standing committee, 21 July 1948.

20 The manuscript was not published till 1994, 40 years after his death.

21 See his reports in MS-Papers 0314/2, ATL.
22 Memo for meeting of 26 July 1950, LFAC Minutes, copy in MS-Papers 0314/3, ATL
23 Beaglehole to Lawlor, 11 July 1948, Lawlor MS-Papers 77-0671/4, ATL.
24 LFAC Minutes, 17 November 1948.
25 In August 1948 Schroder had proposed that where the committee 'promotes or assists publication it should have the right (not always exercised) of requiring the publisher to state, on the title page, or verso or half title, some suitable formula acknowledging the aid of the Fund' (LFAC Minutes, 25 August 1948). The committee enthusiastically endorsed the idea and decided to build up a collection of the works it had subsidised, to be housed in the ATL. The acknowledgement was subsequently made a requirement of publication grants.
26 Handwritten addition to Lawlor's draft annual report, in Lawlor MS-Papers 77-067-5/4, ATL.
27 A.W. Reed to A.H. Reed, 30 November 1950, quoted in Edmund Bohan, *The House of Reed, 1907–1983: Great Days in New Zealand Publishing* (CUP: Christchurch, 2005), p.93.
28 Reeds' edition of Arnold Wall's verse collection *The Pioneers* came in for particular criticism, with *Landfall* complaining about the lack of guiding principles in the selection and ordering of the poems ('Wall is not one of those poets whose every trifle need be preserved with the aid of the public purse') and the book's appearance, likened to 'the deadliest of text-books'. *Landfall* concluded that the Literary Fund would 'hardly increase its reputation by being associated with publications so ill-planned and so unfortunate in appearance' (vol. 3 no. 1, March 1949, 3–4).
29 LFAC Minutes, 20 April 1948.
30 Heenan to Alpers, 17 December 1947, Heenan MS Papers 1132-07, ATL.
31 LFAC Minutes, 21 May 1952: 'the Chairman remarked that from his early reading of Mr. Alpers' MS. it was going to be the work on Katherine Mansfield'.
32 Fairburn to Curnow, 21 November 1947; Fairburn to Brasch, 21 November 1947; Letters 144 and 142 in *The Letters of A.R.D. Fairburn*, ed. Lauris Edmond.
33 Glover, draft letter to Secretary, State Literary Fund, 23 January 1948, copy in Fairburn, MS-Papers-1128-087, ATL. Glover privately summarised the aim of his 'Curnow (Export)

Corporation's project' as being that 'Curnow should leave this country for his country's good' (Glover to Fairburn, 3 February 1948, copy in Fairburn MS-Papers 1124-104, ATL).

34 Brasch to Glover, 28 January 1948, copy in Fairburn MS-Papers-1128-087, ATL.

35 Heenan to Glover, 4 May 1948, Heenan MS-Papers 1132-082, ATL.

36 Unlike Antony Alpers, Curnow was married and had a young family to support and debts to pay off while he was away, which would take up £450. His return boat passage would cost about £160. Then there was his cost of living and other expenses over 12 months. The British Council thought it could find £30 a month while he was at Oxford or Cambridge for a term, and the Carnegie Corporation would take care of his expenses in America.

37 LFAC Minutes, Wellington standing committee, 21 July 1948.

38 LFAC Minutes, 25 August 1948.

39 Ibid.

40 Heenan to Alpers, 11 March 1949, Heenan MS-Papers 1132-07, ATL.

41 Heenan to Schroder, 4 March 1949, Heenan MS-Papers 1132-206, ATL.

42 Schroder to Heenan, 9 May 1949, Heenan MS-Papers 1132-206, ATL; 'Note of an Interview', 26 April 1949, IA 1 158/206/85 (W1894), ANZ; Terry Sturm, phone interview with AM, 29 October 2007.

43 Heenan to Curnow, 8 July 1949, Heenan MS-Papers 1132-042, ATL.

44 Terry Sturm, e-mail to AM, 21 November 2007.

45 For a detailed account from Ballantyne's perspective, see Bryan Reid, *After the Fireworks: A Life of David Ballantyne* (AUP: Auckland, 2004), pp.93–102.

46 This was a not infrequent occurrence; on at least one occasion, Lawlor even managed to put the wrong town, addressing a letter to Invercargill instead of Dunedin.

47 LFAC Minutes, 25 August 1948.

48 These comments are mild compared with what Ballantyne had privately told Henle the previous September, when he described the committee members as being 'typical of the political pipsqueaks and literary hacks who dictate what's what in what passes for Culture in New Zealand', and Allen Curnow's mission as being 'to drink with Day Lewis and Dylan Thomas

and find out how they write poetry', Reid, pp.97–98.

49 Gillespie to Ballantyne, 15 August 1949, Ballantyne MS-Papers 88-012-5/03, ATL.

50 Ballantyne's and Scholefield's comments were quoted verbatim in the *Southern Cross*, 17 August 1949, under the heading 'Charges Denied That N.Z. Writers Get "Raw Deal"', and the *Evening Post* on the same date, under the heading 'State Literary Fund Attacked' and the subheading '"Wildly Inaccurate," Says Chairman'.

51 'The Writer's Lot And State Aid', *Evening Post*, 20 August 1949.

52 'Suggestions for statement re State Literary Fund', Scholefield to Williamson, 25 August 1949, IA 1 86/1 Pt 1, ANZ.

53 *Southern Cross*, 5 September 1949.

54 *Landfall*, 12 (December 1949), 302–03.

55 The Scholarship in Letters started in 1957 at £500.

56 See Roger Robinson and Nelson Wattie (eds), *The Oxford Companion to New Zealand Literature* (OUP: Auckland, 1998), pp.415–16.

57 LFAC Minutes, 3 May 1950.

58 Robinson and Wattie (eds), p.152.

59 Ian Richards, *To Bed at Noon: The Life and Art of Maurice Duggan* (AUP: Auckland, 1997), p.116.

60 Brasch to Bertram, 16 September 1947, Bertram MS-Papers 93-133-07, ATL.

61 *New Zealand National Review*, 1 June 1951, 5.

62 LFAC Minutes, 7 September 1949.

63 Elizabeth Caffin, in Terry Sturm (ed.), *Oxford History of New Zealand Literature*, p.464.

64 LFAC Minutes, 3 October 1951.

65 LFAC Minutes, 4 October 1948.

66 'Suggestions for statement re State Literary Fund', Scholefield to Williamson, 25 August 1949, IA 1 86/1 Pt 1, ANZ.

67 Heenan to Glover, 11 March 1949, Heenan MS-Papers 1132-082, ATL.

68 LFAC Minutes, 1 November 1950.

69 *NZ Truth*, February 1948. Copy in AM MS-Papers 9393-042.

70 *Dominion*, 18 and 19 February, 1948.

71 *John A. Lee's Fortnightly*, 11 February 1948. Lee may have been piqued that the committee had decided not to take up his suggestion to the Government that it subsidise a reprint of his *Shiner* stories. He had earlier written to Parry (29 August 1947) that, given the size and composition of the advisory committee,

'I vision an interminable, academic and very sterile series of debates, with odd flashes of intelligence from an odd member', and predicting that the committee would go 'in search of the safely sterile' and suffer from 'academic constipation' (IA 1 86/1 pt 1, ANZ).

72 LFAC Minutes, 20 April 1948.

73 *Weekly News*, 14 February 1951, 32.

74 *Weekly News*, 14 March 1951.

75 LFAC Minutes, 14 March 1951. The only mention of Holcroft's association with the Literary Fund was in the brief discussion of the advisory committee's membership and made no connection with his position at the *New Zealand Listener*, in which the article appeared.

76 See *NZ New Zealand Listener*, 11 May 1951, 5–7.

77 The full text of his address is in Lawlor MS-Papers 80-063-041, ATL, and was published in his 1954 *Books and Bookmen, New Zealand and Overseas*, a collection of various writings on writers. The response to his comments comes from Peter Simpson's 'A Country in Search of Itself: the 1951 New Zealand Writers' Conference', in Mark Williams (ed.), *Writing at the Edge of the Universe: Essays from the 'Creative Writing in New Zealand' Conference, University of Canterbury, August 2003* (CUP: Christchurch, 2004), pp.123–40, and from Lawlor's own article, 'N.Z. Catholic Attacks Decadence of "New Writing"', in the Melbourne *Advocate*, 28 June 1951, p.9, which gives the impression that Lawlor enjoyed being provocative and even relished the stoush that followed.

78 Melbourne *Advocate*, 28 June 1951, p.9. The link with *Landfall* is implicit and relies on association, though in later correspondence Lawlor made it explicit.

79 'Writers' Conference, Christchurch (May 8 to 11, 1951), Report by Dr G.H. Scholefield', copy in Lawlor, MS-Papers 80-063-041, ATL.

80 Allen to Lawlor, 21 September 1951, Lawlor MS-Papers 80-063-041, ATL.

81 Scholefield, 'Writers'Conference', pp.3–4; Richards, p.147.

82 The conference proceedings were never published (although the organisers approached the Literary Fund for a grant and received a favourable reply). This account is taken from conference coverage by the *Christchurch Star-Sun*, 11 May 1951.

83 Robert Chapman, *Landfall*, 19 (September 1951), 225.

84 Sargeson to Duggan, 4 June 1951, quoted in King, *Frank*

Sargeson, p.313.

85 Cited most recently in Simpson, p.124, and Hilliard, *The Bookmen's Dominion*, p.110.

86 LFAC Minutes, 26 April and 20 June 1951; Professor Ian Gordon, statement in *NZ Truth*, 23 July 1951.

87 Scholefield, 'Writers' Conference', p.4; *Christchurch Star-Sun*, 11 May 1951.

88 Scholefield, 'Writers' Conference', p.5.

89 LFAC Minutes, 20 June 1951.

90 *NZ Truth*, 11 July 1951.

91 *NZ Truth*, 18 July 1951.

92 *NZ Truth*, 25 July 1951.

93 LFAC Minutes, Wellington standing committee, 10 August 1949.

94 Harper to Bodkin, 2 August 1951, IA 1 86/1/4, ANZ.

95 Valedictory tribute by Walter Nash, cited by Tom Brooking in entry on William Alexander Bodkin, *Dictionary of New Zealand Biography, Volume 5, 1941–1960*, AUP/D IA, Auckland, 2000, p.63.

96 LFAC, Third Annual Report, copy in Lawlor MS-Papers 77-067-5/4, ATL.

97 Memo, Holland to Bowden, copy to Bodkin, 13 March 1950, IA 1 86/1 Pt 1, ANZ.

98 Scholefield to Bodkin, 28 March 1950, IA 1 86/1/4, ANZ.

99 LFAC Minutes, 14 February 1951.

100 *Landfall*, 16 (December 1950), 277–78.

101 See LFAC Fourth Annual Report, for year ended 31 March 1951, copy in Lawlor MS-Papers 77-067-5/4, ATL.

3. IGNORANT NON-ENTITIES?: 1952–1955

1 See Robinson and Wattie (eds), *The Oxford Companion to New Zealand Literature*, pp.212, 401–2.

2 See Derek Challis and Gloria Rawlinson, *The Book of Iris: A Life of Robin Hyde* (AUP: Auckland, 2002).

3 See Schroder MS-Papers 0280, Folder 11–20, ATL.

4 R.S. Gormack, *The Nag's Head Press* (Nag's Head Press: Christchurch, 1992), p.37; quoted in, and see also, Gordon Ogilvie, *Denis Glover: His Life* (Godwit: Auckland, 1999), pp.270–74.

5 LFAC Minutes, 20 February 1952; Cole to LFAC, 13 June 1952, in LFAC MS-Papers 0314/2, ATL; LFAC annual report, 1952–

53, draft in Lawlor MS-Papers 77-067-5/4, ATL; e-mail to AM from Christine Cole Catley, 31 December 2007.
6 See Cole MS-Papers 4648/05, ATL.
7 Duggan to Davin, 9 January 1952, quoted in Richards, *To Bed at Noon: The Life and Art of Maurice Duggan*, p.162.
8 Brasch to Secretary, LFAC, 27 February 1952, an AM reference which EC could not find.
9 LFAC Minutes, 21 May 1952.
10 Brasch to Cole, 12 July 1955, Cole MS-Papers 4648-02, ATL. An indication of Moffett's politics can be found in his letter of acceptance to Bodkin, in which he refers to 'the pinko-artistic school of writers' and notes, 'I would hope, at least, to be able to assist in preventing such glaring pieces of political patronage as were handed out under Labour. In this I know I can be assisting your and the Government's aims' (Moffett to Bodkin, 30 October 1951, IA 1 86/1/4, ANZ).
11 LFAC Minutes, 18 November 1952.
12 LFAC Minutes, 17 February 1953. This phrase was crossed out in the minutes.
13 C.R. Allen also applied for a grant for his occasional little magazine, *The Wooden Horse*, after he had an 'unofficial offer' of help from Lawlor (Allen to Lawlor, 16 October 1951, Lawlor MS-Papers 77-067-1/2, ATL). This too was declined a grant by the committee, however.
14 Dennis McEldowney, 'Publishing, Patronage, Literary Magazines', in Sturm (ed.), *The Oxford History of New Zealand Literature*, p.668.
15 LFAC Minutes, 3 November 1953.
16 LFAC Minutes, 21 May and 5 August 1952.
17 LFAC Minutes, 18 November 1952.
18 Sargeson to Lawlor, 11 August 1952, Lawlor MS-Papers 77-067-4/5, ATL.
19 Lawlor to Sargeson, 13 August 1952, Sargeson MS-Papers 0432-75, ATL.
20 Sargeson to Lawlor, 18 August 1952, Lawlor MS-Papers 77-067-4/5, ATL.
21 Richards, p.122.
22 Copy in LFAC MS-Papers 0314/2, ATL.
23 King, *Frank Sargeson*, p.321.
24 Sargeson to E.P. Dawson, 3 September 1953, quoted in King, p.323.
25 LFAC Minutes, 18 May and 17 August 1954.

26 Copy in Sargeson MS-Papers 0432-427, ATL.
27 Michael Beveridge, 'Conversation with Frank Sargeson', *Landfall*, 94 (June 1970), 158.
28 See King, p.327.
29 LFAC Minutes, 15 February 1955.
30 See Robinson and Wattie (eds), pp.373–4.
31 Copy in LFAC MS-Papers 0314/2, ATL.
32 See Robinson and Wattie (eds), p.299.
33 See Elizabeth Caffin, in Sturm (ed.), *Oxford History of New Zealand Literature*, pp.451–2, 463–5. Witheford had also been published in Ian Gordon's *New Zealand New Writing* and was a member of the *Arachne* editorial group in Wellington.
34 LFAC Minutes, 19 May 1953.
35 See Glover to Lawlor, 31 August 1953, Lawlor MS-Papers 77-067-1/2, ATL.
36 See LFAC, Sixth Annual Report, copy in Lawlor MS-Papers 77-067-5/4, ATL
37 See LFAC, Eighth Annual Report, copy in Lawlor MS-Papers 77-067-5/4, ATL. Andrew Sharp's record of grants for 1954/55 varies slightly in that it includes the three poetry publication subsidies to Caxton (for D'Arcy Cresswell, Paul Henderson and J.R. Hervey) totalling £75. In February 1954 the applications were passed to Schroder, Holcroft and Caddick respectively to report on, with Schroder and Holcroft being given the power to act in the absence of both Gordon and the acting chairman, Matthew Oram. These three applications then disappear from the minutes, so it is unclear when they were approved. If they are included in 1954/55, the total amount granted rises to £1900 and the number of publication subsidies to six, totalling £550—still far less than that the £825 given to literary journals.
38 J.H.E Schroder, 'The Place of Publication Subsidies in the Committee's Policy', 23 July 1953, copy in Andrew Mason Ms-Papers 9393-043, ATL.
39 LFAC Minutes, 16 February 1954.
40 Whitcombe & Tombs were also granted subsidies to produce two works of reminiscence: £150 for *Dim Horizons*, an account of growing up in the Kaipara district by Jean Boswell (on the recommendation of Holcroft); and £100 for *Within Sound of the Bell*, by J. Rhoda Barr (on the recommendation of Loudon).
41 LFAC Minutes, 18 November 1952.
42 Copy in LFAC MS-Papers 0314/2, ATL.
43 Copy in LFAC MS-Papers 0314/2, ATL.

44 LFAC Minutes, 10 May 1955. Johnson's letter has not been located.
45 LFAC Minutes, 13 September 1955.
46 LFAC, Eighth Annual Report, copy in Lawlor MS-Papers 77-067-5/4, ATL.
47 *Dominion*, 3 January 1953, 6.
48 Schroder to Smith, 30 August 1955, IA 1 86/1/4, pt 1, ANZ.
49 *Landfall*, 28 (December 1953), 'Notes', 235–37.
50 Harper to Smith, memo, 11 July 1955, IA 1 86/1/4 pt 1, ANZ.
51 Fairway to Harper, memo, 15 February 1955, IA 1 86/1/4 pt 1, ANZ.
52 Johnson to Harper, 28 March 1955, IA 1 86/1/4 pt 1, ANZ.
53 Harper to Smith, memo, 18 July 1955, IA 1 86/1/4 pt 1, ANZ.
54 Smith to Harper, memo, 9 August 1955, IA 1 86/1/4 pt 1, ANZ.
55 Nestor to Smith, 30 August 1955, IA 1 86/1/4 pt 1, ANZ.
56 Blaiklock to Lawlor, 28 March 1957, Lawlor MS-Papers 77-067-1/3, ATL.
57 Lawlor to Schroder, 28 August 1964, Lawlor MS-Papers 77-067-4/5, ATL.
58 Lawlor to Blaiklock, 1 April 1957, Lawlor MS-Papers 77-067-1/3, ATL. The 'literary clique' Lawlor refers to is not named, but was presumably that around Sargeson.
59 Lawlor to Smith, 22 August 1955, IA 1 86/1/4 pt 1, ANZ.
60 This has given rise to an enduring mystery. The Literary Fund application files in ANZ begin in 1955; the best efforts of the staff there could not locate anything earlier, perhaps catalogued under a different name. The application files available (IA 1 86/1/4) begin with part 15, suggesting that there were 14 earlier parts; where are they now?
61 C.A. Sharp, 'Interview with Mr Lawlor', undated (but presumably August 1955), IA 1 86/1/4 pt 1, ANZ.
62 Rachel Barrowman, *The Turnbull: A Library and Its World* (AUP: Auckland, 1995), p.119.
63 Brasch to Bertram, 18 September 1955, Bertram MS-Papers 93-133-07, ATL.
64 Frank Moorhouse, 'The Writer and the State: Patronage, National Security and Secrets', Frederick Watson Fellowship Paper, National Archives of Australia, 2005.
65 *Landfall*, 36 (December 1955), 'Notes', 271.

4. STABILITY, WITH INTERRUPTIONS: 1955–1964

1 LFAC Minutes, 5 March 1957, IA 81 1, ANZ; LF Order Papers, 11 June 1957, IA 2125 86/1/31 1, ANZ.
2 *Landfall*, 28 (Dec. 1953), 235–7; 279–8.
3 *Landfall*, 35 (Sept. 1955), 'Notes', 183.
4 LFAC Minutes, 13 March 1956.
5 *Landfall*, 53 (March 1960), 38, 45.
6 LFAC Minutes, 9 Sept. 1958.
7 LFAC Minutes, 22 Nov. 1960, 7 March 1961.
8 Lynley Hood, *Sylvia! The Biography of Sylvia Ashton-Warner* (Viking: Auckland, 1988), p.160.
9 LFAC Minutes, 19 Feb. 1963; 26 Nov. 1963, IA 1 ACC W2042 7 86/1/31 2, ANZ.
10 LFAC Minutes, 2 Sept. 1960. Letter from PEN asking for increases in the Scholarship to £1250 and the Award for Achievement to £1000.
11 *The Letters of A.R.D. Fairburn*, ed. Lauris Edmond (OUP: Auckland, 1981), Letter 209.
12 LFAC Minutes, 29 Nov. 1955.
13 LF Order Papers, 2 Dec. 1958, ANZ.
14 LFAC Minutes, 28 Aug. 1962, IA 1 W2042 7 86/1/31 2, ANZ.
15 LFAC Minutes, 9 June 1958, IA 81 1, ANZ. This was Glover's last meeting. The receipt of these reports was noted at the meeting on 9 Sept. 1958.
16 LFAC Minutes, 2 Dec. 1958, 24 Feb. 1959, 9 June 1959. The book appeared that year and subsequently won the 1960 Award for Achievement.
17 In a handwritten note dated 1 April 1958, Glover writes, 'Smithyman is a poet, & a bore. He writes like a poet talking in a professor's sleep. Often I just can't follow it, even without nodding off in a trance. But if we must subscribe to oracles practically nobody wants, on the supposition that what bores or baffles us must be poetry, let's squander £40 on him, too.' Capricorn Press, AAC 7536 W5084 110 cul/11/5/5/10, ANZ.
18 LFAC Minutes, 20 Feb. 1962, IA 1 W2042 7 86/1/31/2, ANZ.
19 *Landfall*, 70 (June 1964), 114. See also Paul Millar, *No Fretful Sleeper: A Life of Bill Pearson* (AUP: Auckland, 2010), p.262. An amusing and well-informed fictional account from the publisher's perspective of approaching the Literary Fund for assistance can be found in *Word for Word* (Pegasus: Christchurch, 1960), a novel by Robin Muir, Albion Wright's partner at Pegasus.

20 Janet Hunt, *Hone Tuwhare: A Biography* (Godwit: Auckland, 1998), p.60.
21 Ibid., pp.69–72.
22 Millar, p.250.
23 Paul's Book Arcade, AAC 7536 W5084 111 cul/11/5/42 [undated], ANZ.
24 LFAC Minutes and Agenda, 29 May 1956, IA 1 2125 86/1/31 1, ANZ.
25 LFAC Minutes, 19 Feb. 1963, IA 1 W2042 7 86/1/31 2, ANZ.
26 *Landfall*, letter to Sharp from Brasch, 20 Feb. 1961, AAAC 7536 W5084 109 cul/11/5/3, ANZ.
27 Report of the Special Committee on Moral Delinquency in Children and Adolescents, 1954.
28 LFAC Minutes, 28 Nov. 1961.
29 *Mate*, letter from Dudding, 28 Oct. 1959, AAAC 7536 W5084 109 cul/11/5/5, ANZ.
30 LFAC Minutes, 22 May 1962.
31 See letter from Peter Bland to AM, 20 Oct. 2008, Andrew Mason Papers, ATL. The poem was 'The Nose' and Bland changed 'fucking' to 'bloody', 'putting back the original at a later date'. The unexpurgated poem appeared in his *Selected Poems* (McIndoe: Dunedin, 1987), which received a Literary Fund grant. Its earlier appearance in *My Side of the Story* (Mate Books: 1964), also subsidised, used the *Yearbook* version.
32 See memo from Seath to Cabinet, 10 Sept. 1964: 'an attitude which was in conformity with a request made to the Committee through Professor Gordon by my predecessor, The Hon. Sir Leon Götz, during the tenure of the previous committee', AAFD 811 W4198 53 CAB 76/4/1 1, ANZ. See also Monte Holcroft, *A Sea of Words*, Cape Catley, Whatamongo Bay, 1986, p.83: 'He [i.e. Gordon] admitted, however, that on occasion the Minister of Internal Affairs, Sir Leon Götz, had told the committee it "must tighten up".'
33 LFAC Minutes, 20 Aug. 1963; 26 Nov. 1963.
34 Louis Johnson, 'Poetry Yearbook and the New Zealand Literary Fund', *Comment*, 18 (Jan. 1964).
35 *New Zealand Listener*, 13 March 1964, 8.
36 Holcroft, *A Sea of Words*, pp. 77–88. An earlier account can be found in his *Reluctant Editor: The "Listener" Years, 1949–67* (Reed: Wellington, 1969).
37 *Landfall*, 70 (June 1964), 'Notes', 114–5.
38 L[ouis] J[ohnson], 'Preface', *New Zealand Poetry Yearbook*,

vol. 11 (Pegasus: Christchurch, 1964).

39 'Conversation with an Ancestor' in *Man on a Horse* (University of Otago Press: Dunedin, 1967), in which Baxter comments on one of the poems, 'The Girl in Yellow Jeans'; see *James K. Baxter as Critic*, selected by Frank McKay (Heinemann Educational Books: Auckland, 1978), p.108.

40 'A Little Letter to Auckland Students', *Collected Poems*, ed. J.E. Weir (OUP: Auckland, 1979), pp.291–2.

41 'Signs point to growing pressure on liberty of N.Z. writers', *NZH*, 22 Feb. 1964.

42 See Stuart Perry, *The Indecent Publications Tribunal: A Social Experiment* (Whitcombe & Tombs: Christchurch, 1965).

43 'A Little Letter to Auckland Students'.

44 In 'The New Zealand Literary Fund', *Landfall*, 91 (Sept. 1969), 280.

45 *Landfall*, 61 (March 1962), 'Notes', 3–5; 70 (June 1964), 115.

46 Memo from Seath to Cabinet, 10 Sept. 1964, AAFD 811 W4198 53 CAB 76/5/1 1, ANZ.

47 See Holcroft, *Reluctant Editor*, pp.46–47.

48 V[incent] O'S[ullivan], 'Unfortunate Appointment', *Comment*, 21 (Oct.–Nov. 1964).

49 LFAC Minutes, 19 Feb. 1963.

5. 'A CIVILISED AND CIVILISING INSTITUTION' OR 'AN ESTABLISHMENT OF NEGLECT'?: 1964–1974

1 Dennis McEldowney records, 'He advised me one day, from his long experience as executive officer of committees, that the way to manage them was to make sure you knew more about every topic on the agenda than any one member', *A Press Achieved: The Emergence of Auckland University Press, 1927–1972* (AUP: Auckland, 2001), p.59.

2 *The New Zealand Literary Fund 1946–1970* (Government Printer: Wellington, 1970).

3 *The Mother of All Departments: The History of the Department of Internal Affairs* (AUP/DIA: Auckland, 1997), p.184.

4 *Landfall*, 91 (Sept. 1969), 273–82.

5 Deputy Sec. O'Dea to Minister, 3 Feb. 1970, IA1 W2042 7 86/1/3 4, ANZ.

6 Gordon to G.G. Gibbes-Watson, chairman, QE II Arts Council, 26 May 1967, IA1 W2042 7 86/1/3 4, ANZ; Minutes of the

Golden Kiwi Board of Control meeting, 20 Feb. 1968, IA W2042 7 86/1/3 4, ANZ.

7 Information on the Burns Fellowship kindly provided by Deborah Gale, Arrangement and Description Archivist, Hocken Library, 9 Feb. 2011. The Scholarship in Letters went up to $3000 the following year, 1971/2, a rather delayed response to a recommendation from the committee made on 24 Nov. 1969, LFAC Minutes, IA 1 81 1, ANZ.

8 Gordon to Gibbes-Watson, as above.

9 O'Dea to Seath as above.

10 Gordon to Gibbes-Watson as above.

11 In 'The New Zealand Literary Fund', *Landfall*, 91 (Sept. 1969), 276.

12 Sharp to Gordon, 25 March 1966, IA 1 W2042 7 86/1/3 4, ANZ; LFAC Minutes, 24 May 1966.

13 Sharp to Ray Richards, President NZBPA, 6 Dec. 1966, IA1 W2042 7 86/1/3 4, ANZ.

14 Ray Richards to Harold White, 4 Dec. 1967, IA1 W2042 7 86/1/3 4, ANZ.

15 LFAC Minutes, 27 Feb. 1968.

16 Publishing venues were increasing and occasionally bookshops, magazines or individuals became publishers briefly and put single titles up to the committee (Prometheus Bookshop, *Mate*, Univers Press). A more substantial enterprise, Wellington publisher Price Milburn, chiefly made its success through educational publishing but published James K. Baxter's *Autumn Testament* with Literary Fund assistance in 1972.

17 McEldowney, pp.79–80.

18 Arts Conference 1970, papers, IA 84 6 19, ANZ.

19 LFAC Minutes, 24 Nov. 1969. The 7 proposals accepted by the committee were (a) Publishers and the Alexander Turnbull Library be asked to suggest suitable authors and titles for the Award for Achievement (b) More advertising, press statements etc to inform the public of the Fund's work. (c) Committee will not necessarily assist provincial literary groups but will judge each on its merits (d) Recommend an increase in the Scholarship in Letters (e) Not in favour of providing advisory services to budding writers (f) Literary competitions will not be sponsored. (g) Recommend that the 'normal grant' to authors be increased to $750 and will also be prepared in future to recommend more substantial subsidies to publishers than have been customary.

20 Ibid.
21 Arts Conference 1970, papers.
22 LFAC Minutes, 7 May 1971. A conference of fiction writers at Massey in August resolved that the committee remained autonomous—and got more funds, O.E. Middleton, 'Fiction Writers Confer', *Landfall*, 100 (Dec. 1971), 447; and a *Landfall* editorial in September argued against the change, *Landfall*, 99 (Sept. 1971), 219.
23 Publicity 1971–84, Young Writers' Awards, AAAC W5085 7536 105 cul/11/34, ANZ.
24 Memo from Frean to the LFAC, 20 Oct. 1971, Appendix II to the minutes, 25 Nov. 1971.
25 LFAC Minutes, 17 Sept. 1971.
26 AUP and Whitcombe & Tombs; also Golden Press.
27 Press statement, March 1972, AA AC W5084 7536 105 cul/11/34, ANZ.
28 LFAC Minutes, 25 Nov. 1971, Appendix I, PEN visit, IA 1 81 1, ANZ.
29 Cabinet/ SLF: AAFD 811 W4198 53 CAB76/5/1 1; *Dominion*, 1 May 1972.
30 LFAC Minutes, 22 Feb. 1972.
31 'Poetics of the Impossible', *Big Smoke: New Zealand Poems 1960–1975*, ed. Alan Brunton, Murray Edmond, Michele Leggott (AUP: Auckland, 2000), p.29.
32 *Landfall*, 91 (Sept. 1969), 279.
33 At around $200 an issue.
34 LFAC Minutes, 4 Aug. 1972.
35 Letter from Patricia Godsiff to Mike Jarman, 26 July 1972, IA1 W1893 6 cul 11/4/1 1, ANZ.
36 Ireland and List, LFAC Minutes, 4 Aug. 1972.
37 LFAC Minutes, 27 Aug. 1973.
38 Bernard Gadd to Sec LFAC and reply, July 1973, Subsidies and grants 1973–4, IA 1 W2633 6 cul/11/11/4/1 pt 3, ANZ.
39 Payments and expenses, 10 Oct. 1973, IA 1 W2042 7 86/1/3 4, ANZ.
40 Subsidies & Grants 1973–4, IA 1 W2633 6 cul/11/4/1 pt 3, ANZ.
41 LFAC Meetings, Agenda and Minutes, 1971–77, IA 1 W2633 25 cul 11/3/3, ANZ.

6. A NEW ORDER: 1974–1982

1 Personal communication.
2 Vincent O'Sullivan, personal communication.
3 Memo from Minister, Internal Affairs to Cabinet, 12 June 1974, Payments 1971–73, IA 1 ACC W2633 26 cul 11/3/5, ANZ.
4 See memo, 23 Sept. 1974, Subsidies 1974–5, IA 1 W2633 26 cul/11/4/1 5, ANZ.
5 23 Jan. 1976.
6 See this policy spelled out, LFAC Minutes 27, 28 Feb. 1973, IA 81 1, ANZ.
7 Stead's views were not evident but in replying to Vennell later he said he thought the Fund should be 'wary of "crackpot" groups such as the one at present running CAVE'. Vennell Report. Investigation and Reaction, cul 11/3/10 Pt 1, ANZ.
8 Chan to May, 21 Jan. 1975, IA 1 W2633 28 cul 11/4/8 1, ANZ.
9 Both in NZ Book Awards policy 1975–77, IA 1 W2633 28 cul 11/4/8 1, ANZ.
10 Personal communication, 17 July 2009.
11 David Grant, *On a Roll: A History of Gambling and Lotteries in New Zealand* (VUP: Wellington, 1994), p.238ff.
12 Jock Vennell, personal communication. LFAC Minutes, 30 Aug. 1976.
13 O. St J. Vennell, *Patronage and New Zealand Literature* [the Vennell Report], DIA, Wellington [1977].
14 *NZ New Zealand Listener*, 8 Oct. 1977. Publicity 1974–81, AAC W5084 7536 cul 11/3/4 Box 105, ANZ.
15 Elizabeth Alley, personal communication.
16 *Literary Fund Newsletter*, 4 (March 1978), 1–2.
17 This was eventually published as *Pleasures of the Flesh: Sex and Drugs in Colonial New Zealand 1840–1915* (Reed: Wellington, 1984).
18 See AHI Literary Research Awards: Policy, AANV W4445 7744 Box 249 cul 11/6/4/1, ANZ.
19 Vennell Report, p.20.
20 J.L. Booth, 'Action of Vennell Report', undated [1978], Vennell Report, Investigation and Reaction from Public, cul 11/3/10, ANZ.
21 Magazine policy 1981–, AAAC W5084 7536, Box 105, ANZ.

The formula was:
Production subsidy:
Revenue x print run x 1
Print and bind cost 2
Contributors' subsidy:
Amount paid to contributors x 1/2
Management subsidy:
$1 for every subscription

22 Alistair Paterson to Pat Stuart, 11 April 1981, *Mate*, 1972–81, AAC 7536 W5084 109 cul/11/5/5, ANZ.
23 Memo to the Minister, 29 July 1981, Magazine policy 1981–, AAAC W5084 7536 105, ANZ.
24 LFAC Minutes, 24 May 1977, IA 1 W2633 25 cul 1/3/1, ANZ.
25 Vennell Report, Investigation and Reaction from Public, cul 11/3/10, ANZ.
26 A resolution at the BPANZ AGM in May 1978 confirmed this view, Ann Mallinson to Janet Ward, DIA, 18 May 1978, AAAC W5084 7536 Box 105 cul/11/3/12 1, ANZ.
27 Interestingly, a number of major publishers (such as Collins, Reeds, Whitcoulls) were not consulted.
28 Ann Mallinson, personal communication.
29 Hon. D.A. Highet, speech, 2 Oct. 1978, AAC 7536 W5084 105 cul 11/3/12, ANZ.
30 *Literary Fund Newsletters*, 7, 8.
31 *Literary Fund Newsletter*, 7.
32 Government Publishing Awards for Children's Books—Policy and general 1980–83, AANV W4445 7744 Box 252 cul 11/6/12 1, ANZ.
33 Wendy Harrex, personal communication.
34 Betty Gilderdale, 'Children's literature', *Oxford History of New Zealand Literature*, 2nd ed. (OUP: Auckland, 1998), p.547.
35 The books were by Miriam Smith, Joy Cowley, Patricia Grace and Bill Manhire.
36 *Auckland Star*, 5 Feb. 1980.
37 Ian Wedde to Gillian Martell, 8 Nov. 1985, IBM Writers Award, 1979–88, AANV W4445 7744 Box 252 11/6/11, ANZ.
38 See also letter from C.K. Stead to Hamish Keith, 13 June 1975, proposing a meeting to discuss relations but arguing quite strongly against a full merger: NZ Book Awards policy 1977–8, IA 1 W2633 28 cul 11/4/8 2, ANZ.
39 Elizabeth Alley and Mark Williams, eds, 'Maurice Gee', *In the Same Room: Conversations with New Zealand writers* (AUP:

Auckland, 1992), p.161.

40 Pat Stuart to Gerard Reid, 26 March 1980, Publication policy, AAAC W5084 7536 Box 105 cul 11/3/12 1, ANZ.

7. LAST DAYS OF THE LITERARY FUND: 1982–1988

1 Minutes, PEN Executive Committee, 14 Sept. 1982, 88-227-1/3, ATL.

2 2 Oct. 1982, Sturm Papers.

3 PEN Further records, NZLFAC 1973–1985, 92-066-2/13, ATL.

4 Tony Simpson, personal communication, 25 Oct. 2011.

5 Fiona Kidman, PEN annual report, as quoted in the *New York Times*, 1 May 1983.

6 Sturm reported on the first meeting at the LFAC meeting, 15 Feb. 1984, LFAC Minutes AAAC 7536 W5084 104/ cul/11/3/3 3.

7 Peter Tapsell to Tony Simpson, 4 Jan. 1985, AANV W4445 7744 Box 236 11/4/7 2, ANZ.

8 LFAC Minutes, 16 Aug. 1983.

9 6 July 1987, PEN Papers, 92-066-2/14, ATL.

10 Terry Sturm, 'Literary Fund: August Meeting and Budget, 1988', EC Papers.

11 Ian Wedde to Gillian Martell, for Arts Forum 2000, 3 Nov. 1986, EC Papers.

12 Terry Sturm, 'Literary Fund: August Meeting and Budget, 1988', EC Papers.

13 AAAC 7536 W5084 120/ cul 11/6/6 3, ANZ.

14 See LFAC Minutes, 15 Feb. 1984, letter from Lindsay McCallum.

15 ICI 1978, April 1978, 1A1 W2633 28 cul 11/6/3, ANZ.

16 Keri Hulme, 'Acknowledgements', *Te Kaihau: The Windeater* (VUP: Wellington,1986).

17 Russell Haley to Gillian Martell, ? 1986, Sturm Papers.

18 Manhire to Gillian Martell, 22 Aug. 1985, Overseas Travel Fund for Writers, 1984–87, AANV W4445 7744 Box 104 2/67/6, ANZ.

19 LFAC Minutes, Aug. 1985, Dec. 1985.

20 Non-Fiction Assistance Fund 1984–9, 17 Dec. 1984, AANV W4445 7744 Box243 11/4/14, ANZ.

21 Sturm to Director, MASPAC, 31 Aug. 1988, AANV W4445 7744 Box 243 11/4/14, ANZ.

22 *Hot October*, 1989; *Bonfires in the Rain*, 1991; *The Quick World*, 1992; reprinted together as *An Autobiography* (Bridget

Williams Books: Wellington, 1994).

23 Kate De Goldi, personal communication.

24 Helen Bones, 'The Effect of State Patronage on New Zealand Literature', History Research Project, University of Canterbury, 2005.

25 *New Zealand Listener*, 25 July 1987.

26 Kate Fortune, Report, 1987 Children's Books of the Year Awards, GP Awards for Children's Books, Policy & General, 1983–88, AANV W4445 7744 Box 252 11/6/12 2, ANZ.

27 'By the book', *New Zealand Listener*, 20 Dec. 1986, 20.

28 See LFAC Minutes, May 1984 and March 1986.

29 See Elizabeth Caffin, 'New Zealand Literary Fund Publishing Policy', November 1989, EC Papers.

30 LFAC Minutes, May 1986.

31 Maori Publication Fund, 1983–89, AANV W4445 7744 Box 245 11/5/4, ANZ.

32 Andrew Mason to Rosemary Wildblood, 28 July 1989, Small presses 1987–89, AANV W4445 Box 247 11/5/6, ANZ.

8. INTO THE ARTS COUNCIL: 1984–1994

1 Terry Sturm to Elizabeth Alley, 30 May 1988, Sturm Papers.

2 See discussions in 1970–1 and the Vennell Report investigations in Chapter 5.

3 PEN Minutes, 26 July 1983, PEN Minute Book 1979–84, 88-227-1/3, ATL.

4 Terry Sturm to Ann Mallinson, 12 March 1984, Mallinson Papers.

5 LFAC Minutes, 23 May 1984.

6 LFAC Minutes, 14 Aug. 1984.

7 LFAC Minutes, 11, 12 Dec. 1985.

8 Briefing paper to Sec. DIA by Pat Stuart, 5 Aug. 1987, Appendix. Merger 1986–7, AAAC 7536 W5084 104 cul 11/3/1/1 1, ANZ.

9 Briefing paper to Sec DIA, 5 Aug. 1987, Merger 1986–7, ANZ.

10 Minutes, 10th AGM of the BPANZ, 24 April 1986, BPANZ Papers, 92-104-06/2, ATL. See also Rosemary Stagg, President, BPANZ, to Terry Sturm, 23 May 1986; also File Note, re DIA meeting with BPANZ reps, 20 May 1986, AAAC 7536 104 cul/11/3/1/1 1, ANZ.

11 EC Papers; also Merger 1986–7, ANZ.

12 Gifkins, 'Sales strategies', *New Zealand Listener*, 20 Dec. 1986.

13 Merger 1986–7, ANZ.

14 Terry Sturm to members of the LFAC, 20 May 1986, Merger 1986–7, ANZ.
15 Minister to Terry Sturm, 15 Dec. 1986, EC Papers.
16 Peter Boag to Minister, 9 July 1987, Merger 1986–7, ANZ; Minister to Geoffrey Palmer, 10 July 1987, ibid; Minutes, Cabinet Policy Cttee, 14 July 1987, ibid.
17 NZ Book Awards 1988, AANV W4445 7744 Box 249 11/6/4 4, ANZ.
18 This was granted at a meeting on the same day, 19 May, as the signing of the Heads of Agreement document, to celebrate the transfer, though not necessarily to be permanent.
19 Howard Warner in *Evening Post*, ? July 1988, in Publicity, Literary Fund, 1985–89, AANV W4445 7744 Box 232 11/3/4 2, ANZ.
20 Long afterwards I asked him about his opposition to the move and he agreed he had been unwilling, but that once Internal Affairs supported it, there was no alternative.
21 'Proposed restructuring of Literature Programme', PEN MS-Papers-8782-39, ATL.
22 See, for example, Gordon McLauchlan, 'Who's controlling the arts?', 26 Nov. 1992, NZH; Chris Else (PEN National President) to Jenny Pattrick, 28 Oct. 1992, NZSA Further Papers, 1969–2003, 2004/277/19/2, ATL.
23 Ian Wedde, personal communication.

9. DÉNOUEMENT

1 *Landfall*, 63 (March 1960), 67.
2 Goodman Fielder Wattie Book Awards, Bank of New Zealand, Montana.
3 All of these comments are from personal communication for which I am very grateful.
4 Elizabeth Smither, personal communication.

BIBLIOGRAPHY

UNPUBLISHED SOURCES

Archives New Zealand

Literary Fund (and State Literary Fund) Papers
Literary Fund Advisory Committee Papers
Centennial Historical Committee Papers

Alexander Turnbull Library

David Ballantyne Papers
James Bertram Papers
Lauris Edmond Papers
A.R.D. Fairburn Papers
M.H. Holcroft Papers
Joseph Heenan Papers
P.A. Lawlor Papers
Literary Fund Advisory Committee Papers
Andrew Mason Papers
PEN Papers
Frank Sargeson Papers
G.H. Scholefield Papers
J.H.E. Schroder Papers

In private hands

Elizabeth Caffin Papers
Terry Sturm Papers

Personal communication

Elizabeth Alley
Rachel Barrowman
Maurice Gee
Ray Grover
Wendy Harrex
Witi Ihimaera
Mike Jarman
Fiona Kidman
Jane Kominik
Ann Mallinson
Vincent O'Sullivan
Tony Simpson
Elizabeth Smither
C.K. Stead
Pat Stuart
Jock Vennell
Ian Wedde
Rosemary Wildblood

PUBLISHED SOURCES

Newspapers, journals, etc.

Auckland Star
Christchurch Star-Sun
Evening Post
Landfall
New Zealand Literary Fund Newsletter, 1–20 (1977–1988)
New Zealand Herald
New Zealand Listener
New Zealand Studies
New Zealand Truth
PEN Gazette
Southland Times
Weekly News

Books, articles, etc.

Alley, Elizabeth and Mark Williams (eds). *In the Same Room: Conversations with New Zealand Writers.* AUP: Auckland, 1992.

Barrowman, Rachel. *A Popular Vision: The Arts and the Left in New Zealand, 1930–1950.* VUP: Wellington, 1991.

Bassett, Michael and Michael King. *Tomorrow Comes the Song: A Life of Peter Fraser.* Penguin: Auckland, 2000.

Bassett, Michael. *The Mother of all Departments: The History of the Department of Internal Affairs.* AUP/DIA: Auckland, 1997.

The Dictionary of New Zealand Biography. Vols 3, 4, 5. AUP/DIA: 1998, 2000.

Edmond, Lauris (ed.). *The Letters of A.R.D. Fairburn.* OUP: Auckland, 1981.

Grant, David. *On a Roll: A History of Gambling and Lotteries in New Zealand.* VUP: Wellington, 1994.

Hilliard, Chris. *The Bookmen's Dominion: Cultural Life in New Zealand, 1920–1950.* AUP: Auckland, 2006.

Holcroft, M.H. *A Sea of Words.* Cape Catley: Whatamongo Bay, 1986.

Holcroft, M.H. *Reluctant Editor: The 'Listener' Years, 1949–67.* Reed: Wellington, 1969.

Holcroft, M.H. *The Waiting Hills* in *Discovered Isles.* Caxton: Christchurch, 1950.

Holcroft, M.H. *The Way of a Writer.* Cape Catley: Whatamongo Bay, 1984.

Hood, Lynley. *Sylvia! The Biography of Sylvia Ashton-Warner.* Viking: Auckland, 1988.

King, Michael. *Frank Sargeson: A Life.* Viking: Auckland, 1995.

King, Michael. *Wrestling with the Angel: A Life of Janet Frame.* Viking: Auckland, 2000.

McEldowney, Dennis. 'Publishing, patronage, literary magazines' in *The Oxford History of New Zealand Literature*, 2nd ed. OUP: Auckland, 1998.

McEldowney, Dennis. *A Press Achieved: The Emergence of Auckland University Press 1927–1972.* AUP: Auckland, 2001.

McEldowney, Dennis. *Frank Sargeson in his Time.* McIndoe: Dunedin, 1976.

Millar, Paul. *No Fretful Sleeper: A Life of Bill Pearson.* AUP: Auckland, 2010.

Moorhouse, Frank. 'The writer and the state: patronage, security and secrets'. Frederick Watson Fellowship Paper. National

Archives of Australia, 2005.
Muir, Robin. *Word for Word*. Pegasus: Christchurch, 1960.
The New Zealand Literary Fund 1946–1970. Government Print: Wellington, 1970.
Ogilvie, Gordon, *Denis Glover: His Life*. Godwit: Auckland, 1999.
Richards, Ian. *To Bed at Noon: The Life and Art of Maurice Duggan*. AUP: Auckland, 1997.
Robinson, Roger and Nelson Wattie (eds). *The Oxford Companion to New Zealand Literature*. OUP: Auckland, 1998.
Sturm, Terry (ed). *The Oxford History of New Zealand Literature in English*, 2nd ed. OUP: Auckland, 1998.
Vennell, O. St J. *Patronage and New Zealand Literature*. DIA: Wellington, 1977.

Appendix I: Literary Fund Annual Allocation

1947 £2000

In 1950 the average wage was about £400 a year; £100 in 1950 is equivalent to about $6780 in 2015 prices.

1950/1 Decrease to £1500 (though more than £2500 spent using suspense account).

1951/2 £2000

1955 Retail price not to exceed 3 times the unit cost after a publishing grant.

1956/7 £2500: Introduction of Scholarship in Letters, £500 from Cultural Fund.

1957/8 £2600: Introduction of Award for Achievement, £100 from lottery profits.

In 1960 the average wage was about £15 a week—£750 a year. £100 in 1960 is equivalent to about $7000 in 2015 prices.

1961/2 Increase to £2600 to finance both awards.

1962/3 £3700: £2600 + £1100 from lottery profits for awards (Scholarship in Letters increased to £1000).

1965/6 £3700: £2600 + Queen Elizabeth II Arts Council took over funding of two awards: £1100.

1967/8 £3500: Reduction in allocation to £2400 + £1100: Arts Council refused to fund awards and cost reverted to lottery profits.

1968/9 $7200: Increase in allocation to $5000 (under-expended) + $2200 from lottery profits. Retail price not to exceed 4 times unit cost after a publishing grant.

1969/70 $6200: Allocation reduced to $4000 (although $6236 expended) + $2200; $6000 eventually allocated.

In 1970 the average wage was about $48 a week—$2,400 a year; $100 in 1970 is equivalent to about $1514 in 2015 prices.

1970/1 $9200: $6000 + increase to $3200 from lottery profits (Scholarship in Letters increased to $3000).

1972/3 $17,200: Increase in allocation to $14,000 +$3200 from lottery profits. Scholarship in Letters up to $4000; Award for Achievement to $500 and new bursary for emerging writer $4000.

1973/4 $18,200: Increase in allocation to $15,000 + $3200 from lottery profits.

1974/5 $28,200: Increase in allocation to $25,000 +$3200.

1975/6 $39,200: Increase in allocation to $35,000 + increase to $4200 from lottery profits (Scholarship in Letters up to $6000).

1976/7 $44,200: $35,000 (although $45,000 earmarked earlier) + increase to $9200 from lottery profits.

1977/8 $57,200: Increase in allocation to $53,000 (or $54,000) + $4200 from lottery profits.

1978/9 $106,200: Increase in allocation to $75,000 + $31,200 from lottery profits (extra $20,000* + $7000 for Michael King) (exclusive of $8500 from private companies + $9500 from Victoria University of Wellington and University of Canterbury).

1979/80 $106,200: $75,000 + $31,200 from lottery profits (Scholarship in Letters now $9000).

In 1980 the average wage was about $10,000 a year; $100 in 1980 is equivalent to about $468 in 2015 prices.

1980/1 $113,700: Increase in allocation to $82,500 + $31,200 from lottery profits (exclusive of one-off $20,000 from Telethon).

1981/2 $119,200: Increase in allocation to $88,000 + $31,200 from lottery profits.

1982/3 $123,000: $88,000 + increase to $35,000 from lottery profits.

1983/4 $136,000: Increase in allocation to $101,000 + $35,000 from lottery profits (Scholarship in Letters up to $12,000).

1984/5 $201,000: Increase in allocation to $126,000 + increase to $75,000 from lottery profits (exclusive of one-off $122,500 from Arts & Letters lottery). Scholarship in Letters up to $14,000.

1985/6 $226,000: $126,000 + increase to $100,000 from lottery profits (exclusive of +$16,777 carried forward from 1984–5). Scholarship in Letters up to $20,000.

1986/7 $276,000: $126,000 + increase to $150,000 from lottery profits (exclusive of + $16,000 from Authors Fund). Scholarship in Letters up to $24,000.

1987/8 $300,000: Increase in allocation to $150,000 + $150,000 from lottery profits (exclusive of $16,000 from Authors' Fund and $24,000 from the Minister's special fund, for another Scholarship in Letters, to mark move to QEII).

1988/9 $400,000: $150,000 + increase to $250,000 from lottery profits, exclusive of + $100,000 one-off for move to QEII. Scholarship in Letters now $30,000.

1989/90 $916,402: $133,333 + $34,091 (for extra quarter) from VoteIA; $500,000 + $125,000 (for extra quarter) + $100,000 from lottery profits; $11,000 for QEII central + funds brought forward (NB. Change of government during financial year, so in addition there was a quarter's further funding). Scholarship in Letters up to $36,000.

In 1990 the average wage was about $27,000 a year; $100 in 1990 is equivalent to about $167 in 2015 prices.

1990/91 $1,043,000: allocation $150,000, lottery profits $900,000.

1991/2 $1,121,000 (as for 1990/1 + $40,000 for block grants, $18,000 for Massey Fellowship, $20,000 from Te Waka Toi, $2,000 for inflation).

*Announced December 1978 and to cope with the new bursaries, etc. See *Newsletter* 7.

Appendix II: Award for Achievement

1958 Janet Frame for *Owls Do Cry* (£100)
1959 Ruth France for *The Race*
1960 O.E. Middleton for his collection *The Stone*
1961 Frances Keinzly for *Tangahano*
1962 Errol Braithwaite for *An Affair of Men*
1963 Hubert Witheford for *The Lightning Makes a Difference* and Ruth Dallas for *The Turning Wheel*
1964 Marilyn Duckworth for *A Barbarous Tongue*
1965 Fleur Adcock for *The Eye of the Hurricane* and Hone Tuwhare for *No Ordinary Sun*
1966 Gordon Dryland for *An Absence of Angels*
1967 Maurice Gee for *A Special Flower*
1968 Norman Harvey for *One Magpie for Sorrow*
1969 Janet Frame for *The Pocket Mirror*
1970 None awarded
1971 Noel Hoggard
1972 Nag's Head Press—Bob Gormack
1973 Maurice Gee for *In My Father's Den* ($500)
1974 Joy Cowley for *Of Men and Angels*
1975 John A. Lee
1976 Michael Jackson for *Latitudes of Exile*
1977 Vincent O'Sullivan
1978 Frank Sargeson to mark the completion of his autobiography
1979 Lauris Edmond for the *Young Writers Anthology*
1980 John Weir and Sam Hunt
1981 Eric McCormick for *Portrait of Frances Hodgkins* and general recognition
1982 Bruce Mason

1983 John McIndoe
1984 Vincent O'Sullivan
1985 Margaret Mahy ($1000)
1986 C. K. Stead
1987 James Belich for *The New Zealand Wars*
1988 Fiona Kidman
1989 None appears to have been awarded
1990 Owen Marshall
1991 Bill Manhire
1992 Wendy Harrex

Appendix III: Literary Fund Advisory Committee Members and Secretaries

1947
Sir James Elliott/PEN 'chair'
Dr G.H. Scholefield/PEN
Professor Ian Gordon/PEN
Ngaio Marsh
O.N. Gillespie
J.H.E. Schroder
Ormond Wilson
Pei Te Hurinui Jones
Mrs Craig (Mary) Mackenzie
P.A. Lawlor secretary

1948
Elliott resigned
Prof G.W. von Zedlitz/PEN
Scholefield became chair

1949
Prof G.W. von Zedlitz died
Ngaio Marsh resigned
Sir Joseph Heenan

1950
M.H. Holcroft/PEN

1951
Scholefield resigned
Gordon became chair
All resigned

New committee
Prof Gordon/PEN 'chair'
M. H. Holcroft/PEN
Alan Mulgan/PEN
Matthew Oram, Speaker
John Moffett
Professor Blaiklock
A.E. Caddick
Agnes Loudon
Cecil Hull (died)
Charles Bennett
P.A. Lawlor secretary

1955
Prof Gordon (chair)
Sir Matthew Oram
Agnes Loudon
D.O.W. Hall
O.N. Gillespie (PEN)
Denis Glover (PEN)
Andrew Sharp appointed secretary

1957
Gillespie died
M.H. Holcroft reappointed (first meeting 10.9.57)
Prof Blaiklock reappointed (first meeting 3.12.57)

1958
Prof Gordon (chair)
D.O.W. Hall
Prof Blaiklock
G. Manning (first meeting 9.9.58)
M. H. Holcroft (PEN)
Dr J.C. Beaglehole (PEN) (first meeting 9.9.58)

1961
Prof Gordon (chair)

Prof Blaiklock
Prof J.C. Garrett (first meeting 5.9.61)
Dr Margaret Dalziel (first meeting 5.9.61)
M. H. Holcroft (PEN)
James K. Baxter (PEN) (first meeting 5.9.61)

1964
Prof Gordon (chair)
Prof Garrett
F.W.G. Miller
Dalziel resigned (over *Poetry Yearbook*)
Prof J.C. Reid (first meeting 11.11.64)
Mrs R Mackay (Ruth Gilbert) (PEN) (first meeting 11.11.64)
M.H. Holcroft (PEN) (reappointment criticised by Brasch, Vincent O'Sullivan, others)

1967
Prof Gordon (chair)
Helen Garrett
F. W. G. Miller
Prof Reid
Ruth Mackay (PEN)
W. J. Scott (PEN)
Harold White appointed secretary

1970
Prof Gordon (chair)
Prof R.G. Frean (started 1971)
D.G. Buchanan (started 1971)
Helen Garrett
Pat Godsiff (PEN) (started 1971)
W.J. Scott (PEN)
Mike Jarman secretary, assisted by Pam Hill 1972

1974
Prof C.K. Stead (chair); resigned mid-1976; replaced by Frean
Prof Frean
Roy Parsons
Trevor Reeves
Pat Godsiff (PEN)
Vincent O'Sullivan (PEN), replaced by Bruce Mason in Feb. 1976

Jim Booth secretary from Aug. 1975; from 1976 Pam Hill secretary and Jim Booth executive officer

1976
Prof Frean (chair)
James Bertram
Ian Wedde
Elizabeth Caffin, resigned end 1977; replaced by Elizabeth Alley
David Ballantyne (PEN)
Bruce Mason (PEN)
Jim Booth left mid-1978; Pam Hill replaced by Virginia Silva mid-1977; Silva left Jan. 1978, replaced by Pat Stuart, secretary, from 1978

1979
Prof Ray Copland (chair)
Kevin Cunningham, resigned Aug. 1981; replaced by Alan Roddick
Frank McKay (PEN)
Roger Hall, resigned early 1982; replaced by Prof Terry Sturm
Elizabeth Alley, resigned Aug. 1981; replaced by Ann Mallinson Sept. 1981
David Ballantyne (PEN)
Ann Mallinson became publishing advisor, nominated 1979; appointed Jan. 1980
Chris Rutledge secretary to succeed Pat Stuart who left around Sept. 1981 due to promotion

1982
Prof Terry Sturm (chair)
Prof Copland
Prof C.K. Stead (PEN)
Louis Johnson (PEN)
Ann Mallinson (BPANZ), resigned Aug. 1984
Alan Roddick
Susan Robertson replaced Chris Rutledge as secretary April 1983

1985
Prof Terry Sturm (chair)
Keri Hulme
William Broughton
Elizabeth Caffin (BPANZ)
Louis Johnson (PEN), resigned from Feb. 1988 to take up Katherine

Mansfield Fellowship
Dale Williams (PEN), resigned Aug. 1988
Gillian Martell secretary from May 1985 to Nov. 1986; then Robert Lansdown for one meeting; Jonathan Keate from June 1987 to May 1988

1988: Literature Committee of Queen Elizabeth II Arts Council
Prof Terry Sturm (chair)
Keri Hulme, resigned Nov. 1989; replaced by Witi Ihimaera
William Broughton, resigned Nov. 1990; replaced by Lawrence Jones
Elizabeth Caffin (BPANZ), resigned Aug. 1989; replaced by Wendy Harrex
Elizabeth Smither (PEN)
Dick Scott (PEN)
Rosemary Wildblood, programme manager; Patricia Coe

1991: Literature Committee of QEII
Prof Terry Sturm (chair)
Witi Ihimaera
Lawrence Jones
Wendy Harrex (BPANZ)
Elizabeth Smither (PEN); replaced by Sue McCauley Nov. 1991; Sue McCauley resigned June 1992; replaced by Suzann Olsson
Dick Scott (PEN); replaced by Tony Simpson Nov. 1991

Nov. 1992
Jenny Pattrick (acting chair)
Andrew Mason (on Queen Elizabeth II Arts Council and chair from Feb. 1993)
Witi Ihimaera (resigned March 1993; returned Aug. 1994)
Lawrence Jones (replaced by Elizabeth Smither Aug. 1994)
Jane Connor (BPANZ)
Suzann Olsson (PEN)
Tony Simpson (PEN)

Nov. 1994
Albert Wendt (chair)
Jane Connor
Witi Ihimaera
Suzann Olsson
Tony Simpson
Elizabeth Smither

Appendix IV
Scholarship in Letters

1957 Eric McCormick (£500)
1958 Phillip Wilson
1959 Sylvia Ashton-Warner
1960 Maurice Shadbolt
1961 Marilyn Duckworth
1962 Maurice Gee (£1000)
1963 Noel Hilliard and Redmond Wallis (£500 each)
1964 Janet Frame
1965 O. E. Middleton
1966 Maurice Duggan
1967 Isobel Andrews
1968 David Ballantyne
1969 Gordon Dryland
1970 Maurice Shadbolt
1971 Graham Billing ($3000)
1972 Marilyn Duckworth
1973 Bruce Mason ($4000)
1974 Frank Sargeson
1975 Noel Hilliard
1976 Maurice Gee ($6000)
1977 None awarded, but a second writing bursary instead
1978 Yvonne du Fresne
1979 James McNeish
1980 Ian Wedde ($9000)
1981 Fiona Kidman
1982 Maurice Shadbolt
1983 Jean Watson
1984 Margaret Sutherland ($12,000)

1985 Fiona Kidman ($14,000)
1986 Maurice Gee ($20,000)
1987 Elizabeth Smither ($24,000) + special $24,000 to Maurice Gee for 40-year anniversary
1988 Owen Marshall + additional Scholarship in Letters to Patricia Grace to celebrate merger with QEII
1989 Ian Wedde; Bill Manhire; C.K. Stead ($24,000)
1990 Alistair Campbell; Witi Ihimaera; James McNeish; Maurice Shadbolt ($30,000)
1991 Lauris Edmond; Fiona Farrell-Poole; Maurice Gee; Michael Gifkins; Rachel McAlpine ($36,000); special two-year Scholarship in Letters for 1990: Keri Hulme for 'Bait' and 'On Shadowside'
1992 John Cranna; Yvonne du Fresne; Stevan Eldred-Grigg; Fiona Kidman; Cilla McQueen (now called Leading Writers grants)
1993 Patricia Grace; Lloyd Jones; Elizabeth Smither; C.K. Stead; Hone Tuwhare
1994 Marilyn Duckworth, Gaelyn Gordon, Kevin Ireland, Elizabeth Knox, Renee Taylor
1995 Barbara Anderson; Graham Billing; Fiona Kidman; Brian Turner; Damien Wilkins

Appendix V
University Fellowships

University of Canterbury Writer in Residence

6 months
1979: Michael Morrissey ($6000)
1980: Jennifer Compton ($7,200)
1981: Owen Marshall ($9,500)

8 months
1982: Barry Mitcalfe ($16,000)
1983: Murray Edmond ($18,500)
1984: Margaret Mahy

12 months ($24,000) (became the Ursula Bethell Residency for Creative Writers)
1985: Graham Billing and Keri Hulme
1986: Rachel McAlpine and Kevin Ireland
1987: Mike Johnson
1988: Brian McNeill
1989: Kim Eggleston and Gary Langford
1990: Mervyn Thompson
1991: Bernadette Hall
1992: Fiona Farrell
1993: Sue McCauley
1994: Kate Flannery (De Goldi)

Victoria University of Wellington Writer in Residence

One year $15,374
1979: Joseph Musaphia
1980: Louis Johnson ($17,700)
1981: Vincent O'Sullivan ($22,106)
1982: Witi Ihimaera ($23,940)
1983: Michael King ($24,890)
1984: Ian Wedde ($23,941)
1985: Patricia Grace
1986: Stevan Eldred-Grigg
1987: Lauris Edmond (9 months, up to $27,000)
1988: Fiona Kidman
1989: Maurice Gee
1990: Marilyn Duckworth
1991: Barbara Anderson
1992: Alistair Campbell
1993: Jack Lasenby
1994: Chris Pugsley

Auckland University Literary Fellowship

6 months
1980: Robin Dudding (no LF funding)
1981: Margaret Sutherland ($9,300)
1982: Greg McGee ($9,800)
1983: Michael Gifkins ($11,500)

9 months ($15,750)
1984: Elizabeth Smither
1985: Russell Haley
1986: Sue McCauley
1987: Maurice Shadbolt
1988: Jean Watson ($10,125x2)
1989: Kevin Ireland
1990: Stuart Hoar
1991: Hone Tuwhare
1992: Alan Loney
1993: Shonagh Koea
1994: Peter Wells

University of Waikato Writer in Residence

1991: Tessa Duder
1992: Maurice Shadbolt
1993: Mona Williams
1994: Michael King

Massey University Writer's Fellowship

1993: Anne French
1994: Peter Hawes

Appendix VI: Writing Bursary (intended for 6 months) and ICI Writer's Bursary*

1973 Ivan Bootham and Michael Henderson ($2000 each)
1974 Ian Wedde
1975 Ray Grover
1976 Philip Temple and Jean Watson
1977 Jennifer Compton ($4000); and a second, also of $4000, to Michael Harlow as no Scholarship in Letters given
1978 Elizabeth Smither; a second to Michael Morrissey. ICI ($5000): Michael Heath
1979 Wendy Simons. ICI ($5000): Russell Haley
1980 Jan Kemp. ICI: David Hill
1981 Ian Mune. ICI: Anne de Roo
1982 Peter Hooper. ICI ($6000): Keri Hulme
1983 Mary Logan. ICI: Wendy Simons
1984 Keri Hulme ($6000). ICI ($7000) Alison Gray
1985 Tony Beyer ($8000). ICI ($8000): Riemke Ensing
1986 Joan Rosier-Jones ($10,000). ICI ($9000): Stephen G. Walker
1987 Renée. ICI ($10,000): Elizabeth Knox
1988 Fiona Farrell Poole. ICI: Anne Kennedy
1989 John Cranna. Extra one to Shonagh Koea
1990 Frances Cherry, Apirana Taylor plus an extra one to Tessa Duder; ICI withdrew and that became the Louis Johnson New Writer's Bursary ($15,000): Sandra Arnold; also one additional to Damien Wilkins
1991 Anne French; Michael Harlow ($18,000); Suzann Olsson (LJ New Writer); Norma Michael (Todd Foundation New Writer)

1992 Chris Else; Mervyn Thompson (now called Established Writers grants); Andrew Johnston (LJ) + Annamarie Jagose (Todd)

1993 Jenny Bornholdt; Peter Wells; Bill Payne (LJ); Alison Glenny (Todd) (still $18,000)

1994 Russell Haley, Sheridan Keith; Gabriele Muir (LJ), Maria Wickens (Todd) (all $18,000)

1995 Andrew Johnston; Jean Watson; James Brown (LJ); Debra Daley (Todd) (all $18,000)

* ICI Writer's Bursary was worth $5000 and first awarded in 1978 for 1979. It effectively replaced the Writing Bursary but the LFAC was prepared to offer a second bursary of $4000 as well if the applications warranted it. (See *Newsletter* 4.)

INDEX

References in italics denote photographs and illustrations

n denotes references to endnotes